MACRO MELLOW
RECIPES FOR MACROBIOTIC COOKING

by Shirley Gallinger
&
Sherry A. Rogers, M.D.

D0880424

Library of Congress Catalogue Card Number: 92-60163

ISBN 0-9618821-4-X

Printed in the United States

MACRO MELLOW

TABLE OF CONTENTS

Dedication

Disclaimer

Foreword

Chapter I
Introduction to the Transition Diet   1

Chapter II
Steps on the Path to Better Health   4
Making the Commitment   4
Eliminating the Health Hindering Foods   5
Starting the Diet Transition   6
The Great Balancing Act   8
Yin and Yang Properties   11
Food & Mood   13

Chapter III
The Macrobiotic Diet   15
The Proportion Pie   15
Tools   19
Getting Acquainted with Some New Foods   20

Chapter IV
A Short Course on Whole Foods   23
Land and Sea Vegetables   29
Protein Sources   33
The Wonderful Supporting Cast   35
The Art of Substitution   40

Chapter V
Menu Planning   44
Taming the Sweet Tooth   47

Most Important, the Cook   48
Healthy Cooking for Busy People   49
Opps!! Leftovers   52
Warning!!! Too Much Fat is
    Harmful to Your Health   55

Chapter VI
Monthly Menus   57
Week of Menus for Transition Diet   69
Make Ahead Meals   72
Quick & Easy Meal Suggestions   73

Chapter VII
The Recipes   74
   1.   Grains, the Center of It All   75
   2.   Eat Your Vegetables, Including
         the Sea Vegetables   87
   3.   Proteins, the Body Rebuilders
         (Beans, Tofu, Tempeh, Seitan,
         Seeds, Nuts, Fish, Seafood,
         and Animal Food)   122
   4.   Soup Du Jour   141
   5.   Lighten Up: Salads & Pickles   166
   6.   Give Us Our Daily Bread   191
   7.   Small Pleasures (Appetizers,
         Dips, Spreads, Condiments,
         Sauces, Gravies and Butters)   201
   8.   Just Desserts   239
   9.   Beverages   272
  10.   Super Snacks for Kids
         of All Ages   277
  11.   What's for Breakfast?   283
  12.   The Healthful Lunch   293
  13.   Eating Out: A Survival Lesson   298

Chapter VIII
My Story: How I Became Macrobiotic   300

Chapter IX
Home Remedies for Common Complaints   303

Chapter X
The Garden of Eden   309
The Gardening Calendar   309
Handy Summary of Monthly Garden
    Projects   334

Chapter XI
A Note from the Doctor   337
Medical Aspects of the
    Transitional Phase   337
Nutritional Deficiencies are Rampant
    in the Land of Plenty   346
Prescription Medications Guarantee
    Worse Symptoms   347
Paradigm Shift   348
Know Your Nutrient Levels   349
Guilt   350
Crushing Cravings   352
The Dreaded Discharge   355
Macro Mellowness   356

Resources   357

Books by S.A. Rogers, M.D.   362

Cooking Notes

Index

SHIRLEY'S DEDICATION

To my wonderful husband Don, the love of my life and my best friend, who has always encouraged and supported my efforts to learn and grow and to Sherry and Rob who have given me more opportunities than I ever thought possible even in my wildest dreams.

SHERRY'S DEDICATION

For the readers of The E.I. Syndrome, You Are What You Ate, Tired or Toxic?, and The Cure Is In The Kitchen, it comes as no surprise that my lifelong admiration, adoration, love, gratitude and dedication is to Luscious.

DISCLAIMER

This work is meant only to give you new and fresh ideas and recipes for a healthier diet. If you have medical problems, you should consult your physician.

FOREWORD

In this era, despite an unprecedented number of labor-saving devices, people seem to have less time than ever before. Gone is a great deal of socializing which has often been replaced by a second job or take-home work from the primary job. Gone are quiet and leisurely family meals preceeded by a small grace. In place of this, because of work, school and sports activities, some family members are lucky to be seen by the others for more than 15 minutes a week.

There is usually a time squeeze on Mom, since the super-woman era has allowed her the dubious distinction of being able to work in the home as well as out of the home. She has doubled her work, but not her fun. But with the family scattered and on the run, there is little satisfaction in preparing an elaborate meal which will be eaten alone by some and cold in four minutes by others, or passed up for a fast-food delight in the car. And many women have just plain given up cooking. They have the means to dine out, and feel they deserve it.

Futhermore our increasing reliance on sugars in the diet has left many people too edgy, irritable, anxious, and hyper to be able to derive relaxation and pleasure from cooking, even if they could find the time. The mellow and reflective moments of life seem to have been abandoned for the race to cram as much work into a day as possible. But without our mellow moments, we miss out on those memorable times of rediscovered love, unleashed creativity, increased awareness, the birth of new perspectives, spiritual growth and renewed appreciation.

What this has done to us socially has left the family a less cohesive unit. It also has a negative effect on digestion if we do not dine in a quiet, happy and unhurried atmosphere. But more importantly it has started a silent erosion of our health which is only now being discovered. For by not preparing our own food with whole fresh ingredients of known quality, and by not balancing the meals lovingly in tune with individual needs, we have contributed to the decline in health.

We are the first generation of man to ever eat so many processed foods. These have been deliberately stripped of many vitamins and minerals and the essential fatty acids have been dangerously altered by the process of hydrogenation. Even the U.S. government published a study showing that the average American diet now only provides 40% (less than half!) of the magnesium that we require in a day. And the Journal of the American Medical Association reported that 90% of the Doctors in 1990 never looked for magnesium deficiency. As this is an example of only one of four dozen nutrients needed for health, it is no small wonder that cardiovascular disease (which includes early heart attacks, angina, high blood pressure, palpitations and other cardiac arrhythmias, strokes, Raynaud's phenomenon, phlebitis and more) is the number one cause of illness and death in the United States today.

Magnesium deficiency as well as many other undiscovered mineral, vitamin and essential fatty acid deficiencies are at the root of many degenerative diseases. Nonetheless, just a solo undetected magnesium deficiency, for example, can cause some of these diseases. But the real hooker is that there is no blood test that will adequately diagnose a magnesium deficiency. Fortunately there is a challenge or loading test that will.

Cancer is the number two cause of death and illness in the U.S., after cardiovascular disease. One of the vitamins that is very important in protecting us from cancer is vitamin E. It sits in the cell membrane or "shell" and grabs dangerous chemicals that try to pass into the cell and attach to our DNA (genetic material) and turn on the genetic message to make cancer cells.

But vitamin E is removed from most of our foods so that they will not go bad and they will last for months in our pantry. For example white bread flour and cooking oils are so processed as to often contain no vitamin E. And they are some of the best sources of it. Since we are the first generation of man ever exposed to such an unprecedented number of chemicals, we are more in need of protective vitamin E than ever. But instead, we are also the first generation eating less of it. So it is no surprise that cancer is on the rise (and the second cause of illness). And, of course vitamin E is also very essential in preventing cardiovascular disease (the number one illness) as well as cancer (the number two illness). And this is just an example of how only one of over four dozen nutrients factors into the scheme of disease.

At the Northeast Center for Environmental Medicine, specializing in environmental medicine and nutritional biochemistry, we both see in Syracuse, New York, people from literally all over the world who have conditions that have resisted all that medicine can offer. By finding the dietary and environmental triggers and hidden biochemical (nutrient) defects, we have been fortunate to have seen some of the most "impossible" cases get well.

But because multiple chemical sensitivities is such a severe problem for many of our folks, years ago we began an intensive search to help the body unload its toxic burden of chemicals or to detox. We found that a macrobiotic diet was the answer for ourselves and hundreds of our patients.

The E.I. Syndrome was written to show folks how to diagnose and treat the wide range of environmental illnesses, from asthma, migraines, depression, and "brain fog" to colitis, arthritis, chronic fatigue, and more. You Are What You Ate was written to show them how to begin eating macrobiotically, then Tired Or Toxic? was written to explain the vitamin and mineral levels that should be checked, how to do the specialized tests, and even where to find them. It also gave over 30 scientific reasons why macrobiotics is so healing, complete with the biochemical and medical references for doctors.

I thought I could hang up the word-processor then, that our mission had been completed. I was wrong. We quickly saw that there were at least two more books that were needed. For the seriously ill person, we needed a sequel to the macro primer (You Are What You Ate), for no one had ever spelled out exactly what the strict healing phase diet was and how to pull it off on a daily basis. Hence, the birth of The Cure Is In The Kitchen.

But there was still another need that had not been addressed. Many people could not even begin the diet until they had figured out what to feed the rest of the family who had no intentions of ever going on a macrobiotic diet. We needed a book that would show folks how to prepare nutritious foods using the macrobiotic principles and ingredients, but it had to be cleverly disguised so they would be unaware that they were eating anything that was good for them. The person eating the diet for healing purposes was in need of ways to use the basic "grains, greens and beans" in a disguised form in the family's daily diet.

Obviously a book of this sort also makes a great start for the person who wants to ease into macro, as well as for the person who never intends to eat macrobiotically but would like to eat healthier and feel better. For example, it is the perfect diet for the person with high cholesterol or triglycerides, not to mention the diet for the person who has had bypass surgery and knows statistically that it is only a matter of a couple of years before the new vessels also plug up and the procedure will need to done all over again. For a modified macrobiotic diet is the only scientifically proven way to reverse heart disease even when all that medicine and surgery have to offer has failed (Ornish, Lancet, 1990).

I had some great titles for this book, like "What the Hell to Feed the Rest of the Family Who Hates Macro" or "The save Your Ass Cookbook", all of which were rejected. There were some other drawbacks such as my not being a very good or innovative cook in general.

Shirley, on the other hand, with over forty years experience in feeding a family of five plus much entertaining, loves cooking and is wonderful at it. As she started getting absorbed in this project, she would bring her creations into the office for us to try. She would create dinners for us with our non-macro husbands, Don and Lucious, that were terrific. We knew then that her creativity had to be unleashed and her talents shared.

Shirley came to the office 15 years ago. She is one of the most nurturing, kind, most compassionate nurses I will ever have the privilege of knowing. Besides her work at the office she is an avid perennial and organic food gardener who has guided me through the years. Active in the local nature group, hiking, camping, and motor cycling, she is still on the ski patrol after 27 years. And at nearly 63, she took a month off from the office to motorcycle across the U.S. to Colorado. This is the kind of activity that comes from a diet optimally high in nutrients.

As for her culinary talents and improvisational adaptability, I've seen her cook a four dish macro meal out of a suitcase in a hotel room in Australia. And as the self-appointed taster, I can certainly vouch for the recipes in this book that they are tasty: yet she has made them simple enough for even a doctor to follow. She has guided hundreds of our patients to better health with these meals, and now we would like to help you enrich your own personal and family health with whole unprocessed foods that possess much higher nutrient value than the standard American diet (appropriately abbreviated SAD). At 63 she is free of symptoms and medications, and looks and acts optimally healthy, the way we were meant to be. As versatility is also a bench mark of health, it should not come as a surprise that as active and energetic as she is, she also has a deep reflective, loving, spiritual and mellow side as well. We would like to share our ideas with you so that you too, can become macro mellow.

Sherry A. Rogers, M.D.   Syracuse, New York
                                          1991

CHAPTER I

INTRODUCTION TO THE TRANSITIONAL DIET

****

"Tell me what you eat and I will tell you what you are."
Brillat - Savarin, Physiologie du Gout
****

Why on earth do we need another cookbook? Because we need a cookbook that will take the mystery out of macrobiotics. We need to demystify yin and yang, acid and alkaline, balancing your foods, macro cooking methods in general, and to modify the recipes to suit our American tastes. And why is macrobiotics so necessary in the first place? Because it is the only scientifically proven method to reverse heart disease, arteriosclerosis, and cancer (Ornish, Lancet, 1990, D. Ornish, M.D., Dr. Dean Ornish's Program for Reversing Heart Disease, Random House, 1990; A. Satillaro, M.D., Recalled By Life, Avon Books, 1982. S. Rogers, M.D., The Cure Is In The Kitchen). But because it is so time consuming as well as difficult, many cannot do it. Moreover, many do not need to be so strict. Yet they would like to get some of the health benefits of the macrobiotic diet. Hence a transition diet, bridging the gap from the standard American diet (SAD) to the strictest healing phase of the macrobiotic diet, fills the gap.

The transition diet fills many other needs. For the person who is ill and must do the strict phase, he has two problems. (1) His cooking needs must be factored into the cooking needs of the rest of the family, most of whom may not want to touch macrobiotic food with a ten-foot fork. It is difficult to have two separate kitchens, one for the SAD (standard American Diet) and one for macro. It is much easier and more economical if the same ingredients can be shared by both. Like wise, (2) the person on the strict phase does not want to eat the same foods each day. Now when he has made a big batch of grain or beans, he is able to transform these into delicious meals for the family. This is the essence of this book.

And for the average person, who has no one in the family who must eat the strict healing phase of macrobiotics, this transition phase diet is the perfect upgrade of the SAD which is needed to reverse chronic disease like arthritis, high cholesterol, high blood pressure, heart disease, or any myriad of other degenerative diseases.

If you are merely thinking about improving your diet in general or forestall the inevitable onset of degenerative disease, you will want to start with the transition diet. The transition diet will introduce you to new foods and emphasize good nutrition instead of empty calorie, processed foods. The transition diet can be a step towards a macrobiotic diet or it may be all you will need at this time, but it is a big step in the right direction.

If you have decided to do the macrobiotic diet for health reasons, you can start with the transition diet and ease into it, but going " cold turkey" and jumping in feet first is possible and may even be preferable if you have the right mind set, or are sick enough, and are willing to devote some time and energy to healing your body, mind and soul. The word macrobiotics literally means (macro-large and bio-life). It is not just a diet although the diet is extremely important, but it is also a way of life. It is not a religion. Macrobiotics, like environmental medicine, emphasizes clean air, clean water, clean food, work and exercise, mental activities such as hobbies, art, reading, writing, music, work, volunteering or anything that keeps you active and interested in life.

It also emphasizes mellowness: relaxation, massage, chiropractic manipulation, acupressure, acupuncture, and above all, the powers of the mind and a positive outlook on life, good relations with all the other people in your life and to be grateful and thankful for all that you have been given, even adversity, as this will help you to grow stronger. It certainly is a very positive way of looking at life and a giant step in improving your own life.

The gardening portion of this book is written for the persons who want and need to have control of furnishing their own organic fresh vegetables throughout the year. It will also give you a healthy amount of good exercise and sunshine. Even apartment dwellers can raise some fresh produce on a balcony or windowsill. The beginning gardener can go slowly and learn as the garden grows. Even if you do not plan to garden, I urge you to read this section to learn about farmers' markets, stocking up for the winter and how to find wild foods which are free to all. Modern food growing methods have depleted the soil and poisoned the produce. Modern food processing has transformed real food into chemical imitations. We need to take control of our food supply for our own and our family's health.

Above all, we want you to enjoy this book and use it daily.

Underline, turndown the corners of the pages, change the recipes to suite your own tastes. It's your book now and we hope you will use it with the same joy we found in writing it for you.

CHAPTER II

STEPS ON THE PATH TO BETTER HEALTH

****
"Disease is the retribution of outraged nature."
Hasea Ballou
****

MAKING THE COMMITMENT

Since you are reading this book, I already know that you are "on the quest" for ways to improve your health. The interesting thing about health is that as your own health improves, it sends out ripples to your family, friends, and co-workers, who then also become more health conscious.

Good health is composed of many things. First of all it is not merely lack of disease. Diet is extremely important but it is only one part of the whole. Good health requires clean air, clean water, clean food, exercise, love and laughter, artistic expression, good relationships with your family and friends, interesting work or hobbies, enthusiasm for life, a spiritual belief and being at peace with yourself. In other words, being mellow enough to have it all together, physically, mentally and spiritually.

If you are presently suffering from poor health it is not too hard to make up your mind to change your ways and make the commitment, but as your health improves it is easy to back-slide. In order to prevent this you really need to have a basic understanding of the importance of the diet and lifestyle changes you will be making. You also need to clarify in your own mind the reasons why you personally are making this commitment.

The reasons people have for changing to a grain and vegetable diet are varied. Some do not believe animals should be slaughtered for food, many believe to reduce world-wide hunger and starvation we need a vegetarian diet for all. Others see a macrobiotic diet as the way to health and happiness. For whatever reason, for true success you must be fully committed. Start a notebook now. Write down a statement of your commitment and then map out a plan. List your goals for today, this week, this month, three months, six months and a year. As you reach your goals, write them in your

4

notebook and continue using your goals for as long as you need them to meet your commitment to a healthier lifestyle. It is not always easy, but it certainly is worthwhile, as you will find.

Almost everyone back-slides along the way. Be kind to yourself, it's not the end of the world. Just climb back on board and get on track again.

ELIMINATING THE HEALTH HINDERING FOODS

The next step on the path to health is to eliminate the foods which have been proven to be health hindering. The list is long. First eliminate all junk foods. You probably already know what they are; soft drinks, candy and salted and high fat snacks such as commercial corn chips, potato chips, crackers, etc.

The second step would be to eliminate alcohol, drugs (unless prescribed by your doctor as "necessary for your health"), sugar in all forms including white and brown sugar, molasses, corn syrup and artificial sweeteners, also chocolate and caffeines such as coffee, cola drinks, and black tea. You also should eliminate strong spices such as black pepper and cayenne pepper.

The third step would be eliminating all processed foods which include most of the local supermarket staples. Processed foods are any which have been altered by man through adding, deleting, or altering any of the components of the food. Milling and bleaching grains for bread and then fortifying them with vitamins is just one example. You should also totally eliminate hydrogenated fats such as margarines, solid vegetable shortenings, heat pressed oils and processed foods which contain these products. You do have to read labels. Best of all, by merely using whole unadulterated foods for 99% of your cooking, you will eliminate the hidden processing that strips and adulterates commercial foods.

Fourth, eliminate red meat, these include beef, lamb, pork, and veal. Also, eggs except for very limited use.

The fifth step would be to eliminate all dairy products; butter, cheese, cream, ice cream, milk and yogurt.

The sixth step is to discontinue, or greatly reduce, the consumption of tropical produce such as bananas, Brazil nuts, cashew nuts, coconuts, dates, figs, grapefruit, oranges, papayas, avocado and the nightshade family of vegetables which include white potatoes, tomatos, peppers, eggplant and tobacco. A transition macrobiotic

5

diet allows a limited amount of some of these more extreme foods on special occasions, once you have achieved your goal of being healthier.

If you have succeeded with steps 1-6, you are basically doing a macrobiotic diet but you also may be thinking there is nothing left to eat. Trust me; there is much more to eat, and the rest of this book is devoted to helping you learn how to plan and cook meals that create balance and health.

STARTING THE DIET TRANSITION

Food is such an important part of life; it's social, it's family traditions, and most of all it's a life-time of habits, of likes and dislikes which we have all cultivated from high chair to high school, right up until today. We have been brain washed by everybody from Mom's "drink your milk" to modern television's ads pushing everything from sugared cereals, orange juice, soft drinks, pizza and TV dinners. Food today for many is quick and easy; eating on the run, take outs, going out, or cooked at home from a package. Not exactly what mother nature had in mind for all of us with her bounty, and a far cry from the foraging of our forebearers. Changing the way we eat is not an easy task, but with the commitment which you have made, it is possible. There are several ways to start.

If you are presently suffering from E.I. (Environmental Illness) you need to do the yeast free diet and/or the rare food diet first to discover any hidden food sensitivities and to see just how good you can feel. (Read The E.I. Syndrome for details, from this same publisher). Both of these diets are diagnostic tools and are not meant to be lifetime diets. By doing either of the diets you have already eliminated the junk food and most of the health hindering foods.

The next step is to eliminate from your diet all red meats, and greatly reduce the use of egg and dairy products. At the same time you will start to increase your intake of whole grains, vegetables and beans. You might even dabble in some seaweeds, tofu, miso, and tamari sauce. At this point you will still have poultry and fish and some of the tropical fruits and vegetables. One good way to start is to eliminate all animal foods from your breakfast and lunch. Dinner could include animal food but you will start to gradually introduce some totally vegetable main courses on a regular basis, always keeping in mind your goal and commitment of better health for yourself and your family.

The next step to a transition macrobiotic diet is pretty easy once you have gotten this far. The only foods you eliminate now are the eggs, dairy, poultry, tropical fruits and vegetables from the non-macro list on a regular basis. Hopefully, if a macrobiotic diet was your goal, you have already been reading and learning about food balancing, cooking methods and general theory. The next chapter will explain these concepts in more detail.

Changing your diet changes your lifestyle to some degree. There is no getting around the fact that there is more cooking involved which means more time in the kitchen. Food shopping methods will also change. Most of what is sold in the supermarket is not what you should consume for a healthful diet. The farmers' markets, local farms, your own garden, health food stores and mail order suppliers will become your sources of real food. Hopefully you will also be able to have a garden and raise some fresh vegetables. Opposition by family members and friends can also be a problem. Of course they love you and worry if you start losing weight, but when they see your health, energy and happiness improving, they will soon see that this is a necessary but transient step in the journey to wellness. And not everyone needs to lose weight on this diet. When someone insists you need red meat to survive, just tell them that the steak they are eating came from an animal that only eats grass and grains and look what happened to him. Develop your sense of humor. It will breeze you through a myriad of adversities.

Some people will use the macrobiotic diet as a healing mode, some will love it and live with it for the rest of their lives. Others will heal and then branch out. But assuredly you will forever be changed for the better, knowing you are what you ate. How far you go in changing your diet is up to you. Any of these steps is a step in the right direction.

THE GREAT BALANCING ACT

"Everything in nature is a cause from
which there flows some effect."
Spinoza

Everything in nature is a balancing act including the foods we eat. The universe is constantly changing to stay balanced. Day changes to night, the sun rises and sets, the seasons change, the moon waxes and wanes and controls the ocean tides, sunshine follows rain and vegetation grows and dies and commits its remains to rebuild the soil. All of these cycles are endless. As part of the universe our bodies are constantly changing and doing a balancing act. We change from young to old, from awake to asleep, hungry to full, happy to sad, energetic to lethargic, work to play, and these are only the changes that we can easily observe.

Just think of the countless changes that are happening inside out bodies to keep us balanced and alive. Our heart contracts and expands to pump blood to every cell, our lungs contract and expand to provide oxygen to the circulating blood, muscles contract and expand so we can move to work and play. We hardly think of these things unless we have heart disease, asthma, or muscle damage which prevents one of these functions from operating properly.

An even greater balancing act goes on at an even more unnoticed level. Our bodies constantly change to keep our chemical balance. If we become too acid or too alkaline we are in serious trouble. Our red blood cells which carry oxygen to every part of our body die and are replaced by new ones constantly. If they are not balanced we become anemic. White blood cells are constantly at war with the invaders of bacteria and germs that try to take over our bodies. If they lose the war, we become out of balance and ill. There are literally thousands of balancing acts being played out by our bodies every second of life whether we are awake or asleep. The body instinctively knows what we need in order to maintain status quo and does everything possible to keep us in balance. This wonderful, amazing body of ours can take the foods we eat and change them into the fuel which keeps all of these balancing systems working. The human body builds and repairs itself and maintains many automatic chemical and electrical control systems.

8

The digestive system is a truly amazing fuel refinery which can take raw materials we eat and change them into glucose "fuel" to keep the engine running. As with gasoline, the beginning product and the process determine whether we run on super premium high test or just poke along on a low grade regular. Balanced fuel for the human refinery consists of carbohydrates, proteins, vitamins minerals, fats, water and roughage. Vegetables and fruit contain all of these components and can be a complete diet if properly combined. Animal foods are high in protein and fat. Both vegetable and animal protein can be converted by the body into amino acid building blocks which repair and produce every cell in our bodies. Carbohydrates provide fuel for energy. Vitamins and minerals from our daily foods are the regulators needed for growth and control of many body functions. When we become vitamin or mineral deficient, the balancing act is thrown out of order and we can become severely ill with vitamin deficiency diseases which lead to a wide array of symptoms which are often misdiagnosed or undiagnosed.

Let's follow a meal through the digestive system. As the teeth cut and grind the food, the salivary glands release digestive enzymes which start breaking down carbohydrates. Another enzyme, ptyalin, found in the saliva splits the molecules of starch into smaller molecules of sugar. This is the reason that the longer you chew whole grains, such as brown rice, the sweeter it tastes.

The chewed food is next sent to the stomach. The stomach is a very well muscled, small hollow, J-shaped organ about ten inches long. The stomach muscles are important because they are needed to finish breaking up every piece of food into tiny particles. The lining of the stomach produces digestive enzymes such as hydrochloric acid and several other enzymes such as rennin, lipase and pepsin, which all have special jobs to do in the digestive process. The rennin curdles milk, lipase splits fats, the hydrochloric acid helps change minerals to promote their absorption, and splits proteins into their component amino acids.

After anywhere from three to five hours the stomach contents are released into the small intestine. The first part of the small intestine is called the duodenum, and more digestive juices are added along with pancreatic fluids and bile from the liver.

The pancreatic fluid contains a number of enzymes that act on all kinds of foods. Proteins are broken down into amino acids, large sugar molecules are changed into simple sugars and fats are reduced to fatty acids in preparation for absorption into the blood and lymph systems.

Bile contributes to the digestive system by emulsifying fatty foods and making them easier to absorb. Most of the small molecules of sugar, amino acids and fats are absorbed by the body from the small intestine.

The remaining contents of the small intestine then pass into the large intestine and are excreted by the body as feces. The water which is absorbed through the walls of the large intestine is sent to the kidney and is excreted by the body as urine. Food products which were carried by the blood vessels from the small intestine are delivered to the liver which processes them into fuel to be available on demand by the body. The liver also stores some vitamins and minerals for the blood system. Our amazing digestive system can usually process any type of food we put into it but a poor diet will eventually break down the system and put us out of balance. The food we eat literally becomes us.

The macrobiotic beliefs, developed from oriental medicine, characterize all the universe from the largest entity to the most minute particle according to classifications which are called yang "contractive" and yin "expansive". As you begin to understand this theory, you will understand how the choices of foods control the balance in our lives. The following charts will help to explain this theory. Keep in mind that yin attracts yang, yang attracts yin, while yang repels yang and yin repels yin. Some examples of attraction are man and woman, spirit and matter, and the positive and negative poles of magnets. Samples of repelling are oil and water, the two positive poles or the two negative poles of a magnet. Nothing is ever totally yin or totally yang and nothing stays the same in the universe. There is constant movement and change to create balance of the whole.

THE YIN & YANG PROPERTIES

Attribute	Contractive (Yin)	Expansive (Yang)
size	smaller	larger
density	thicker	thinner
length	shorter	longer
texture	harder	softer
weight	heavier	lighter
shape	more contractive	more expanded
	harder	fragile
climate	tropical	arctic
season	summer	winter
humidity	drier	wetter
light	lighter	darker
position	more inward	more outward
	central	peripheral
direction	horizontal	vertical
function	assimilation	dispersion
	organization	decomposition
sex	male	female
organ	compact,	hollow,
structure	condensed	expansive
attitude	active,	gentle,
	positive	negative
biological	animal	vegetable
dimension	time	space
movement	more active	more inactive
	-faster	-slower
catalyst	fire	water

11

THE YIN & YANG OF FOOD

CONTRACTIVE
(Yang)

EXTREME YANG
Red Meat
Eggs
Hard, salty cheeses
Salt

MODERATE YANG
Poultry
Rabbit
Fish
Seafoods

BALANCED
Whole grains
Beans
Local vegetables
Seeds
Local nuts
Seasonal fruits

EXPANSIVE
(Yin)

MODERATE YIN
Dairy foods
Tropical fruits,
nuts & vegetables
Night shade family
ie: white potatoes
    tomato, egg   Fruit juices
    plant, peppers

EXTREME YIN
Alcohol
Drugs
Sugar
Coffee
Black tea

COOKING

FUEL

Yang   Yin

Wood   Coal   Gas   Electric
Charcoal   Microwave

METHOD

Grill	Bake	Pressure	Steaming	Pickling
Deep fry		cooking	Boiling	Pressed
		Stir fry		salad
				Raw

TASTE

Salty	Bitter	Hot	Sour	Sweet

A balanced diet consists of combining proper proportions of foods with proper cooking and seasoning methods to create balance in our bodies, according to the season, our health, activity, and mental state. More detailed information on Yin and Yang can be found in The Book of Macrobiotics The Universal Way of Health, Happiness and Peace, by Michio Kushi, available through Japan Publications, Inc., Kodansha, International USA, Ltd., through Harper and Rowe Publishers, Inc., 10 East 53rd St.,New York, NY 10022.

FOOD AND MOOD

****

"The food that enters the mind must be watched as closely as the food that enters the body."

Patrick J. Buchanon,
Right From the Beginning (Little, Brown)
****

As the food we eat affects us physically, it also seems reasonable that it would affect our moods. Once again it all comes back to balance, yin and yang, and learning to listen to the body. When we understand this we can make the necessary changes in our diets to bring our status back to the center of the seesaw, as our body is constantly working to keep all systems balanced. A steady diet of extreme foods will lead to mood swings. Eating foods from the center creates balance, renews energy, relieves stress and creates less dramatic moods. Sugar, caffeine, tropical fruits and alcohol can

13

create cravings for meat, eggs, cheese and salt. We usually over-compensate and then the strong cravings for sweets and alcohol return again. So up and down you go on the food seesaw, causing your body to work very hard to keep everything in balance. By eating more whole grains and vegetables you can break this up and down cycle, smooth out your moods and create an evenly balanced disposition which will allow you to accomplish your goals and enjoy life to the fullest.

The yin foods are expansive and fuel for our mental, psychological and spiritual activities and create relaxation and looseness. Eating too many yin foods can at first make you feel energized and elated, but then comes the crash and you may feel spacey, confused, depressed, helpless or hysterical. The ultimate yin experience is a drug addict. The yang foods are contractive and fuel for our physical activity, focused work, purposefulness and tension. Excessive consumption of yang foods such as meat, eggs, salt and strong hard cheeses will at first make you feel aggressive and competitive, but eventually a steady diet of those foods will create impatience, stubbornness, frustration, irritation, and you may become resentful, insensitive, compulsive, angry and even violent. Can you begin to understand why some children are hyperactive, and why some people become difficult to deal with in life?

CHAPTER III

THE MACROBIOTIC DIET

****

"The external harmony and progress of the entire human race is founded on the internal harmony and progress of every individual."

Maharishi Mahesh Yogi

****

A macrobiotic diet is a way of eating that eliminates the health hindering foods discussed previously and emphasizes the diet based on the whole grain, vegetables and supplementary foods eaten in proper proportions. It does not count calories. It does emphasize organic, locally grown and seasonal foods as much as possible. It also emphasizes various cooking methods to prepare the foods for our own personal needs according to the season and our health. Whole grains are emphasized and should constitute approximately 50% of the diet. Vegetables, including sea vegetables, comprise 25% of the diet, while beans and various bean products comprise 10% and soups comprise 5%. In addition to these basics, the balance of 10% is comprised of a supplemental group composed of seeds, nuts, fish, seafood, and fruit. This supplemental group also includes seasonings, shoyu sauce, tamari sauce, miso, umeboshi plums, natural sweeteners such as rice syrup and barley malt and various other condiments and beverages.

The Proportion Pie

Turning these percentages into daily meals will give you a well balanced diet that can be transitional or totally macrobiotic. The choice is yours on how carefully you cut the pie.

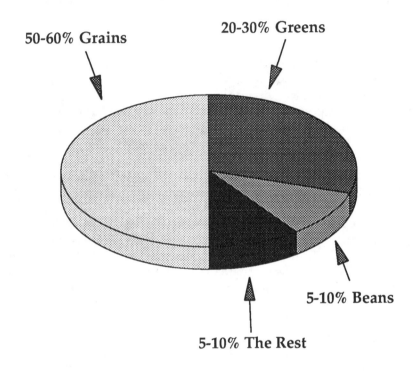

50-60% Grains

20-30% Greens

5-10% Beans

5-10% The Rest

Diagram from <u>You Are What You Ate</u>, Sherry A. Rogers, M.D., Prestige Publishing, Syracuse, NY (1987).

These proportions can be worked into a varied and delicious diet which will help to keep you centered on the seesaw of foods. Proper choice of food and a wide variety of foods are very important to keep your body in balance and to be sure that you receive all the nutrition you need. The contractive and expansive energy of the foods can be changed by the cooking methods which are used. Fire and water are the catalysts used in cooking. Fire has a contracting effect, water has an expanding effect. A good macrobiotic cook can use these catalysts to balance the opposite energies and produce a healthful diet. A thoughtful cook can even modify the temperament and moods of the rest of the household through the choice of foods and balance. Roasting and grilling over an open fire are the most extreme forms of contraction and if we go too far the food will turn to ashes. Food soaked in water is the most expansive and if left soaking too long will eventually decompose. Cooking methods which combine these energies such as boiling, steaming and pressure cooking are the most commonly used on a daily basis. A small pinch of salt or salty seasoning such as shoyu sauce, tamari, miso or umeboshi plum are usually added during cooking to cause some slight contraction to offset the effects of the watery or expansive energy. Drying and pickling foods increases the contractive energy of the foods. Oil creates an expansive energy and is used in only very small amounts to conduct heat and to release the energy in the food. We can summarize the effects of factors used in cooking and natural food processing as follows:

Contractive Yang Energy:
It is accelerated by high temperature, "more fire", less water, greater use of pressure, longer cooking time, aging, less oil or no oil, drying, and less bacterial or yeast activity.

Expansive Yin Energy:
It is accelerated by lower temperature, "less fire", more water, less salt, less use of pressure, shorter cooking time, freshness, more use of oil, soaking, greater bacterial or yeast activity, or fermentation.

The diet sometimes needs to be altered for certain situations. On the contracted or compact ends of the human growth scale, elderly people, babies and young children need balancing yin, hence they require less grain and need softer foods and more sweet tasting vegetables with a minimum amount of seasonings. Teens and adults can tolerate more seasoning and more crisp and solid foods. Persons who are grain sensitive will need to eat a larger proportion of vegetables and rely on non-grains such as quinoa, buckwheat, teff, amaranth and wild rice to start with. If you have problems read the chapter "What If I'm Too Allergic?" in The Cure Is In the Kitchen, S.A. Rogers, M.D., Prestige Publishing, Syracuse, N.Y. 1991.

In planning your daily menu, keep these points in mind:

1. Proportions - Aim for 50% grain, 25% vegetables, 5% soup, 10% beans, and 10% in the form of extras. This does not have to be at each meal but should be accomplished at least throughout the day.

2. Variety - Aim for a variety of grains and vegetables. Try to have some type of root vegetable, fresh leafy green vegetable and a small amount of sea vegetable in some form, daily. Two servings of each are even better.

3. Seasonings - sesame salt ("gomashio"), can be used daily as well as sea vegetable condiments. Sea salt is used for cooking. When you can tolerate fermented seasonings such as tamari sauce, shoyu, miso, rice vinegar and umeboshi vinegar, they will add much flavor to your foods. Umeboshi plums are a standard seasoning and excellent to alkalinize your system. Fresh ginger is an unlimited use seasoning which is especially warming in the winter season. It is also suggested that everyone have a small amount of natural pickles daily.

4. Season - Aim for locally grown seasonal foods. Hot weather emphasizes more fresh, lightly steamed or boiled vegetables, raw salads, less cooking time, less salt and oil. Colder weather emphasizes hardy, rich dishes, stews and thick soups, more protein such as beans, and more oil and salt.

5. Time of Day - Beans, hardy vegetables and stronger seasonings are preferred for your main dinner meal. A simple breakfast and lunch are recommended to keep you from feeling heavy and sluggish throughout the day.

6. Personal needs - Those doing heavy physical labor or strenuous exercise require more protein and hardier, richer dishes than someone who has a sedentary lifestyle.

7. Leftovers - Let's start calling them planned-overs. Extra grain

can be re-heated, added to soups, stirfried, made into grain
burgers, put in a casserole, made into a loaf, added to salad
and used as a filling for stuffed squash, tortillas or burritos
(macrobiotic style, of course!). Extra beans can be re-heated,
made into soup, mashed for a bean spread, added to a
vegetable stew, made into a salad, refried with onions and
used to fill tortillas or burritos. The possibilities are only as
endless as your imagination.

TOOLS

****
"My iron pots and pans like cathedral
bells chime."
W. Manderfield, Driftings
****

Most kitchens are already equipped with standard utensils
which will get you started. Stainless steel is highly preferred over
aluminum or non-stick coated pots and pans. It lasts a lifetime and is
an excellent investment and does not put aluminum and teflon into
your system. Corning Ware and Pyrex glass are also recommended.
An old fashioned cast iron skillet is an excellent addition to your
kitchen. It is indestructible if treated right and is superior for frying.
Cast iron also adds needed iron to your diet every time you use it.
One tool which you will want to add to your kitchen is a pressure
cooker. The Aeternum brand is made of stainless steel. It is
extremely safe as the lid fits inside the pot and is virtually accident-
free when used correctly.
You also need a stainless steel steamer basket (bain-marie).
This is usually a folding basket, widely available, which adjusts to
different pan sizes. It is inexpensive and very useful for cooking
fresh vegetables and reheating food.
Mesh strainers are needed in several sizes for everything
from draining washed grains and beans to cooked greens, and a small
size for a tea strainer.
A good vegetable knife is essential for cutting and preparing
all these wonderful vegetables. Wooden spoons for cooking are light,
easy to use and do not scratch your pots or pans. A good natural
fiber vegetable brush is necessary as organic vegetables are usually

19

scrubbed well and not peeled before cooking. A vegetable grater is essential for grating daikon, ginger and other vegetables. Invest in natural fiber mats of bamboo to cover foods while they are cooling and to use when making nori rolls.

You also need a method of grinding seeds and nuts and for making sauces. An electric blender, food processor, a mortar and pestle or a Japanese suribachi (that's a bowl) and surikogi (the pestle), will all do the job. A flame tamer (heat deflector) is used to prevent foods from burning, especially grains.

The last items on the list are glass containers for storing grains, beans, nuts and seeds. It is important to keep these supplies dry and cool. Refrigerated would be preferred if possible. You can use canning jars or purchase jars with rubber gaskets and snap top locks as these are available at discount stores. Okay, we have the tools. Let's start cooking!

GETTING ACQUAINTED WITH SOME NEW FOODS

****

"All tastes are acquired tastes. We are born with a taste for nothing except human milk."

Ewell Gibbons

****

Aduki - A small red bean, also adzuki.

Agar-agar - Sea vegetable, "macrobiotic jello".

Amazake - A liquid made from fermented sweet rice, used as a sweet beverage, sweetener or for dessert; available commercially or can be made at home.

Arame - A sea vegetable.

Arrowroot - Finely ground flour used as a thickener, similar to corn starch.

Bancha - A tea beverage, which aids digestion and good for daily use. Available as green leaves or brown twigs.

Barley malt - A grain sweetener, thick, dark-colored fermented liquid.

Burdock - A long, thick, dark-skinned, white root from the good old burdock weed, used as a cooked vegetable.

Couscous - Partially refined, cracked wheat, cooks quickly, good for summer cooking and grain desserts.

20

Daikon -The radish family; a long, thick, very large, white root, very sweet when cooked; grated raw it is pungent and a digestive aid to accompany oily or greasy foods or animal food.

Ginger - Flesh colored knobby root, hot pungent flavor, adds zesty flavor to cooking.

Gomashio - Sesame salt condiment, easy to make.

Grain coffee - Coffee substitute made from roasted grains, usually a combination of at least five different grains.

Hijiki - Sea vegetable.

Kanten - Like agar-agar but in a solid block form instead of flakes, another form of gelatin, a sea vegetable.

Kasha - Roasted buckwheat groats.

Kombu - Sea vegetable.

Kukicha - A non-caffeinated, light and satisfying, roasted twig tea.

Kuzu - A starch made from the root of the kuzu plant, is an excellent thickener for gravies, sauces and desserts. Also called kudzu.

Lotus root - Root of the water lily family, used fresh, dried and seed forms.

Mirin - A sweet rice cooking wine.

Miso- Salty paste made from fermented soybeans or rice, with or without other grains, flavors soup and many other dishes, excellent food for restoring beneficial flora to the intestinal system.

Mochi - Pounded sweet rice, made into cakes and eaten fresh or dried for later use, available commercially, very chewy and sweet tasting.

Mugicha - Tea made from roasted barley.

Nishime - Method of cooking vegetables with minimum amounts of water.

Nori - Sea vegetable, is pounded into sheets, essential for nori rolls, sushi.

Rice syrup - A natural grain honey derived from rice.

Rice vinegar - Mild smooth vinegar made from rice.

Sea palm - Mild sea vegetable from the Pacific Ocean.

Seitan - Wheat gluten, boiled with flavorings, a meat substitute.

Sesame salt (gomachio) - Combination of roasted sesame seeds and sea salt, ground together, used daily for seasonings and protein, calcium and vitamin E.

Shiitake - A mushroom variety available fresh and dried. Used for soup stock and vegetable dishes.

Soba - Japanese buckwheat noodle.

Somen - Japanese wheat noodle, very thin.

Shoyu - Another name for high quality soy sauce; naturally fermented from soybeans and wheat. Not to be confused with poorer quality soy sauces with added alcohol, colorings or corn syrup.

Tahini - A butter made from ground sesame seeds.

Tamari - Naturally made soy sauce made from fermented soy beans, traditionally wheat-free. Some varieties contain mirin, an alcohol. Read ingredients.

Tekka - Condiment made from burdock, carrot, lotus root, ginger, miso, sesame, roasted until it turns a dark brown to black, available from macrobiotic food suppliers, sprinkled over grains or vegetables for flavor.

Tempeh - Cakes of fermented soybeans, must be well cooked, excellent source of vegetable protein, food meat substitute in soups, stews and many other dishes.

Tofu - White cake made from soybeans and water, also called bean curd, available fresh or dried, good vegetable protein, can be used fresh as a dairy substitute, can be cooked by many different methods, takes on the flavor of the food it is cooked with; very versatile.

Udon - Japanese wheat noodle.

Umeboshi - Salty pickled plum (actually an apricot) very alkalizing, aids digestion, can be obtained in whole form, paste or as a vinegar.

Wakame - Sea vegetable.

Yannoh - Grain coffee.

CHAPTER IV

A SHORT COURSE ON WHOLE FOOD

"A healthy body is a guest-chamber for the soul; a sick body is a prison."

Bacon, The Advancement of Learning

GRAINS

Grains are the basis of the diet, 30-60% of each meal. General instructions: all grains should be kept in airtight containers and stored in a cool, dry place. Grains should be checked for foreign material such as stones and chunks of dirt and then washed well in several changes of water before cooking. For best flavor, grains should be cooked in pure spring water. A pinch of sea salt for each cup of grain is a general rule of thumb. The most common method of cooking grains is boiling on top of the stove. Pressure cooking is recommended in macrobiotic cooking to increase the energy of the food. Grains can also be baked in a covered casserole. For most recipes the water and salt are brought to a boiling point and then the washed grain is added. When the water returns to a boil, the heat is reduced to low, the pot is covered tightly and it is cooked for the recommended amount of time. (See Chart) To prevent burning, a flame tamer is used. Grains are usually prepared with proportions of one part grain to two parts of water, but more or less water can be used to obtain the texture you desire. Feel free to experiment. Each cup of raw grain makes about 3 cups of cooked grain. For a variety of flavors, grain can also be dry roasted for 10 to 15 minutes in a dry frying pan until it releases a nutty fragrance. At this point add hot water and continue cooking as usual. Grains that are soaked before cooking are sweeter, cook faster and are more digestable.

Soak rice from 1-8 hours.
Soak whole oats, wheat, spelt, rye and barley for 4-8 hours.
Millet, buckwheat, quinoa, teff, and amaranth do not require soaking as they have a thinner shell and cook quickly.

Unsoaked grains are more chewy and separate. Soaked grains are more sticky, especially if pressure-cooked.

      i.e.   Soaked and pressure cooked rice
             is best for nori rolls and rice balls.

Salt is used in cooking grains to help break down the grain and makes it sweeter tasting. Salt is alkaline-forming and balances the acid-forming grains. Salt should be added after soaking, and preferably after grain has come to a boil.

To cook a soaked grain, bring to a boil over medium heat to full pressure or to a boil. Reduce heat to low and cook for recommended time. For long cooking times use a flame tamer under pot to prevent burning. Do not uncover pot while cooking. When cooking time is up, stir grain from top to bottom to fluff up. Cover again and let rest for 5-10 minutes before serving.

GRAIN COOKING CHART

Grain	Soaking Time	Cooking Time
Brown rice	1-8 hrs,	50 minutes optional
Wild rice		45 minutes
Barley	4-8 hrs	1 - 1 1/2 hrs
Millet	Do not soak	30 mins
Whole oats	4-8 hrs	Several hrs or overnight on very low heat
Steel cut		30 mins oats
Rolled oats		10-20 mins
Wheat berries	Minimum 3 hrs	60 mins
Bulgar		15-20 mins

Couscous		1-10 mins
Spelt	1-8 hrs	1 hr
Rye Berries	1-8 hrs	1 hr
Buckwheat (Kasha)		30 mins
Amaranth		30 mins
Quinoa		30 mins
Teff		20-30 mins

Brown Rice

Brown rice comes in several forms, short grain, medium grain, long grain, sweet and basmati, and special flavored rices. Short grain brown rice is the standard type for daily use in the temperate climate. It contains the most minerals and gluten. Medium grain rice is slightly larger and also is fine for regular use. Long grain rice is best for warmer climates but can be used occasionally during the warm weather, for fluffy salads and for desserts such as rice pudding. Sweet rice is very sweet, glutenous, and high in protein. It is usually reserved for making mochi and for special occasion uses, but it can be mixed with short grain rice, half and half, for variety. Sweet rice is also fermented to make amasake beverage. Basmati is very flavorful and aromatic rice for occasional use.

Barley

Look for whole hulled barley or pearl barley, but not pearled barley which is a milled and refined product. It tastes somewhat bland and can be added to soups, stews, casseroles, combined with other grains or used as a stuffing for squash or cabbage rolls. It has a light cooling effect and is excellent for warm weather use. Hato barley is a form of wild barley which is excellent for regular use. It has a different flavor and texture and is very flavorful when mixed with other grains or cooked by itself.

Millet

Millet is a small round golden grain, fluffy when cooked, warming to the body, somewhat dry when cooked. Usually served with a sauce or gravy or cooked with a moist vegetable such as squash or cauliflower. Cooked millet can also be formed into loaves and patties which hold their shape for re-heating. Millet is the most alkalizing grain.

Oats

Oats are excellent as a breakfast cereal, as they cook up soft and creamy, contain more fat than other grains and produce a warming effect. Oat flour is excellent for baing cookies and desserts, as is oatmeal. Please avoid instant oatmeals, which are processed.

Rye

Rye is not usually used as a cooked grain but it is very tasty. Rye flour is used for breads and crackers.

* Many people are sensitive to the following grains and may need to avoid them for a period of time:

* WHEAT - Whole grain wheat is very hard and must be soaked before cooking. It is called wheat berries in this form.

*BULGAR - Whole wheat that has been partially boiled, dried and ground. Makes good pilafs and salads.

*COUSCOUS - Made from wheat that has been refined and cracked, but not bleached. It is used for summer salads or desserts.

*SPELT - is also a wheat derivative.

26

*WHEAT FLOUR - Whole wheat flour used to make breads, crackers, baked goods, pasta and noodles. As it is not a whole grain, it should be used in moderation. Flour comes in several different varieties. A whole wheat bread flour and a whole wheat pastry flour are the ones you will use the most.

*CORN - Corn comes in many varieties and is a native American staple. Sweet corn on or off the cob is a summer favorite, stone ground corn meal and corn flour are used in tortillas, corn breads and muffins. Corn meal can also be used as a cereal or to make polenta. Popcorn is a great macrobiotic snack -no salt or butter, please.

NON-GRAIN "GRAINS"

The following are the non-grain grains because wheat, a member of the grass family of grains, is the backbone of the American diet, many people have developed an allergy to it, once sensitive, they often also react to other members of the grass family, like rice, rye and corn. But there are other grains that are not "true grains" in that they are not in the grass family. These products are not (botanically speaking) true grains or members of the grass family, and so are often tolerated by grain or grass family-sensitive people. You could easily rotate these if you are extremely grain sensitive.

Amaranth
Amaranth was a sustaining food of the Aztec Indians. It has been transplanted to the United States and is grown here now. It grows like a grain and it looks like a grain and is utilized like a grain, but it is not a true grain. In the biological classification of foods, it is the amaranth family alone.

It also is sometimes known as vegetable amaranth and the young leaves are harvested and cooked much as we prepare spinach; The seeds can be combined and cooked as a regular grain with one part of grain and two parts of water to make a cereal. The flavor is somewhat strong. It can be ground into a flour which can be used as a substitute for wheat flour by about 25%. Amaranth is very high in fiber and protein and it contains amino acids that the true grains are low in, such as lysine, methionine and cysteine, and yields a high

27

quality usable protein. It has a high content of minerals and trace minerals.

Buckwheat
It is the hardiest of the non-grains, grows in cold climates, also known as kasha. It can be obtained whole, in coarse or fine granules, roasted or unroasted. It is very warming, energizing and strengthening to the body and is excellent for use in the winter. It can be used as a main dish, loose or in croquettes, as salad or cereal, as noodles ("soba"), and as a flour for pancakes, cookies and more.

Quinoa
Pronounced "keen/wa". Is a South American grain used by the Indians. It cooks quickly and has an interesting nutty taste, is high in fiber, up to 20% protein, and is light and delicious. It must be washed well before cooking. It is excellent for a variety of uses and you will find many recipes in the book which use this grain.

Teff
This originated in Ethiopia. It is a very tiny seed, high in minerals and protein and is nutritionally superior to wheat. It can be used as a cereal grain or ground into a flour for flat bread or used in quick breads, muffins, cookies. It is now grown in the United States and is becoming widely available. Teff has an interesting flavor and texture when cooked.

Wild Rice
Not a true grain, is expensive but adds delicious flavor and wide variety to your menus. It can be mixed half and half with regular rice for delicious pilaf.

Broken Grain Products
Limit use to two to three times per week. Whole grains are preferred. Breads, unyeasted, sourdough, yeast free rice bread, tortillas, essene (a sprouted wheat or rye, pounded and baked), noodles, (whole wheat, udon and somen) puffed grains (dry cereals and rice cakes) and grits (usually corn). Seitan (wheat "meat"), is the gluten of whole wheat flour which is washed out and cooked in a flavored sauce and can be used as a meat substitute in prepared dishes. Fu is puffed dried seitan. Flakes of rye, wheat, rolled oats and rolled barley are all available for use as cereals.

<u>Flour Products</u>
    Crackers, cookies, pie crusts, pancakes, baked desserts, breads and pasta from many of these grains, especially wheat, barley, brown rice and oats.

LAND AND SEA VEGETABLES

****
"Variety is the very spice of life that gives it all its flavor."
Cowper, The Task
****

    Vegetables compose 25-30% of your diet. Use a wide variety of leafy, round and root vegetables. Carrot, onion, parsnips, turnips, and squashes are the sweet root vegetables, seasonal and locally grown are the best choices.

Regular Use Vegetables

Leafy	Round	Root
Bok choy	Broccoli	Burdock
Carrot tops	Brussel	Carrot
Chinese	sprouts	Celery root
cabbage	Green	**Daikon
Chives	cabbage	radish,
Collard	Cauliflower	fresh or
greens	Kohlrabi	dried
Daikon tops	Onion	**Lotus root
Dandelion	Pumpkin	fresh or
greens	Squashes	dried
Endive	acorn	Dandelion
Escarole	butternut	root
Kale	buttercup	Leeks
Mustard	Delicato	Radish
greens		red & white
Rappi		Rutabaga
Parsley		Scallions
Radish tops		Shallots
Romaine lettuce		Turnip

29

*   Available at oriental groceries.

**   In dried form, available by mail from NEEDS, Goldmine Natural Foods and Trader's Ark catalogues and other macrobiotic food suppliers (see resources).

Additional Vegetables
(More fragile, expansive, used less frequently)

Leafy	Round	Root
Lambs quarters	Celery	Jerusalem
Leaf lettuce	Cucumber	Artichoke
Head lettuce	Beans	Beets
Sprouts	green	Salsify
Swiss chard	yellow wax	
	Cabbage	
	purple	
	Green peas	
	Mushrooms	
	Red onion	
	Snow peas	
	Summer squash	
	yellow, patty	
	pan, spaghetti	
	Zucchini	

Special Occasion

Leafy	Round	Root
Beet greens	Artichoke	Sweet
Spinach	Eggplant	potato
New Zealand	Fennel	White
spinach	Okra	potato
	Peppers	Yam
	yellow, red	
	& green	
	Tomato	

Cooking Methods For Vegetables

boil	steam	oil saute
water saute	stir fry	blanched
waterless	stew	pressed
(nishime)	bake	salads
roast	broil	raw salads
		pickled

Note: In the recipe section you will find many recipes using all of these different methods.

Sea Vegetables

All sea vegetables contain large amounts of minerals, which include trace minerals needed for our health. Aim for a minimum of 1-2 tablespoons, daily, in your meals. They are easy to slip into soups, cooked beans and vegetables, salads, desserts, the old favorite nori rolls and rice balls, and in many other ways, such as condiments. You will find them in many of the recipes. Lets get to know them better.

Agar-Agar
"The macrobiotic jello", made from a sea vegetable, comes in a flaked form. Dissolves easily in a hot liquid and adds no flavor of its own to the prepared dish, has a cooling effect on the body and lubricates the digestive tract.

Arame
Excellent cooked with root vegetables, or used in a boiled salad. Is especially good for the spleen, pancreas, and stomach.

Dulse
Can be eaten raw or cooked. Excellent in salads and sandwiches, high in iron and supportive to the spleen.

Hijiki
The strong one. Expands to four times its original size when soaked in water. Requires longer soaking and cooking than

31

most other sea vegetables. The stronger taste is mellowed by long cooking. It is strengthening to the intestines, assists in absorption and assimilation of food.

Kanten

Another style of agar-agar. Comes in bars which are dissolved in hot liquid.

Kombu

Used to make soup stock and cooked with beans to aid digestion. Supportive to the kidney and adrenal functions. High in sodium alginate, a radiation protective factor.

Nori

The most familiar. Used to make nori rolls, sushi, and rice balls. Can be made into a condiment and eaten plain. Best if toasted briefly before using.

Sea Palm

Mild taste and texture. Excellent in salads, can be made into a condiment. Supportive to the spleen, pancreas and stomach.

Wakame

Very mild flavor. Cooks quickly. Can be crumbled into soup, used in salads and vegetable dishes. Supportive to the liver and nervous system.

Now that you know about them they don't sound nearly as frightening, do they? They will soon become good friends.

PROTEIN SOURCES

****

"We are indeed much more than what we eat, but what we eat can nevertheless help us to be much more than what we are."

Adelle Davis

****

Beans, tofu and other soy foods, grain products, seeds, nuts, fish, seafood, animal food. This group is 5-10% of the diet.

Beans

Regular Use	Occasional Use
Aduki	Anasazi
Garbanzo	Black eyed peas
(chick peas)	Black turtle
Lentils	Great northern
green	Pinto
Black soybeans	Mung
	Navy
	Red lentil
	Soybeans
	Split peas
	green,
	yellow

Occasional Bean Substitutes
Tofu
Tempeh (fermented soyfood)
Soy milk
Grain products (high protein)
Seitan (wheat meat)
Fu (dried seitan)

Nuts	and	Seeds
*Almonds		*Sesame seed
Chestnut		Sunflower seed
** Peanuts		Pumpkin seed
Pine nuts		Squash seed
Pecans		Lotus seed
Walnuts		Flax seed
(nut milk)		(seed milk)

Avoid all tropical nuts such as Brazil, cashew, coconut, macadamia, and pistachios.

* Tahini - sesame butter
* Almond butter
** Peanut butter

* All starred items are to be used very sparingly as they are high in fat.

** Peanuts are questionable because they usually contain mycotoxins. Also it is very easy to eat too much of any high fat food, especially peanut butter.

Animal foods and their products:
Avoid in general all mammal meat
  (i.e. beef, lamb, veal, rabbit, etc)
Red meat
Chicken
Turkey
All fowl
Dark oily fish
Eggs
All dairy products
  (milk, cheese, yogurt, ice cream, etc.)
Wild game

Fish: Occasional Use
Cod
Flounder
Halibut
Trout
Red snapper
Sole
Scrod
White meat fish
Dried bonita flakes
    (seasoning broths or use in soups, sauces, etc)

Seafood: Occasional Use
Clams
Lobster
Oysters
Scallops
Shrimp

If you decide you need some animal protein it is best to use organically grown free range poultry, rabbit or wild game.

THE WONDERFUL SUPPORTING CAST

****
"Supermarkets are all right but it's much more fun to shop for food in nature."

Ewell Gibbons
****

FRUITS

Usually prepared cooked from dried or fresh fruit. Fresh fruits may be used in season.

Occasional Use:
Apples
Apricots
Berries - blackberry, blueberry, elderberry, raspberry, strawberry
Cantaloupe

35

Cherries
Currants
Grapes - raisins
Peaches
Pears
Plums
Watermelon

Avoid or very limited use if you live in Northern temperate climate:
All tropical fruits - bananas, coconut, dates, figs, grapefruit, oranges,
pineapple, kiwi, mango, papaya. A small amount of lemon and lime
juice may be used for cooking.

OILS, SEASONINGS, CONDIMENTS AND COOKING INGREDIENTS

****

"Condiments are like old friends -highly thought of, but often taken
for granted."
            Marily Keaton, Food Editor, Look, Jan. 29, 1963.
****

OILS

Flaxseed oil (refrigerated, do not heat or use for cooking, great for
            salads.)
Unrefined sesame oil (use minimal heat)
Virgin olive oil (cooking and salad dressings)
Unpressed corn oil (baking)
Cold pressed (Hains), preferably organic:
            Walnut
            Almond
            Sesame
            Safflower
            Sunflower
            Soy
            Canola

SEASONINGS

Unrefined Sea Salt

Natural miso (many varieties)
1. White or mellow style chick pea for beginners and in warm weather (less fermented).
2. Darker variety (barley, chick pea, hato, red; more flavor, fermented for longer period).

Wheat-free Tamari (check label to be sure is also alcohol-free)

Shoyu Sauce (check label to be sure is alcohol-free)

Umeboshi plums and paste

Umeboshi vinegar

Brown rice vinegar

Mirin - a sweetened rice wine

Fresh ginger root, grated and squeezed, keep frozen for easy grating. Use juice for most purposes.

Horseradish - Wasabi is a very hot ground horseradish powder mixed with water and used sparingly.

Culinary herbs (use sparingly)
Basil, bay leaf, caraway seed, celery seed, coriander, dill, mint, lovage, oregano, poppy seed, sage, summer savory, rosemary, tarragon, thyme, turmeric

<u>Special Occasion Seasonings:</u>

Anise	Cayenne pepper	Pure vanilla
Cinnamon	Carob	extract
Cumin	Black pepper	Pure almond
Nutmeg	White pepper	extract
Paprika	Mustard	

<u>Thickeners:</u>
Kuzu (strengthening effect)
Agar-Agar (relaxing effect)
Arrowroot

SWEETENERS

Amasake
Rice syrup
   (yinnie)
Barley malt syrup
Pure maple syrup

Fruit juice
Cooked fruit
Dried fruit

CONDIMENTS

Recipes in recipe section:

Sesame salt (Gomashio)
Sea Vegetable powder (roasted)
Sea vegetable powder with sesame seeds
Tekka

PICKLES

Use small amount of pickled products daily to aid digestion, assimilation and develop good intestinal flora. 1 tsp to 1/2 cup daily.

Regular Use:
      Salt brine pickles
      Bran pickles
      Miso pickles
      Sauerkraut
      Tamari pickles
      Olives

Avoid:
      Commercial dill and garlic dill
      Special pickles-
         Apple cider pickles
         Wine vinegar pickles

BEVERAGES
****

"Water is the only drink for a wise man."
Thoreau, Walden
****

Pure spring water
Pure well water
Bancha tea
Kukicha - twig tea
Roasted barley tea (Mugicha)
Grain coffee
Dandelion root tea
Kombu tea
Mu tea
Safflower tea

Special Occasion Beverages:
Vegetable juices of allowed vegetables
    (freshly prepared)
Mineral water
Beer
Sake (rice wine)
Local organic wine

THE ART OF SUBSTITUTION OR LEARNING NEW WAYS OF COOKING FOR FUN, FLAVOR, ALLERGIES AND HEALTH

****

"The discovery of a new dish does more for human happiness than the discovery of a new star."

Brillat - Savarin

****

*See recipes

Replace	Substitute
Dairy	Soy milk *Almond milk *Sesame milk *Sunflower milk *Grain milk
Sour Cream	*Tofu sour cream
Whipped cream	*Sweet dessert topping
Ricotta cheese	*Tofu "Ricotta" cheese
Cheese sauce	*Macaroni & cheese *Comfort Casserole *Pasta Primavera
Butter	Unrefined vegetable oil, flax, corn and sesame
Yogurt	*Soy yogurt
Cheese	*Tofu cheese

Beef stock	*Rich vegetable stock seasoned to taste with dark miso or shoyu/tamari sauce
Chicken stock	*Light vegetable (including sea vegetables) stock seasoned with mellow miso or chickpea miso
Cornstarch	Kuzu 1 1/2 tbl to 1 cp liquid for gravies 2 tbl to 1 cup liquid for jelling
	Arrowroot 1 tbl per cp water for medium thick sauce, prolonged cooking will thin sauce
Baking Powder	Rumford (aluminum free) *Corn free baking powder
Egg (For baking purposes)	3 tbl stewed and pureed dried apricot in blender
1 egg	1 x 1 x 2 square of tofu blended with water to egg consistency (good binder for cookies, grain burgers, and no-meat loaves)
	*Flaxseed
	1 tbl Lecithin granules dissolved in 2 tbl liquid

Sweeteners:
Cane sugar
Brown sugar
Corn Syrup
Molasses

Rice syrup (yinnie)
Barley malt syrup
(good substitute for
molasses)
Maple syrup
Maple syrup granules
(dehydrated maple syrup)
Dried Fruits
(raisins, currants

apricots, apples,
dates)
Fruit juices and
concentrate (apple,
apricot, pear,
grape, apple cider)
Fresh fruits
Honey

Vinegar (cider,
grain, or wine)

Brown rice vinegar
Umeboshi vinegar

Lemon or lime juice,
freshly squeezed
Vitamin C crystals
1 tsp to 1/4 cp water

Wheat Flour Substitutes for the Wheat Sensitive
Each substitute equals 1 cup wheat flour

Amaranth flour
> High in nutrients and protein 3/4 cp with 1/4 cp brown rice, oat, soy or arrowroot for baking. 7/8 cp amaranth flour = 1 cp wheat flour but makes a very heavy finished product.

Arrowroot
> 3/4 cp or 1/2 cp & 1/2 cp of another flour or nut meal, great thickening agent.

Barley flour
1 1/4 cp - very good in pancakes and baked goods but closely related to wheat. Contains gluten.

Brown rice flour
7/8 cp - or 1/2 brown rice flour and 1/2 oat flour in cookies piecrust. Contains no gluten.

Buckwheat flour
3/4 cup. Good in pancakes, baked goods and breading.

Chickpea flour
3/4 cp. Good in flat bread, cookies and as thickening agent.

Oat flour
1 cp - good in cookies, pancakes muffins, breading and thickening agent, can be ground in home blender from oatmeal.

Soy flour
1 1/3 cp. Very heavy if used alone, can be combined with another flour (25% soy and 75% alternate flour) to increase lightness and protein in pancakes and baked goods.

Nuts and Seeds
1/2 cp & 1/2 cp another flour or starch. Grind seeds or nuts in blender. Good in crackers & piecrusts. Combine with other flours for baked goods.

Remember you can freshly grind your own flours in a blender or processor from the whole grain.

CHAPTER V

MENU PLANNING

****

"Thou should eat to live; not live to eat."

Cicero

****

Try to plan a week at a time to be sure you are meeting seasonal needs and to cook in quantity when appropriate. By planning ahead you will know when you need to soak beans or prepare a pot of soup. Pre-planning also helps with planned-overs and shopping, since you can check to see that you have needed supplies and purchase only what you need for the week, thereby eliminating waste. Planning ahead saves time and money in the long run.

Proportions have been explained before, but just a quick review. Grains and vegetables are the basis of the diet and should constitute 3/4 of the meal. The rest of the meal would include a choice of beans, seeds, nuts, sea vegetables, condiments, fruits and beverages. You would not include every item in each meal.

It is usually easiest to select the grain or special grain vegetable dish that you are planning and work from there to select other foods which compliment the center of the meal. If you are serving a fish or seafood meal that would become the center of the meal that you would want to compliment.

Aim to keep the meal simple but tasty. Too many fancy combinations of foods are not pleasing to the taste or the digestive system. Try to limit fancy dishes to a maximum of two per meal.

Vary the textures of foods such as creamy, chewy, firm and crisp and try to furnish all five flavors in a meal. "Sour, bitter, sweet, sharp-pungent and salty." Aim for a variety of colors. A mono-colored meal is very boring. Think of green, yellow, orange vegetables; black, red, green or white beans; white, tan or brown grains; black sea vegetables; bright crisp vegetables; pickles and fruits of many colors.

Usually the daily meals of breakfast and lunch are quick and simple with a larger and more varied dinner. Some people prefer a two meal system with a brunch meal and a dinner. No matter what your meal schedule, there are certain daily minimum requirements

44

which you should try to follow. This is a list of daily basic needs which can be expanded according to your own needs.

One serving of clear simple miso soup
One serving of another bean or vegetable soup
Two to three servings of whole grain
One serving noodles, bread or another grain
Two servings of sea vegetables
One serving of oil
Two servings of leafy, green vegetables
One serving of a yellow vegetable
One to two servings of root vegetables
Zero to one serving beans or bean product such as tofu or tempeh
One to two servings of pickles
Two to three servings of tea or grain beverage, if desired.

Condiments such as sea salt, sesame salt, miso, shoyu, tamari sauce, umeboshi plums and vinegar, rice vinegar and other natural seasonings can be used daily, as well as grated or chopped carrot, daikon, parsley and scallions and also unlimited use of fresh grated ginger root.

Weekly, you could add two to three servings of nuts or seeds, one to two servings of fish or seafood, two to three servings of raw salad in the summer, one to two servings of blanched or pressed salad in the winter, three to four seasonal fruits, two to three servings of sugar-free grain sweetened desserts.

If your diet is in good balance you should rarely have cravings. Cravings are a sign that your body gives to alert you to change your diet, so listen closely and try to remember what you have been over-eating. Try to tune in to what you are really craving. Is it sweet, sour bitter, salty, crunchy, creamy, or is your diet too strict and boring? Learning new recipes is the cure for the latter. Often you crave what your body is trying to get rid of, or if you are under a lot of stress, anxiety or tension you maybe reaching for a sweet to calm yourself.

For special cravings:	Try to neutralize with:
Bitter	grain coffee burdock dandelion mustard greens chickory or endive
Salt	miso, shoyu, tamari, umeboshi
Sour	Often sour will take away sweet cravings lemon, sauerkraut, rice vinegar. A squeeze of lemon juice over your cooked vegetables for example.
Sweet	Baked winter squashes, well cooked onions, carrots or parsnips, onion butter, carrot butter, apple butter, mochi (pounded sweet rice squares), fruit desserts with rice syrup or barley malt sweetenings, amasake (rice milk). Also try above sour remedy.

Very specific cravings:
*SEE RECIPES

Bread	noodles, sourdough breads, *CORN BREAD MUFFINS
Cheese	*TOFU CHEESE, *TOFU SOUR CREAM, *SCRAMBLED TOFU, bean spreads and pate, *TOFU MACARONI AND CHEESE
Crunchy	popcorn, rice cakes, granola or dry brown rice cereals
Meat	tempeh, seitan, *LENTIL NUT LOAF, *MEATLESS TOFU BALLS

TAMING THE SWEET TOOTH

The sweet taste is a necessary part of any diet and is easy to obtain without resorting to highly processed sweeteners such as white sugar, brown sugar, corn syrup and artificial sweeteners. The macrobiotic diet furnishes the sweet taste by using, first of all the sweet vegetables such as hard winter squashes, pumpkin, carrots, onions and cabbage, in cooked dishes or as a butter type spread (*See recipes). Azuki beans, chestnuts, and sesame tahini also contribute to a sweet flavor.

People who have hypoglycemia or a raging sweet tooth need to start using squash soup daily.

Sweet Squash Soup

1/2 Cup cubed hard squash (butternut, buttercup, acorn, skin included if organic)
1/2 Cup diced onion
1/2 Cup diced daikon radish or green cabbage
1/2 Cup diced carrot
4 Cups spring water
Pinch sea salt or 3" piece of kombu sea vegetable

Bring to a boil, reduce heat, and simmer gently until vegetables are tender.

This can be eaten as a soup at any time of the day. In warm weather, pour off the juice and drink at room temperature and use the cooked vegetables as a side dish. Try some anytime the sweet tooth dragon strikes.

If these foods do not tame your sweet tooth, you can use small amounts of apple juice or sweet cider, applesauce or other cooked apple desserts such as a baked apple. Cooked breakfast cereals two or three times a week can have added a small amount of raisins and sunflower seeds or walnuts added for sweetness and texture or fresh, seasonal and locally grown fruit. Blueberries and other fruits can be made into wonderful pancake syrup (see recipe). If all these methods fail, you can still obtain and even sweeter flavor by using rice syrup, barley malt syrup or real maple syrup in small amounts.

People in excellent health could even use small amounts of honey or molasses.

47

MOST IMPORTANT, THE COOK

****
"Every day you do one of two things: build health or produce disease in yourself."

Adelle Davis
****

In this book, there are many recipes for you to try but every one of them lacks one ingredient: you and your skill. For without it, nothing will come out right. All of the finest organic food in the world is worth very little without the skill of the cook--you. You are a VIP, (very important person). Some people love to cook and some hate to cook. I hope you, at least, like to cook, or can learn to appreciate how mellow relaxing and therapeutic it can be for you. For you hold the health of your family and yourself in your hands.

Macrobiotic cooking is an art that you can easily learn. The first lesson is attitude toward cooking. A calm happy, mellow cook can create delicious healing foods. Foods cooked with love nourish the body and the soul. Planning your meals ahead for a few days, helps you avoid the stress of having nothing planned or prepared ahead. It avoids the struggle to come up with a meal when you are tired and too hungry to resist the temptation of fast food.

Soft music in the background or an open window with birds singing outside can be very calming as you are cooking. Even a quick walk to the garden for fresh vegetables or herbs can give you a great burst of enthusiasm for cooking.

A clean, neat orderly kitchen equipped with the proper pots, pans and utensils also helps to make cooking a pleasure. Arrange your work area so that the tools you use are close by. Have a special place for everything and always return it to that spot after use. In that way you will not waste time looking for a certain item that you need.

Learn the art of cutting and cooking vegetables in many different ways to give variety and color to your meals. You can become a kitchen magician in the use of planned-overs. Planned-over bean dishes make great soups and spreads with the addition of vegetables and vegetable stocks. Planned-over soups make wonderful aspics by adding agar-agar or kanten and jelling. Variety

48

is the key, almost any firm dish can be made into a soup and any soup dishes can be transformed into a jellied salad or a thick sauce. Start with a stock jar. Save all the cooking liquid from steamed and boiled vegetables as a basis for soups and sauces. The sweet veggies such as carrot, parsnips and squashes make especially good stock. When it is time to clean the refrigerator you can use up the leftover uncooked greens and root vegetables that are starting to fade, to create your own stock. In all types of fine cooking, a good stock is the secret to delicious recipes. See the recipes for light stock and rich stocks. Cooked grains can be turned into burgers, casseroles, and an endless number of other delicious things.

A well cooked meal, beautifully served, to the people you love in a happy, serene and thankful setting is gourmet cooking at its finest.

As you develop your cooking skills, don't be afraid to experiment with a recipe. Your tastes might be different and recipes can easily be altered to suit your family or yourself. Plan time for cooking and devote your energies to preparing health-giving foods. In this era we all work hard and tend to give cooking last priority. But it is here that real health begins. It is the most rewarding investment you could ever make in your own health and the health of your family.

HEALTHFUL COOKING FOR BUSY PEOPLE

We are all busy people but the same principle applies if you are cooking for one or more. The main principles are organization and pre-planning. If you follow these suggestions you can have a complete macrobiotic dinner on the table in less than one hour from the time you get home from work, complete from soup to nuts. It may take a few days to get into the routine but here is how it works.

It's morning, time to shower, dress, eat breakfast and head for work. While you are waiting for your breakfast to cook, measure out, wash and put your rice to soak in the pan that you will be cooking it in along with the water and salt. Place the pan on the burner you will use to cook it but don't turn it on. I am hoping that you prepared your lunch last evening as you cleaned up the kitchen after dinner. Grab your lunch and go to work. When you get home from work, say "hello" to the family and go straight to the kitchen. Turn on the burner under the rice. (Change your clothes and get

49

comfortable).

Back to the kitchen now. The rice should be at the boiling point. Cover tightly and reduce the heat. Set your timer for 50 minutes and begin the rest of the dinner. If somehow you forgot to prepare the rice, there is still time to do millet, buckwheat, quinoa or teff which only take about 30 minutes to cook. Prepare enough grain for dinner along with planned-overs for tomorrow's breakfast and lunch.

I bet there are no cooked beans on hand so you could have a tofu or a tempeh dish. Both of these are quick to prepare and full of good vegetable protein. Make a note to wash and put beans to soak with kombu when cleaning up the kitchen, or cook up some that don't need soaking, such as lentils or aduki beans. Most beans do require soaking so you have to plan two steps ahead to have them soaked and ready to cook when you are home to cook them. They could be soaking during the day and you could cook them in the evening during or after dinner for a supply for the next couple of days.

Vegetables are easy. Start any longer cooking root vegetables now. Make enough for tomorrow's packed lunch. Now wash and prepare your leafy greens that will be boiled, steamed or sauteed. Prepare enough for tomorrow's breakfast. Have empty containers ready. When veggies are done, steal a few of each and some cooking liquid from them. Cover and refrigerate. This is the base for tomorrow's breakfast miso soup. Pressed salads or quick pickles can be prepared on the weekend when you have extra time. They keep well for several days and will always be ready to round out a meal. Organic sauerkraut is a good pickle substitute of you don't have any pickles ready.

Weekends are a great time to prepare some sweet treats, such as oatmeal cookies or fruit kanten, applesauce or other healthful desserts.

Well, we almost have a complete dinner except for sea vegetables and condiments. Quickly toast a sheet of nori and crumble it over your serving of rice or vegetables. Make notes to prepare some sea vegetable condiments or plan to cook sea vegetables with root vegetables for dinner tomorrow evening.

Sit down and relax: chew everything very well and enjoy. Clean up the kitchen, pack the grain and root vegetables for lunch along with any special treats you might have stashed away. You should also have a bowl of grain and a container of leafy greens for breakfast plus the container for making miso soup.

It's morning again, wake up and breakfast is practically ready. Pour the soup broth into the pan and place over a low heat. In another pan, place the grain with a small amount of water to reheat over a low burner. Get out your bowl and spoon. Your soup should be almost hot now, add diluted miso and simmer a couple of minutes, then pour into a bowl and enjoy. Rinse out the bowl and add the hot grain, garnish with seaweed condiment and sesame salt and eat along with planned-over room temperature greens. Bring a cup of bancha tea for the ride to work.

Now stop to think - Do I need to put beans or grains on to soak for tonight? If so, do it now. Get dressed, grab the lunch you fixed last evening and head out to work with a full happy stomach.

Back home again. I'll bet you are getting into the routine. Put the long cooking items to on to cook, change your clothes and start on the rest of the dinner, planning enough for planned-overs for breakfast and lunch tomorrow. This is so easy you might even want to bake some apples for dessert tonight or do a special sea vegetable dish. Don't forget the pickles and condiments. maybe a pot of tea, and especially don't forget to get ready again for tomorrow.

This method works. I know, because I have been using it for two years and believe me, I'm a busy person.

Weekends are a great time to experiment with some special recipes to dazzle your friends and family and prepare pressed salads, soups, pickles and condiments and desserts which will keep for several days.

The first few weeks or months of macro cooking can be frustrating because three is so much to learn. But the commitment to better health for you and your family will make it all worthwhile, and soon you will find that this good food is adding quality hours to your day which is well worth the time spent in the kitchen.

Look in the recipe section for quick and easy recipes and for ways to add lots of variety to your menus, as you become more and more organized and into the two step, plan ahead thinking.

REMEMBER ROME WASN'T BUILT IN A DAY

OOPS! LEFTOVERS

Throughout this book we have emphasized <u>Planned Overs</u>, but there will always be the times when plans don't go exactly right and you end up with the dreaded leftovers. Actually we should look at leftovers as an opportunity for some creative cooking.

My favorite doctor has always wanted a cookbook that has suggestions for using up items that are leftover after you purchased them for a special recipe and only used a portion of the ingredients. Here are some ideas to stimulate the creative cook.

Grains	Stuffed Acorn Squash (good with rice, barley, buckwheat, or quinoa)
Rice	Nori Rolls
	Rice Balls
	Risotta Verde
	Whole Grain Rice Bread
	Celebration Salad
	Whole Meal Salad
	Fried Rice w/Tofu
	Tofu-Rice Croquettes
	Special Rice Pudding
Millet	Scrambled Tofu w/Millet
	Goldilock Porridge
Bulgur	Tabouli Salad
Quinoa	Shrimp Fried Quinoa
	Quinoa Souffle
	Fit for a Queen Quinoa
Cooked Beans: Pinto	Bean Salad w/Spring Veggies

Garbanzo	Pasta w/Greens & Beans
	Hummus
	Creamy Garbanzo Soup
	Grain, Green & Bean Soup
	BBQ Burgers
Lentils	Lentil Salad
	Lentil Soup
	Lentil Walnut Loaf

Remember any cooked bean can be turned into a delicious soup by lightly sauteing onion or leek, adding beans and vegetable broth and simmering. Season to taste.

Tofu	Tofu Mayonnaise
	Tofu Sour Cream
	Almond Dip
	Curry Dip
	Olive-Walnut Dip
	Spring Chive Dip
	Hijiki Salad w/Tofu Dressing
	Green Goddess Dressing
	Mock Egg & olive Salad
	Tofu Veggie Sandwich Spread
	Scrambled Tofu
	Quinoa Souffle
	Spring Green Pea Soup
	Sweet Dessert Topping
	Dessert Shortcake
	Gingerbread Cake
	Apricot Whip
	Pumpkin Pie
Soy Milk	Lemon Sauce w/Dill
	Lemon Dessert Sauce
	Sweet Potato Muffins
	Almond Custard
	Mocha Pudding
	Buckwheat & Barley Pancakes
	J.A. Vichyssoise

Soy milk, rice milk or nut milks can be used in any way you would use dairy milk in a recipe.

Stale Bread	Tofu Burgers
	Harvest Stuffing
	Bread Pudding
	Quinoa Souffle
Mushrooms	Onion-Mushroom Gravy
Fresh	Pressed salads
Vegetables	Blanched salads
	My Garden Stew
	Summer Minestrone
	Rainbow Stir-Fry
	Summer Vegetables w/Kuzu
	Ginger Sauce
Green Beans	Summer Green Bean Salad
	Green Beans Almondine
Cucumbers	Fresh Cucumber Pickles
	Kosher Dill Pickles
Corn	Summertime Corn Soup
Root	Autumn Baked Vegetables
Vegetables	Sunshine Turnips
Summer	Summer Squash Soup
Squash	Summer Couscous w/Squash
	Summer Squash Special
Winter	Butternut Surprise Soup
Squash	Stuffed Acorn Squash

Greens	Creamed Greens
	Eat Your Greens Pie
	Escalloped Cabbage
	Green Leaf Rolls w/Dumplings
	Mediterranean Greens
	& Beans

If you have more from your garden than you think you can possibly use try all of the above suggestions. Don't forget to make soup stocks and green vegetable drink as well as sweet vegetable drinks.

WARNING!!!
TOO MUCH FAT IS HARMFUL TO YOUR HEALTH

****
Life is not to live, but to be well.
Martial
****

Basically the MACROBIOTIC as well as the TRANSITION diets are low fat diets, and as we have learned these are the kinds of diets we need to prevent 20th century diseases. Dr. Dean Ornish recommends that we limit our total fats to between 15 to 35 grams a day according to our height and proper weight and between 5 and 12 grams of saturated fat per day to reverse heart disease. Most Americans eat over 100 grams of fat a day and much of that is saturated fat. Saturated fat comes mainly from animal sources, so that by greatly reducing or eliminating animal protein the total fat in your diet can be easily reduced. We all do need some fat in our diet but it is very easy to get enough, the problem is that we get too much. Grains, beans, vegetables, sea vegetables, fruits have very little or negligible amounts of fat. The foods high in fat are animal foods such as meat, milk, cheese, cream, and salad dressings.

In the Macrobiotic or Transition diet, the fats that you will need to be aware of (and calculate for daily total) are those from oils, nuts, seeds, tofu and other soy products.

OILS 1 TBL
14 grams fat

NUTS 1 OZ.
Almonds	15 grams fat
Chestnuts	trace of fat
Filberts	19 grams fat
Hazelnuts	18 grams fat
Peanuts	4.5 grams fat
Pecans	19 grams fat
Walnuts	20 grams fat

SEEDS 1 OZ
Pumpkin	6 grams fat
Sesame	5 grams fat
Sunflower	14 grams fat

NUT & SEED BUTTERS 1 TBL
Almond butter	8 grams fat
Peanut butter	16 grams fat
Tahini	8 grams fat

TOFU 2 1/2x1 3/4 x1"
5 grams fat

SOY MILK 1 Cup
5 grams fat

Other foods to be aware of are green olives at 4.9 grams fat for 10 and 6.5 grams fat for 10 black olives. Coconut and palm oils are also high in saturated fats, but you will not be using these products on a healthful diet.

As you can see it is easy to eat too much fat unless you are very aware of what you are eating. Try keeping track of your fat intake for a few days to see how easy it is to eat much more than we need for our health.

CHAPTER VI

MONTHLY MENUS

JANUARY

****

"Every day you do one of two things: build health or produce disease in yourself."

Adelle Davis

****

Seasonal Foods	Cabbage, carrots, onions, leeks, winter squash, pumpkin, turnips, rutabaga, sprouts, apples, pears.
Cooking Methods	Stewing, simmering, pressure cooking, baking, frying. Use a stronger seasoning, more salt. Miso, tamari, shoyu, salty condiments. Use more buckwheat, short grain brown rice, sweet rice, oats, whole wheat berries. More ginger root, beans, tempeh, seitan, oils, nuts and seeds.

SPECIAL MENU

GINGERED LEEK & LENTIL SOUP

CREAMY NOODLE CASSEROLE

PRESSED CABBAGE SALAD

BAKED APPLES

Planned-overs	Cook enough of all dishes for next day's lunch. (with variations)

57

FEBRUARY

****

"Thou should eat to live; not live to eat."

Cicero

****

Seasonal Foods

Carrot, onion, leek winter squash, turnip, rutabaga, sprouts, apples, pears.

Cooking Methods

Simmering, stewing, pressure cooking, slow baking.
Emphasize soups, stews, oven baked entrees, buckwheat and ginger.

SPECIAL MENU

MY GARDEN STEW W/ROOT VEGGIES

BUCKWHEAT PILAF

SAUTEED KALE WITH CHICK PEA GARNI

HEAVENLY PEARS

Planned-overs

Cook extra stew for tomorrow's lunch. Stew will carry well in a wide mouth thermos. Cook extra chick peas for hummus and pita sandwiches.

MARCH

****

"Variety is the very spice of life, that gives it all its flavor."

Cowper - The Task

****

Seasonal Foods	Carrots, onions, winter squash, sprouts, kale, cabbage, apples, dried fruits. More fresh produce available in the stores. Most of stored vegetables have been used.
Cooking Methods	Less long cooking and frying. Fewer baked entrees, less oil and nuts.

SPECIAL MENU

CREAMY GARBANZO SOUP

DYNAMIC DUO

GERMAN STYLE TEMPEH & CABBAGE

BLANCHED VEGETABLE SALAD WITH ARAME

AND

SESAME DRESSING

APPLE CRISP

Planned-overs	Cook extra garbanzo beans and DYNAMIC DUO for BBQ BURGERS tomorrow.

59

APRIL

****

"If we now consider typical American meals with a critical eye, we see innocent stupidity elevated to an art."

Adelle Davis

****

Seasonal Foods

Chives, scallions, wild leafy greens, Jerusalem artichokes, dried fruits.

SPECIAL MENU

FRENCH ONION SOUP

QUICHE FOR ALL SEASONS
WITH
BROCCOLI & CARROTS

BROWN RICE

GREEN SALAD
WITH
LEMON-OIL-HERB DRESSING

FILLED OAT BARS

Planned-overs

Make extra rice for NORI ROLLS tomorrow, and there should be extra OAT BARS for your lunch bag.

MAY

****

"For a man seldom thinks with more earnestness of anything than he does his dinner."

Samuel Johnson

****

Seasonal Foods   Scallions, parsley, spring greens, asparagus, Jerusalem artichokes, strawberries.

Cooking Methods   Less baking and long sauteing. More raw salads. Less oil, nuts, salt and salty condiments. Less flour products.

SPECIAL MENU

LEMON MISO SOUP

SHRIMP FRIED QUINOA

STEAMED ASPARAGUS

STRAWBERRY DREAM

Planned-overs   Cook extra quinoa for FIT FOR A QUEEN QUINOA tomorrow.

JUNE
****

"The body is a test tube. You have to put in exactly the right ingredients to get the best reaction out of it.

Jack Youngblood
****

Seasonal Foods

Parsley, chives, kale, scallions, broccoli, collards, mustard greens, watercress, radishes, asparagus, strawberries.

Cooking Methods

Boiling, steaming, quick saute. More raw salads and pressed salads. More jelled dishes and more expansive foods. More grain and bean salads.

SPECIAL MENU

LIGHT MISO SOUP WITH SCALLIONS & PARSLEY

BROCCOLI-WALNUT STIR FRY
OVER
BROWN RICE

ROSY SALAD

ALMOND CUSTARD
WITH
FRESH STRAWBERRIES

Planned-overs

Prepare extra rice, salad and dessert for tomorrow.

JULY
****
"An ounce of prevention is worth a pound of cure."
Benjamin Franklin
****

Seasonal Foods   Parsley, chives, scallions, fresh leafy greens, radishes, summer squash, green beans, raspberries, blueberries, cantaloupe, watermelon and fresh herbs.

SPECIAL MENU

COOL CARROT SOUP W/DILL

TABOULI SALAD

STEAMED GREEN BEANS

FINGER SALAD
SCALLIONS, RADISHES, CELERY
CARROT STICKS
AND
HUMMUS DIP

CANTALOPE WITH BLUEBERRIES

Planned-overs   Prepare extra soup and salad for next day's lunch at home or away.

63

AUGUST
****

"Most illness arise solely from long continued errors
of diet and regimen."

Avicenna

****

Seasonal Foods

Sweet corn, cucumbers,
tomatoes, peppers, summer
squashes, peaches, plums,
cantaloupe, watermelon.

SPECIAL MENU

RICE SALAD WITH SHRIMP

LENTIL PATE

FRESH CORN ON THE COB

SUMMER SQUASH SPECIAL

CUCUMBER-WAKAME SALAD

WATERMELON SLICES

Planned overs

Cook extra lentil pate to use as
a sandwich filling or to turn
into a delicious soup.

SEPTEMBER

****

"In general, mankind, since the improvement of cookery, eats twice as much as nature requires."

Benjamin Franklin

****

Seasonal Foods   So many! All the fresh garden produce plus locally grown peaches, pears, apples, pears and grapes.

Cooking Methods   Start using more bean stews, sauteed vegetables, waterless cooking methods. Use slightly more salt and oil and fewer raw foods. More lightly boiled salads and a wide variety of greens, root vegetables, squashes and cooked fruits.

SPECIAL MENU

SUMMERTIME CORN SOUP

GINGER BAKED FISH

RICE PILAF

GREEN SALAD
WITH
VINAGRETTE DRESSING

PEACH PIE

Planned-overs   Make extra soup and rice for tomorrow's lunch.

OCTOBER

****

"Live within your harvest."

Persian proverb

****

Seasonal foods

Cauliflower, broccoli, winter squashes, onions, leeks, Brussel sprouts, pumpkin, root vegetables pears, grapes.

Cooking methods

Longer cooked vegetables.
More bean dishes and soups.
More oil and salt.
More millet and rice.
More round vegetables   (squashes, pumpkin, Brussel sprouts, cabbage).

SPECIAL MENU

BUTTERNUT SURPRISE SOUP

WILD & TAME RICE PILAF

LENTIL/WALNUT LOAF

AUTUMN BAKED ROOT VEGGIES
WITH
GINGER

HIJIKI SALAD
WITH
CREAMY GARLIC DRESSING

APPLE CRUNCH PIE

Planned-overs

Cook extra soup, rice,
LENTIL/WALNUT

NOVEMBER

****

"Earth who gives us our food
Sun who makes it ripe and good
Dearest Earth and Dearest Sun
Joy and love for all you've done"
Traditional Grace

****

Seasonal Foods

Winter squashes, pumpkin, leeks, onions, carrots, turnip, rutabaga, Jerusalem artichokes, kale, Brussel sprouts, apples, pears.

Cooking methods

Longer cooking, baking, frying. More oil, salt, miso, and nuts. Fewer raw salads and fresh fruits.

SPECIAL MENU

CREAMY SPLIT PEA SOUP

STUFFED ACORN SQUASH

THREE COLOR VEGGIE COMBO

PUMPKIN PIE

Planned-overs

Make extra soup for tomorrow's lunch.

DECEMBER

"He who has health, has hope: and he who has hope, has everything."
Arabian Proverb

Seasonal foods   Onion, carrot, leek, turnip, rutabaga,
                                  winter squashes, pumpkin, fresh
                                  sprouts, apples, dried fruits.

SPECIAL HOLIDAY MENU

TAMARI BROTH WITH GARNISH

NATURAL TURKEY OR HUBBARD SQUASH
WITH
HARVEST STUFFING

GLAZED ONIONS

STEAMED BRUSSEL SPROUTS

CRANBERRY RELISH MOLD

STEAMED PUDDING
WITH
LEMON SAUCE

Planned-overs   Steamed pudding will keep well for
                                  several weeks if kept refrigerated.

68

WEEK OF MENUS FOR TRANSITION DIET

*MAKE EXTRA FOR PLANNED-OVERS
DESSERTS ARE OPTIONAL
USE BEVERAGE OF YOUR CHOICE

MONDAY

Hot Oatmeal w/
  Raisins, Sunflower
  Seeds & Cinnamon
  Nut or Soy Milk

Noodles in
  Vegetable Broth
Nori Rolls
Raw Veggies
*Oatmeal Cookies

*Gingered Leek & Lentil Soup
*Brown Rice
Steamed Broccoli
*Blanched Root Vegetables
w/Green Goddess Dressing
Dried Fruit Compote

TUESDAY

Miso Soup
  w/Veggies
Toasted Sourdough
  Bread
Choice of Spreads:
Sweet Vegetable,
Tahini or Almond
  Butter

Leek & Lentil Soup
Leftover Brown
  Rice w/Blanched
  Root Veggies &
Umeboshi Vinegar
Chopped Parsley &
  Chives
Oatmeal Cookie

*Creamy Garbanzo Soup
*Dynamic Duo
Cauliflower Bouquet
German Style Tempeh
Warm Carrot Salad
*Applesauce
Cook Extra Garbanzo for BBQ Burgers
Tomorrow

69

WEDNESDAY

Tofu French Toast
w/Whole Wheat Bread
Real Maple Syrup
or Apple Butter

Creamy Garbanzo
Soup
Noodle Salad
w/Vegetables
& Green Goddess
Dressing
Applesauce

*Summer Minestrone
BBQ Burgers
*Baked Beans
Cabbage Salad w/Celery Seed
Corn Bread Muffins
Apple Crisp

THURSDAY

Quick Miso Soup
Whole Grain Cooked
Cereal
Nut or Soy Milk
Corn Muffins

Summer Minestrone
BBQ Burger or
Baked Bean
Sandwich
Apple Crisp

*Creamy Pea Soup
*Golden Loaf
Onion Gravy
Steamed Carrots
Lemon-Sesame Sauce
Blueberry Pie

70

FRIDAY

Quick Miso Soup
Pan Fried Golden
  Loaf w/Onion
  Gravy or Pure
  Maple Syrup

Creamy Pea Soup
Soyburger or
Tempeh Sandwich
Natural Dill
  Pickle
Fresh Fruit

Kombu Broth w/Carrot & Scallions
Ginger Baked Fish
Rice Pilaf
Cauliflower & Broccoli Combo
Grated Daikon & Carrot w/Tamari Sauce
Apricot Whip

SATURDAY

Wholegrain Cooked
  Cereal w/Sunflower
  or Pumpkin Seeds
*Basic Oat Bran
  Muffins

Quick Miso Soup
Corn Tortillas
  w/Bean Filling
Sprouts & Umeboshi
  Vinegar

Meatless Tofu Balls w/Italiano Red
Sauce over Whole Wheat Spaghetti
Sourdough Bread
Green Salad w/Lemon-Oil-Herb Dressing
Mocha Pudding

SUNDAY

Whole Grain Pancakes
or Buckwheat Barley
Pancakes with Blue-
berry Sauce or
Real Maple Syrup or
Apple Butter

Quick Miso Soup
Mock Egg & Olive
Spread in Pita
Pocket Bread
w/Lettuce or
Sprouts
Pickles

Vegetable-Barley Soup
Stuffed Acorn Squash
(quoina, onion, sunflower seeds,
scallions, mushrooms, tamari)
Boiled Daikon Root w/Kale
Sweet Potato Muffins
Heavenly Pears

MAKE AHEAD MEALS

* MAKE AHEAD

SUMMER

FALL

*Kombu Broth w/Tofu
& Scallions
*Tabouli Salad or
Rice Salad
Quick Saute Summer
Squash
Peach Dream
Coucous Cake
*Cool Barley Tea

*Lentil Soup
*Fried Brown Rice
w/Onions &
Carrots
Steamed Broccoli
*Dried Fruit
Compote

WINTER	SPRING
Creamy Split Pea Soup	*Lemon Miso Soup
*Stuffed Acorn Squash	*Med-Grain Brown
Steamed Greens	Rice
*Sunshine Salad	*Lentil Stew
*Oatmeal Raisin Cookies	Steamed Dandelion
	or Mustard Greens
	*Strawberry Dream

QUICK AND EASY MEAL SUGGESTIONS

Simple Millet	Pasta W/Greens
w/Veggies	& Beans
Steamed Kale	Boiled Carrots
Macro Macaroni	Quick & Easy
& Tofu Cheese	Bulgar Pilaf
Steamed Greens	Steamed Broccoli
	or Brussel Sprouts
Summer Couscous	Corn on the Cob
w/Squash	Teriyaki Tofu
Green Salad	Broccoli
Stir Fry	Udon or Soba
Vegetables over	Noodles w/Broth
Brown Rice	Vegetables of
	choice
Stuffed Squash	Scrambled Tofu
Sauteed Greens	w/Millet
	Carrots
	Steamed Greens
Stir Fried Rice	Broiled Fish
w/Onion & Tofu	Quick Fried Rice
Steamed Greens	& Onions
	Green Salad

CHAPTER VII

THE RECIPES

1. GRAINS, THE CENTER OF IT ALL

2. EAT YOUR VEGETABLES, INCLUDING THE SEA VEGETABLES

3. PROTEINS, THE BODY REBUILDERS
   (BEANS, TOFU, TEMPEH, SEITAN, SEEDS, NUTS, FISH, SEAFOOD, AND ANIMAL FOOD)

4. SOUP DU JOUR

5. LIGHTEN UP: SALADS & PICKLES

6. GIVE US OUR DAILY BREAD

7. SMALL PLEASURES
   (APPETIZERS, DIPS, SPREADS, CONDIMENTS, SAUCES, GRAVIES AND BUTTERS)

8. JUST DESSERTS

9. BEVERAGES

10. SUPER SNACKS FOR KIDS OF ALL AGES

11. WHAT'S FOR BREAKFAST?

12. THE HEALTHFUL LUNCH

13. EATING OUT: A SURVIVAL LESSON

Abbreviations used:
Cp = cup   F = degrees Fahrenheit
Lb = pound   Med = medium size
Oz = ounces   Qt = quart
Tbl = tablespoon   Time = hours:minutes
Tsp = teaspoon   WW = whole wheat

1. GRAINS, THE CENTER OF IT ALL

Grains are the center of the diet and should be anywhere from 30-60 % of the daily intake. Usually grain is served plain with various condiments for variety. Here are some good grain combinations to try:

1/2 cp Short grain brown rice & 1/2 cp sweet rice
1/2 cp Short grain brown rice & 1/2 cp barley
1/2 cp Long grain brown rice & 1/2 cp wild rice
3/4 cp Short grain brown rice & 1/4 cp millet
1/2 cp Buckwheat groats & 1/2 cp quinoa
1/2 cp Buckwheat groats & 1/2 cp bulgur

You can also vary the grains by dry roasting or soaking for several hours before cooking. To dry roast a grain before its regular cooking, merely measure and wash it as usual, then roast it in a fry pan until it is dry and has a nutty aroma. These methods are also good methods to make the grains more digestible. People who seem to be sensitive to certain grains can sometimes tolerate them cooked by these methods or by combining two different grains. Also some grain-sensitive people tolerate them when ground into flours and made into pancakes or muffins, but not when eaten as whole grains.

The recipes in this section are for times you want to do something a little special with your daily grains.

SPECIAL GRAIN DISHES

AUTUMN APPLE RICE
 PILAF
BARLEY PILAF
DYNAMIC DUO
GOLDEN LOAF
MOCK MASHED POTATOES
POLENTA

QUICK & EASY
 BULGUR PILAF
SIMPLE MILLET
 W/VEGETABLES
SUMMER COUSCOUS
WILD & TAME RICE
 PILAF

VERY SPECIAL HINT:
Protect your newly purchased grains and flours by freezing overnight to kill any little critters which might grow and multiply in your pantry.

AUTUMN APPLE RICE PILAF

Serves: 4-6   Time: 00:50

1 CP WATER
1 CP APPLE JUICE
1 CP SHORT GRAIN BROWN RICE
1 TSP OIL
1 TSP RICE SYRUP
PINCH OF SEA SALT
2 MED SIZED RED APPLES
1/2 CP THINLY SLICED CELERY
1/3 CP CHOPPED WALNUTS

1. Wash rice.

2. Bring apple juice, water, rice syrup, oil and salt to a boil and add rice.

3. Reduce heat, cover tightly and cook over low heat until all liquid is absorbed (approx. 50 minutes).

4. Chop nuts, slice celery and prepare apples by quartering, removing core and chop coarsely.

5. When rice is cooked add the apple, celery and nut and heat thoroughly.

6. Apples and celery may be blanched before adding to rice if less chewy dish is preferred.

Comments: _Serve with baked squash and dark green vegetables._

BARLEY PILAF

Serves: 4   Time: 00:60

1 CP UNCOOKED BARLEY
2 CP SPRING WATER OR LIGHT VEGETABLE STOCK
1 TBL OIL
1 MED ONION, CHOPPED
1/4 CP CHOPPED WALNUTS
DASH CINNAMON (OPTIONAL)
SEA SALT TO TASTE
CHOPPED PARSLEY OR SCALLIONS FOR GARNISH

1. Heat oil in 1 quart size saucepan and saute the chopped onion until transparent.

2. Add barley and saute briefly.

3. Add light vegetable stock or spring water with dash of sea salt.

4. Bring to boiling point, cover tightly and simmer over low heat for 50-60 minutes or until barley is tender.

5. Stir in chopped walnuts and dash of cinnamon. Check for seasonings and adjust as needed.

6. Serve with chopped scallion or parsley garnish.

Comments: Nice variation from rice, can be combined with other grains. Try 3/4 cp barley and 1/4 cp wheat berries.

DYNAMIC DUO

Serves: 4   Time: 00:30

1 CP BUCKWHEAT
1 CP QUINOA
4 CP SPRING WATER
PINCH SEA SALT

1. Place water and salt in large saucepan and place over med heat while you prepare the grains.

2. Wash and drain each grain separately combine and dry roast in a heavy skillet until toasty.

3. When grains are roasted and water is boiling combine all.

4. Reduce heat and simmer for 20 minutes.

5. Allow to rest for 5-10 minutes. Stir grains and allow to rest another 5 minutes before serving.

Comments: Wonderful cold weather grain combo, hearty and tasty. Planned-overs make great burgers.

GOLDEN LOAF

Serves: 4   Time: 00:30

1 CP MILLET
1/4 CP QUINOA
3 CP SPRING WATER
PINCH OF SEA SALT

1. Wash grains well and drain.

2. In large saucepan or pressure cooker combine grain, water and sea salt. According to cooking method you are using either cover and simmer for 40 minutes or bring to pressure and cook for 40 minutes.

3. When grains are cooked transfer immediately while still warm to loaf pans. Pack in well and smooth top with a wet spatula.

4. Let cool at room temperature then refrigerate.

5. When ready to use turn out of pan and slice.

6. Saute in skillet either dry or using a small amount of oil.

7. Use as a base for gravy style dish or serve with apple butter or maple syrup.

Comments: _Loaf is formed by chilling the cooked ingredients. This keeps very well for several days._

MOCK MASHED POTATOES

Serves: 3-4   Time: 00:30

1 CP MILLET
1/2 SMALL CAULIFLOWER SLICED THINLY
2 1/2 CP SPRING WATER
PINCH SEA SALT

1. Wash millet and drain well.

2. Bring water and sea salt to a boil.

3. Thinly slice the cauliflower.

4. Combine all ingredients and bring to boil, reduce heat and simmer
   for 25 minutes. May be pressure cooked if preferred.

5. Remove from heat and mash well with a potato masher.

6. Add a little hot water if too thick.

Comments: _Serve with onion gravy for a real treat._

POLENTA

Serves: 4-6   Time: 00:30

6 1/3 CP SPRING WATER
1 TBL SEA SALT
2 CP YELLOW CORNMEAL

1. Lightly grease a 2 to 3 quart oven proof bowl.

2. Bring water and salt to a brisk boil in a 3 quart saucepan.

3. Reduce heat to medium low and gradually add cornmeal in a fine
   stream while whisking constantly to prevent lumps from forming.
   Boil gently for 20-25 minutes stirring often with a wooden spoon
   until very thick but still pourable.

4. Pour into prepared bowl and spread level with a rubber spatula or
   back of wooden spoon.

5. Let stand for about 10 minutes until firm to touch and the polenta
   starts to pull away from the sides of the dish.

6. Invert onto a serving plate.

7. Cut into wedges to serve.

8. If cooking for one or two recipe can be divided into a small
   casserole dish and a loaf pan.

Comments: Serve with a bean dish for complete protein. Can be sliced and
fried for breakfast.

QUICK & EASY BULGUR PILAF

Serves: 4   Time: 00:30

2 SHIITAKE MUSHROOMS (OPTIONAL)
1 MED CHOPPED ONION
2 TSP OIL
2 CP SPRING WATER
1 CP BULGUR WHEAT
1-2 TBL SHOYU/TAMARI SAUCE
1/4 CP FRESHLY CHOPPED PARSLEY
1/4 CP CHOPPED ROASTED ALMONDS

1. If using dried mushrooms, start soaking.

2. Chop onion and saute in oil until it becomes transparent, 3-4 minutes.

3. Add sliced mushrooms and saute a minute longer. Add water, shoyu and bulgur and bring to a boil. Cover tightly and remove from the heat.

4. Let sit for 15 minutes or until all liquid is absorbed.

5. Mix in chopped parsley and almonds and fluff the mixture.

6. Serve while hot.

Comments: *Fast and easy to prepare. Leftovers can be reheated or turned into bulgur burgers.*

SIMPLE MILLET WITH VEGETABLES

Serves: 4   Time: 00:30

1 CP MILLET
2 1/2 CP SPRING WATER
1/3 CP SUNFLOWER OR PUMPKIN SEEDS
2 CARROTS
1 PARSNIP
2 SCALLIONS OR 1 SMALL ONION
PINCH SEA SALT

1. Wash millet and drain well.

2. Combine with water and sea salt in large saucepan or pressure
   cooker and place over high heat.

3. Slice or chop vegetables and add to mixture.

4. Add sunflower or pumpkin seeds to mixture. Cover and cook for
   20-30 minutes. If using pressure cooker bring to pressure first
   before you start timing cooking period.

5. Stir well and check for seasoning before serving.

6. Can be garnished with green scallions or chopped parsley.

Comments: Easy and delicious.

SUMMER COUSCOUS WITH SQUASH

Serves: 6   Time: 00:20

1 TBL OLIVE OIL
2 CP SHREDDED ZUCCHINI
2 CP SHREDDED YELLOW SUMMER SQUASH
2 CP LIGHT VEGETABLE STOCK
1 1/2 CP COUSCOUS
1/3 CP MINCED FRESH PARSLEY
1-2 TBL LEMON JUICE
SEA SALT AND/OR TAMARI TO TASTE

1. Heat oil in a large skillet over medium heat.

2. Add shredded squashes.

3. Stir-fry for 8-10 minutes until liquid released from the squash evaporates.

4. Add broth, bring to a boil and stir in the couscous.

5. Cover tightly, remove heat and let stand for 5 minutes or until the broth is absorbed.

6. Stir in minced parsley, lemon juice and seasonings of choice.

7. Spoon into serving dish, fluff with fork and garnish with more chopped parsley if desired. Recipe can be halved or doubled.

Comments: _Great fast and easy main dish for a hot summer day._

WILD & TAME RICE PILAF

Serves: 4   Time: 00:50

2-4 DRIED SHIITAKE MUSHROOMS SOAKED IN 1 CP
    HOT WATER
1/2 CP LONG GRAIN BROWN RICE
1/2 CP WILD RICE
1 1/2 TSP OIL
1 ONION OR SMALL LEEK
PINCH SEA SALT
2 CP WATER/VEGETABLE STOCK
1 TBL SHOYU OR TO TASTE
CHOPPED FRESH PARSLEY

1. Soak mushrooms in hot water for 20 minutes. Fresh shiitake mushrooms may be used in place of the dried if available.

2. Wash brown rice and wild rice and drain well.

3. Roast grains in a heavy skillet until dry and beginning to brown.

4. Place in casserole.

5. Drain mushrooms and slice into thin strips or pieces. Discard tough stems and reserve for use in soup stock.

6. Add water or vegetable stock, shoyu and salt.

7. Cover casserole tightly and bake in 350F oven for one hour or until all liquid has been absorbed.

8. Stir in the chopped parsley, cover and let rest for 5-10 minutes before serving.

Comments: *Roasting grains and then baking gives hearty flavor.*

2. EAT YOUR VEGETABLES, INCLUDING SEA VEGETABLES

There are endless ways to prepare vegetables. They can be steamed, blanched, boiled, baked, deep fried, grilled, and used in salads, soups, pickles, as well as the standby vegetable side dishes. Vary the way you cut and cook vegetables for variety and please don't be afraid to try some unusual vegetables. You may be pleasantly surprised as you add a new food to your menus.

You will want to use seasonal vegetables as well as locally grown (and organic when possible) for the best nutrition and health for your family.

You can work the sea vegetables into soups, stews, salads, and main dishes until the family becomes accustomed to them and learns to really like them.

HINTS:
Do you have more dark leafy greens from your garden than you can possibly use? Boil them in fresh spring water. Discard the greens, and lightly season the "green juice" and use as an energy drink as a source of magnesium and other minerals.

Dried corn silk makes a delicious tea.

Soup stock made from the inner leaves of sweet corn is very sweet and delicious. Don't forget to add raw corn cobs, too.

Store your fresh parsley like a bouquet of flowers. Place stems in water, cover lightly with plastic or cellophane bag. Secure loosely with rubber band and store in refrigerator, will stay fresh and crisp for several days.

If the family balks at sea vegetables try to cook them in soups and then put soup through the blender before serving. You will have a delicious creamy soup with loads of hidden nutrition.

NEW VEGETABLE DISHES

ARAME W/ROOT VEGETABLES
AUTUMN BAKED VEGETABLES
CABBAGE & ARAME WITH MUSTARD SAUCE
CAULIFLOWER BOUQUET
CREAMED GREENS
ESCALLOPED CABBAGE
GINGERED CARROTS & SNOW PEAS
GLAZED ONIONS
GOLDEN STUFFED ONIONS
GREEN BEANS ALMONDINE
KOMBU VEGETABLE BAKE
MEDITERRANEAN GREENS & BEANS
MY GARDEN STEW
RAINBOW STIR FRY
ROASTED J.A. & ONIONS
SPECIAL CABBAGE ROLLS
STUFFED ACORN SQUASH
SUMMER SQUASH SPECIAL
SUMMER VEGETABLES W/KUZU GINGER SAUCE
SUNSHINE TURNIPS
SWEET SOUR CABBAGE
THREE COLOR VEGGIE COMBO
WILD GREENS

VERY SPECIAL HINT: When trying a new vegetable on the family, try to disguise it in a casserole or soup, until they become accustom to the flavor.

ARAME WITH ROOT VEGETABLES

Serves: 4-6   Time: 00:30

1 CP ARAME, SOAKED
1 TBL OIL
1 LARGE ONION CUT INTO CRESCENTS
2 LARGE CARROTS CUT INTO MATCHSTICKS
1 CP SPRING WATER
2 TBL SHOYU/TAMARI SAUCE

1. Soak arame in water to cover for 10-15 minutes. It will swell to 2 cups.

2. Prepare onion and carrots. Drain arame.

3. Heat oil in large skillet and saute onion for 2 minutes.

4. Add drained arame and saute for 2 minutes.

5. Add carrot, stir and saute for 2 minutes longer.

6. Add water and shoyu sauce. Bring to boil, reduce heat to a simmer. Cover with lid ajar so liquid can evaporate.

7. Simmer for 25-30 minutes.

8. Increase heat toward end of cooking time if liquid has not entirely evaporated.

9. Serve immediately while hot.

Comments: Very sweet flavor. Planned-overs are good at room temperature.

AUTUMN BAKED VEGETABLES

Serves: 4   Time: 00:45

2 LARGE CARROTS
2 LARGE PARSNIPS
8 VERY SMALL ONIONS
3-4 INCH PIECE DAIKON
2-3 PURPLE TOP TURNIPS
1 VERY SMALL RUTABAGA
1 TBL GRATED FRESH GINGER (OPTIONAL)

1. Preheat oven to 350F.

2. Scrub vegetables and cut into 1 inch pieces.

3. Place in a oven proof casserole with a tight fitting lid.

4. Grate ginger and squeeze juice over the vegetables. Add 2 tbl water and cover tightly.

5. Bake for 30 to 45 minutes or until tender but not mushy.

Comments: _Use a variety of root vegetables. Very sweet tasting and very warming on a cold day._

CABBAGE-ARAME IN MUSTARD SAUCE

Serves 4-6   Time: 00:20

1 TBL OIL
1 SMALL HEAD CABBAGE
2/3 CP ARAME

SAUCE:
1/2 TBL MUSTARD POWDER
2 TBL SHOYU SAUCE
1 TBL MIRIN

1. Combine ingredients for sauce and set aside.

2. Soak arame in cold water while you prepare the cabbage.

3. Slice the cabbage into thin slivers and saute in the oil for 1-2 minutes, add drained arame and saute 1 minute longer.

4. Cover and steam until just tender.

5. Add sauce, stir well and let simmer another minute or so to blend flavors.

6. Serve immediately or transfer to a salad bowl and let cool to room temperature to serve as a salad.

CAULIFLOWER BOUQUET

Serves: 4-6   Time: 00:30

1 WHOLE CAULIFLOWER
1 CP BECHAMEL SAUCE WITH LEMON JUICE
SOURDOUGH BREAD CRUMBS

1. Preheat oven to 350F.

2. Trim and steam whole cauliflower until just barely tender.

3. Place cauliflower upright in a casserole dish.   Cover with the bechamel sauce and sprinkle with bread crumbs.

4. Bake 20 minutes until top is golden brown.

Comments: *Nice for a special occasion but easy enough to do any time.*

CREAMED GREENS

Serves: 2-4   Time: 00:30

1 LB FRESH GREENS (KALE, COLLARDS, SPINACH, SWISS CHARD OR OTHERS)
1 SMALL ONION OR SHALLOT
1 TBL OLIVE OIL
1 1/2 TBL OAT FLOUR
1/4 TSP SEA SALT
DASH OF NUTMEG
3/4 CP HOT VEGETABLE STOCK OR SPRING WATER
(1/4 TSP HERBAMARE SEASONING IF USING WATER IN PLACE OF STOCK)

1. Wash greens and chop finely.

2. Steam briefly until bright green and wilted. Drain thoroughly in mesh strainer. Press firmly to extract as much liquid as possible. Set aside while you prepare cream sauce.

3. Peel and mince onion or shallot.

4. In a 1 qt saucepan heat oil and saute onion or shallot until transparent.

5. Add oat flour, sea salt and nutmeg and mix well. Add hot stock gradually while stirring to avoid lumping, until mixture comes to a boil.

6. Simmer for 1-2 minutes and then add chopped greens and cook over low heat until greens are hot.

7. Serve immediately.

Comments: Will satisfy those cravings for something creamy. People will eat greens this way that never did before.

ESCALLOPED CABBAGE

Serves: 4-6   Time: 00:45

4 CPS COARSE CHOPPED CABBAGE
1 CP SPRING WATER
2 TBL OIL
1 MED ONION, CHOPPED
2 TBL WHOLE WHEAT FLOUR
1/2 LB TOFU
1/2 TSP SEA SALT
1 TBL OIL
1 TBL RICE VINEGAR
SOURDOUGH BREAD CRUMBS

1. Preheat the oven to 350F.

2. Parboil the chopped cabbage in 1 cup of water for 5 minutes.

3. Saute the onion in oil until limp. Sprinkle the flour and salt over the onion and stir well.

4. Drain off the cabbage cooking water and add gradually to the onion flour mixture while stirring to form a creamy thick sauce.

5. Blend or beat until smooth, the tofu, oil, and vinegar.

6. Combine the cabbage, sauce, and tofu mixture and pour into a 1 1/2 pint baking dish.

7. Top with bread crumbs and bake for 30 minutes or until lightly browned. Serve hot.

Comments: _Easy to make but very good tasting._

GINGERED CARROTS & SNOWPEAS

Serves: 4   Time: 00:30

2 LARGE CARROTS
1/2 TSP LIGHT OIL
PINCH SEA SALT (OPTIONAL)
1/4 CP SPRING WATER
1/4 LB SNOW PEAS
2 TBL MIRIN (RICE WINE)
1/2 TSP FRESH GINGER JUICE
2 TBL KUZU
1 TBL SPRING WATER

1. Cut carrots on the diagonal into 1/8 inch slices, then cut each slice into 2 or 3 lengthwise slices.

2. Heat oil in skillet, add carrots and salt and saute briefly.

3. Add water, cover and cook until tender-crisp.

4. Add snowpeas, toss with carrots and cook about 30 seconds to 1 minute until peas are a bright green color.

5. Uncover and remove from heat.

6. Pour off any liquid and reserve in a measuring cup. Add mirin and water to equal 1/3 cup.

7. Dissolve kuzu in 1 tbl water and add to the reserved 1/3 cup of stock.

8. Pour over vegetables, bring to boil and stir until sauce thickens and becomes translucent.

9. Add ginger juice and simmer for 1 minute. Serve immediately.

Comments: Don't overcook vegetables, should be brightly colored.

GLAZED ONIONS

Serves: 4-6   Time: 00:20

1 LB SMALL WHITE BOILING ONIONS
1 TBL OIL
SPRING WATER AS NEEDED
2 TBL RICE SYRUP

1. Peel onions.

2. Heat oil in a large skillet and gently saute onions until lightly browned.

3. Cover with fresh spring water and bring to boil. Reduce heat and cook for 5-10 minutes or until just tender. Don't overcook.

4. Drain off liquid and reserve for soups.

5. Remove onions to a bowl and add rice syrup to skillet. Heat gently until it liquefies. Add onions to skillet and simmer slowly turning often until all are lightly glazed.

6. Remove to serving bowl and serve.

Comments: Nice for holiday dinners, but good anytime and easy to do.

GOLDEN STUFFED ONIONS

Serves: 6   Time: 00:45

6 LARGE ONIONS
1 CP UNCOOKED MILLET
2 1/2 CP SPRING WATER
PINCH SEA SALT
1 MED BUTTERNUT SQUASH (4 CP UNCOOKED, CUBED)
6 PARSLEY SPRIGS
1 CP WATER
1 TBL KUZU
1 TBL SHOYU SAUCE

1. Peel onions and steam over a rack in a large kettle for 10 minutes. Drain and set aside to cool.

2. Bring millet, water, salt, and squash to a boil in medium size saucepan. Reduce heat, cover and simmer for 30 minutes.

3. When millet is ready, mash with potato masher to a smooth consistency.

4. Hollow out the onion, leaving a 1/2 inch shell. Chop the reserved onion pulp and measure out 1 cp and add to the millet-squash mixture. Any leftover onion can be used in soups, etc.

5. Fill each onion shell with the stuffing mix.

6. Place onions in a baking dish with about 1/4 inch of water on the bottom.

7. Preheat oven to 400F.

8. Prepare sauce by dissolving kuzu in water, add seasonings and simmer until clear and thick. Spoon a tbl of sauce over each onion and bake for 15 minutes. Serve hot with parsley garnish.

Comments: _Very sweet and satisfying as well as pretty to look at._

GREEN BEANS ALMONDINE

Serves: 4-6   Time: 00:20

2 LBS FRESH GREEN BEANS
1/2 TSP SEA SALT
1 TSP GRATED GINGER (OPTIONAL)
1 TBL LEMON JUICE
1/4 CP SLIVERED ALMONDS

1. Wash beans and cut into 1 inch pieces.

2. Combine beans with salt and ginger, and steam with a small amount of water until tender. Approx. 10-15 minutes.

3. Toss with fresh lemon juice an add slivered almonds.

4. Any leftovers go well in a salad. Serve hot.

Comments: *Delicious and great to serve for special dinner party.*

KOMBU VEGETABLE BAKE

Serves: 3-4   Time: 00:60

12 INCHES OF KOMBU COOKED AND CUT INTO SQUARES
1 CARROT SLICED DIAGONALLY
1 TURNIP, DICED
1 CP SHREDDED CABBAGE
1/4 CP SPRING WATER
1 TSP GRATED GINGER
1 TSP SHOYU/TAMARI SAUCE

1. Preheat oven to 325F.

2. Lightly oil a covered casserole dish.

3. Cut cooked kombu into one inch squares and place in casserole.

4. Combine water, ginger, and shoyu or tamari sauce. Lightly sprinkle kombu with about 1 tbl of mixture.

5. Prepare rest of vegetables and add in layers, sprinkling each layer with sauce as they are added to the casserole.

6. Cover and bake for 45 minutes. Serve hot.

7. Garnish with freshly chopped parsley if desired.

Comments: Kombu should be cooked before starting the recipe.

MEDITERRANEAN GREENS AND BEANS

Serves: 2-4   Time: 00:15

1/2 TBL OLIVE OIL
1 CLOVE GARLIC MINCED
1 SMALL BUNCH KALE
1/2 CP COOKED GARBANZO BEANS
PINCH SEA SALT (OPTIONAL)
3 TBL SPRING WATER
TAMARI SAUCE TO TASTE

1. Heat oil in a large skillet.

2. Add minced garlic and saute briefly. Do not let brown.

3. Add chopped kale and saute for 2-3 minutes.

4. Add cooked beans and water.

5. Cover and cook just until greens are tender.

6. Add tamari sauce to taste and serve.

Comments: _Also good with other hearty greens._

MY GARDEN STEW

Serves: 4   Time: 00:45

2 TSP LIGHT SESAME OIL
2 MED ONIONS, DICED
1/2 CP MILLET
4-6 CP SPRING WATER
DASH SEA SALT
1 BAY LEAF
2 CP CUBED WINTER SQUASH OR CUBED SUMMER SQUASH
2 CP SLICED CARROTS, PARSNIPS, DAIKON, RADISH, OR PEARL
ONIONS, OR ANY OTHER FAVORITE ROOT VEGETABLE.
1 TBL CHICKPEA MISO
1/2 CP VEGETABLE STOCK
1 INCH PIECE OF FRESH GINGER
SHOYU/TAMARI SAUCE TO TASTE

1. Heat oil in a large saucepan and saute the diced onion until it is
   transparent.

2. Wash the millet and drain well.

3. Add water, sea salt and bay leaf and bring to boiling point. Stir in
   the millet and root vegetables. If using summer squash, do not
   add until the last 5 minutes of cooking. Winter squash should be
   added with root vegetables. Bring to a boil, lower heat and
   simmer gently for 20-30 minutes until vegetables are tender.

4. Dissolve the miso in a small amount of the cooking liquid and
   return to the saucepan. Simmer gently for 5 minutes.

5. Grate ginger root and squeeze the juice into the stew. Remove the
   bay leaf.

6. Serve in large soup plates with garnish of chopped parsley and/or
   chopped scallions. The millet naturally thickens the stew.

Comments: Vegetables can be varied by what is in season.

RAINBOW STIR-FRY VEGETABLES

Serves: 6-8   Time: 00:15

1 1/2 LB BRUSSELS SPROUTS TRIMMED AND HALVED
2 CP CAULIFLOWER FLORETS
4 THIN CARROTS THINLY SLICED
3 TBL SAFFLOWER OIL
4 MINCED SHALLOTS
1 CP SHREDDED RED CABBAGE
1/2 CP SPRING WATER
SEA SALT TO TASTE

1. Cook sprouts and cauliflower in salted boiling water for about 4 minutes.

2. Add carrots and cook 1 minute.

3. Drain, reserve cooking liquid for other uses. Cool quickly by rinsing with cold water. Drain well.

4. Heat oil in skillet over medium-high heat. Add shallots and saute for 1 minute.

5. Add cabbage and cooked vegetables and stir-fry for 2 minutes longer.

6. Add water or reserved cooking liquid and cook stirring constantly until crisp-tender, 3-5 minutes.

7. Season to taste and serve.

8. Minced fresh parsley makes a nice garnish.

9. Recipe can be halved for a smaller group.

Comments: _Special party dish._ _Also wonderful way to use up the garden bounty._

ROASTED J.A. & ONIONS

Serves: 4   Time: 00:30

1 LB JERUSALEM ARTICHOKES
1/2 LB SMALL BOILING ONIONS
1 CLOVE GARLIC
1/2 TBL OLIVE OIL
SEA SALT TO TASTE
MINCED PARSLEY TO GARNISH

1. Scrub Jerusalem artichokes very well.

2. Peel onions and place both in a flat baking dish.

3. Peel garlic and either mince finely or put through a garlic press and sprinkle over the vegetables in baking dish.

4. Brush lightly with olive oil and bake for 25-30 minutes at 350F.

5. Be careful not to overcook or the artichokes will become mushy.

Comments: Nice fall through winter dish and even early spring.

SPECIAL CABBAGE ROLLS

Serves: 4   Time: 00:30

8 LARGE CABBAGE LEAVES
3/4 CP BUCKWHEAT GROATS
1 1/2 CP SPRING WATER
PINCH SEA SALT
1 TBL CURRANTS
3/4 CP CHOPPED CELERY
1/2 CP SAUERKRAUT, CHOPPED (OPTIONAL, BUT NICE)
1/4 CP ROASTED SUNFLOWER SEED

SAUCE
1 CP SPRING WATER
2 TSP KUZU
1/2 CP SLICED ONION OR LEEKS
1 TBL MIRIN
1 TBL SHOYU SAUCE

1. Steam cabbage leaves until soft and set aside to cool.

2. Cook buckwheat in spring water and salt for 30 minutes or until tender. Combine cooked buckwheat with currants, celery, sauerkraut and sunflower seeds.

3. Divide mixture equally between 8 leaves and fill cabbage leaf with mixture. Fold sides of leaf and then ends to form an envelope. Secure with toothpick and set aside.

4. Prepare sauce by combining the water, kuzu, onion or leeks, mirin an shoyu sauce in a large saucepan. Stir over med heat until mix is clear and onions are cooked, about 5 minutes.

5. Serve hot with garnish of your choice.

Comments: Leftovers can be eaten cold or reheated for lunches. Delicious and warming.

STUFFED ACORN SQUASH

Serves: 2-4   Time: 00:45

1-2 ACORN SQUASH ACCORDING TO NUMBER OF SERVINGS
2 CP COOKED GRAIN (RICE, BARLEY, BUCKWHEAT, OR QUINOA ARE ALL GOOD)
2-4 CHOPPED SCALLIONS
2 TBL ROASTED SUNFLOWER SEED
1 STALK CHOPPED CELERY
SHOYU/TAMARI SAUCE TO TASTE

1. Preheat oven to 350F.

2. Wash squash and slice in half. Remove seeds.

3. Place cut side down on a baking pan. Add 1/4 cp water to pan and bake at 350F degrees for 30 minutes.

4. Combine grain, vegetables, sunflower seeds and shoyu sauce.

5. Remove squash from oven and turn right side up. Fill cavity with prepared filling and return to the oven for 15-20 minutes until hot and lightly browned. If there is extra filling, bake it in a small casserole and serve as a side dish with the stuffed squash.
Serve hot.

Comments: Simple and delicious. Can be multiplied to serve as many as you need. Good way to use planned-over grains.

105

SUMMER SQUASH SPECIAL

Serves: 4-6   Time: 00:20

2-3 SMALL YELLOW SQUASH
1-2 TSP OLIVE OIL
FINELY CHOPPED FRESH BASIL AND OREGANO (DRIED CAN
BE USED IF FRESH IS NOT AVAILABLE)
GRATED PARMESAN SOY CHEESE (OPTIONAL, BUT GOOD)

1. Wash and cut squashes in half lengthwise. Remove seeds from
   squash halves to make a cavity.

2. Place squash halves cut side down in large skillet. Add 1/2 cp
   spring water and steam gently for 4-5 minutes or until just tender.

3. Remove from skillet and place in oven proof dish cut side up.

4. Brush lightly with oil and sprinkle with herbs and soy Parmesan
   cheese, if using. Center can also be filled with other vegetables if
   desired.

5. Place under broiler and broil until lightly browned.

6. Remove and serve hot or cool. Can serve as picnic vegetable at
   room temperature.

*Comments: Summer time special. Easy to prepare, pretty to look at, and
delicious to eat.*

SUMMER VEGETABLES W/KUZU SAUCE

Serves: 4-6   Time: 00:30

3-4 CARROTS
2-3 SMALL YELLOW SQUASH
1/2 HEAD CAULIFLOWER
1 TSP GRATED GINGER
1 TBL KUZU DISSOLVED IN
2 TBL SPRING WATER
CHOPPED PARSLEY FOR GARNISH

1. Scrub carrots and cut into one inch diagonal chunks.

2. Put 1 cp spring water in bottom of 3 quart saucepan. Place metal steaming basket in pan and add carrots. Place over high heat and bring to boil.

3. Steam carrots while preparing other vegetables.

4. Wash squash and cut into 2-3 inch diagonal chunks. Set aside. Wash cauliflower and break into one inch size florets.

5. When carrots are almost tender add squash and cauliflower to the steaming basket and cook until all are tender but not mushy.

6. Remove vegetable to a large serving dish. Remove steamer basket.

7. Bring juice to a boil and add juice of grated ginger.

8. Combine kuzu with 2 tbl water and stir into hot liquid. Cook until thickened and clear, add additional water if too thick.

9. Pour over vegetables and garnish with chopped parsley. Serve.

Comments: Very pretty as well as a delicious way to use up those squashes.

SUNSHINE TURNIPS

Serves: 4-6   Time: 00:20

1 1/2 LB PURPLE TOP TURNIPS
1 TBL MILD OIL
JUICE OF 1/2 FRESH LEMON
SEA SALT TO TASTE
CHOPPED FRESH PARSLEY

1. Scrub turnips and cut into 1/4 inch slices. Cut slices into 1/4 inch sticks.

2. Drop into boiling salted water and cook for 10-15 minutes or until tender. Drain well and save liquid for soups.

3. Toss with oil, lemon juice, salt, chopped parsley and serve while hot.

4. If on a strict healing diet, you can omit the oil.

Comments: You never knew turnips could taste so good.

SWEET SOUR CABBAGE

Serves: 4-6   Time: 00:15

1 MED SIZED CABBAGE SHREDDED
2-3 TBL WATER
1/2 TSP SESAME OIL
1/2 TSP UMEBOSHI PASTE
1 TBL MIRIN

1. Shred cabbage finely.

2. In wok or large skillet, heat water and oil.

3. Stir-fry cabbage for 3-4 minutes until wilted and just barely tender.

4. Combine umeboshi paste and mirin and add to mixture. Stir and mix until well blended.

5. Serve immediately.

Comments: *Quick, easy and delicious*

THREE COLOR VEGGIE COMBO

Serves: 4-6   Time: 00:30

3-4 MED SIZE CARROTS
1/2 MED SIZE CAULIFLOWER
3-4 CP THINLY SLICED KALE
1-2 TSP UMEBOSHI VINEGAR
SEA SALT

1. Scrub carrots and cut into 1/2 inch chunks.

2. Place in steamer basket over 1 cp hot water.

3. Steam while preparing rest of vegetables. Wash and separate the cauliflower into florets. Wash kale and cut into thin strips.

4. When carrots are almost tender, add the cauliflower and steam for 5 minutes.

5. Add the kale and steam until bright green and all vegetables are tender.

6. Drain off liquid and reserve for soups.

7. Add umeboshi vinegar to taste and sea salt if desired. If on a strict healing diet this combo tastes great even without the vinegar.

Comments: Dish for all seasons, beautiful to look at and delicious.

WILD GREENS

Serves: 3-4   Time: 00:15

2 QT FRESH DANDELION GREENS
1 CP BOILING WATER
1/4 TSP SEA SALT (OPTIONAL)
CHOPPED CHIVES AND/OR FRESH PARSLEY MAKE A NICE
GARNISH

SAME RECIPE CAN BE USED FOR LAMBS QUARTERS, NETTLES
AND OTHER WILD VEGETABLES.

DANDELION CAN ALSO BE USED RAW IN SALADS OR ADDED
TO SOUPS.

1. Wash greens in cold water and cut into small pieces.

2. Bring water and salt to a boil in large pan and add greens, cover
   and cook until greens turn a bright green.

3. Drain well.

4. Save liquid for soups or as a vegetable drink.

5. Garnish with chives and/or parsley and serve hot.

Comments: _Wild greens are strengthening and fun to obtain yourself._

3. PROTEINS, THE BODY REBUILDERS

Plain beans are great but here are some great meatless tastes. EXPERIMENT!! I'll bet you'll find some that your family will truly enjoy and even ask for again, because they are similar in taste to some of your old high fat meat meals.

ADUKI-SQUASH COMBO
BBQ BURGERS
BARLEY LENTIL LOAF
BOSTON BAKED BEANS
BROCCOLI-WALNUT STIR FRY
BUCKWHEAT NOODLES W/SCALLOPS
CREAMY NOODLE CASSEROLE
FRIED RICE W/TOFU
GERMAN STYLE TEMPEH W/CABBAGE
LENTIL-WALNUT LOAF
LENTIL PATE LOAF
LENTIL STEW
MACRO MACARONI & CHEESE
MARINATED BROILED RED SNAPPER
MEATLESS TOFU BALLS
ORIENTAL FISH STEW
PASTA W/GREENS & BEANS
QUICHE FOR ALL SEASONS
ROSY BEAN ROLL
SEITAN STROGANOFF
SHRIMP FRIED QUINOA
SWEET & TANGY TEMPEH
THREE WAY RICE & LENTILS
TOFU RICE CROQUETTES
TOFU SWISS STEAK
TRANSITION TURKEY

HINTS:
To produce tender and digestable beans, wash and soak, generally overnight, then discard soaking water. Add fresh spring water, a 3-inch piece of kombu, and cook. Add salt and/or shoyu sauce 10 minutes before beans are tender. Beans will be tough if salt is added

at beginning of cooking.

Tempeh is reportedly a source of B12 which is often missing in the vegetarian diets. Tempeh should always be well-cooked. Steam for at least 20 minutes before using in a salad or spread.

Tofu is a complete protein. Pressing tofu will make it firmer and more absorbent. Freezing it will create a chewy texture.

ADUKI-SQUASH COMBO

Serves: 6-8   Time: 01:30

1 CP ADUKI BEANS
1 SMALL BUTTERNUT SQUASH
1 ONION
1 STALK CELERY
1 3-INCH PIECE KOMBU
SEA SALT & TAMARI TO TASTE

1. Wash and soak aduki beans and kombu for 3-5 hours.

2. Prepare vegetables by scrubbing and peeling as needed.

3. Cut kombu into small diced pieces and layer in order: kombu, celery, onion and squash.

4. Add beans on top of the vegetables. Pour fresh spring water down side of pan to just cover beans. Bring to boil, reduce heat, cover and simmer for 1 hour.

5. Uncover pot and cook at medium temperature until excess moisture has cooked away and mixture is soft and creamy.

6. Add sea salt and tamari and check for seasoning. Adjust as needed.

7. Serve hot or cool as a side dish.

8. Leftovers can be thinned with vegetable broth to make a delicious soup.

Comments: Great sweet taste and smooth texture.

BBQ BURGERS

Serves: 6-8   Time: 00:30

2 CP COOKED DYNAMIC DUO
1 CP WELL DRAINED GARBANZO BEANS
1/4 CP SUNFLOWER SEEDS
1/4 CP TAHINI
1 LG OR 2 MED CARROTS, FINELY GRATED
1 MED ONION, GRATED
1 LG STALK CELERY, GRATED
2 TSP TAMARI OR TO TASTE
1/2 TSP SEA SALT
1/4 CP BEAN JUICE OR BROTH
1/4-1/2 CP BUCKWHEAT FLOUR

OPTIONAL FLAVORING CHOICES:
2-4 TBL FALAFEL MIX
HERBS TO YOUR TASTE

1. Mash beans and combine with grains, sunflower seeds, finely grated carrot, onion and celery.

2. Add tamari, sea salt, bean juice or vegetable stock and mix together very well. Mixture will be quite wet and mushy at this point.

3. Add buckwheat flour gradually until mixture will hold together when formed into a patty.

4. Either fry in lightly greased skillet or bake on oiled pan in a 350F oven for 30 minutes.

5. If you prefer a spicier mixture, add either the falafel mixture or herbs and spices of your choice.

6. Serve hot with gravy or sauce, or cool as a sandwich filling.

Comments: _Great way to use leftovers in a sandwich or with gravy._

BARLEY-LENTIL LOAF

Serves: 4   Time: 00:60

1 CP BARLEY, SOAKED
1/2 CP RED LENTILS, SOAKED
1/4 CP SUNFLOWER SEEDS
4 CP SPRING WATER
1/4 TSP SEA SALT
1 BAY LEAF (OPTIONAL)

1. Wash and soak the barley and lentils for several hours or overnight.

2. When ready to prepare, preheat the oven to 350F.

3. Combine the drained barley and lentils, sunflower seeds, fresh water, sea salt, and bay leaf in a saucepan and bring to a boil. Simmer for 5 minutes and then pour into a greased loaf pan.

4. Cover tightly and bake for one hour.

5. Cool slightly and serve with parsley garnish or a parsley-scallion sauce.

Comments: Remember to soak barley and lentils ahead of time.

BOSTON BAKED BEANS

Serves: 6-8   Time: 06:00

2 CP NAVY OR PEA BEANS
8 CP SPRING WATER (4 CP TO SOAK & 4 CP FOR BAKING)
4 INCH PIECE OF KOMBU
1 SMALL ONION
2-3 TBL BARLEY MALT SYRUP
1 TSP DRY MUSTARD
1 TSP SEA SALT
2-3 WHOLE CLOVES (OPTIONAL)

1. Wash and soak beans overnight with kombu.

2. Drain and place in saucepan with 4 cp of fresh spring water. Bring to a boil and skim off any scum which forms. Simmer for 5 minutes. Remove from heat and drain liquid and reserve.

3. Place kombu in the bottom of a bean pot. Add peeled onion stuck with whole cloves, if using. Add beans to pot.

4. In a small dish combine the barley malt syrup, salt, dry mustard. Slowly add 1 cp reserved bean cooking liquid. Pour over the beans in the pot and additional bean cooking liquid to cover the beans by about one inch.

5. Cover pot and cook in a 300F oven for 4 to 6 hrs. Check occasionally and add more cooking liquid if needed.

6. Serve when dark brown and tender.

Comments: Great for picnics. Slow cooking for 6 hrs or more develops flavor and tenderness.

BROCCOLI-WALNUT STIR-FRY

Serves: 4   Time: 00:20

1 LB FIRM TOFU
2 TBL OIL
1 CP SPRING WATER
PINCH SEA SALT
2 CARROTS, THINLY SLICED
2 CP BROCCOLI FLORETS
2 ONIONS THINLY SLICED
1 CP MUSHROOMS (OPTIONAL)
1 CP ROASTED WALNUT HALVES
1 TBL KUZU
2 TBL SHOYU SAUCE

1. Drain tofu very well. Cut into 1 inch cubes and brown in 1 tbl oil in wok or large skillet.

2. Bring 2 cp of water with pinch of sea salt to a boil, drop in the thinly sliced carrots and broccoli florets and cook for one minute.

3. Drain well and reserve the cooking water.

4. Remove the tofu from the wok and set aside.

5. Add 1 tbl of oil to the wok and saute the thinly sliced onions until soft over medium heat. Add mushrooms and walnuts.

6. Increase heat to medium high and add carrots and broccoli. Stir and add tofu cubes.

7. To the reserved vegetable juice, add shoyu and blend in 1 tbl kuzu.

8. Add mixture to wok and stir until thick, clear and bubbling.

9. Serve over hot brown rice.

Comments: _Loaded with good protein._

BUCKWHEAT NOODLES W/SCALLOPS

Serves: 2-3   Time: 00:30

1 CP WATER
1 TBL LEMON JUICE
1/2 LB BAY SCALLOPS
1 TSP GRATED GINGER ROOT
1 TBL RICE VINEGAR
1 TSP BARLEY MALT SYRUP
1 TBL OLIVE OIL
1 TBL TAMARI SAUCE
1 TBL MIRIN
6 OZ BUCKWHEAT NOODLES
2 TBL CHOPPED CHIVES

1. Bring water and lemon juice to a boil, add scallops. Reduce heat and simmer 2 to 3 minutes. Drain and place in large salad bowl.

2. Combine the ginger root, vinegar, oil, tamari sauce, and mirin in a small jar and shake well. Set aside.

3. Cook 6 oz of soba noodles according to the package directions. Drain and cool until lukewarm.

4. Add to scallops.

5. Pour on dressing and toss gently, add the chopped chives and toss again and serve at room temperature.

Comments: Wonderful late summer dinner with fresh vegetables.

CREAMY NOODLE CASSEROLE

Serves: 5-6   Time: 00:45

4 CP COOKED BUCKWHEAT NOODLE
2 MED ONIONS SLICED THIN
1 STALK CELERY SLICED THIN
1/2 HEAD CAULIFLOWER BROKEN INTO SMALL FLORETS
1 CARROT SLICED THIN
1 TBL LIGHT SESAME OIL
5 CP SPRING WATER
2 HEAPING TBL KUZU
1/4 CP TAHINI
1/2 TSP SEA SALT
2 TBL TAMARI OR TO TASTE
PARSLEY OR CHIVES TO GARNISH

1. Saute the onions in oil until they are limp, but not browned.

2. Add carrot and celery and saute for a few minutes.

3. Add cauliflower and water and bring to a boil and simmer until the vegetables are tender.

4. While vegetables are cooking, prepare the sauce by combining the tahini, tamari and kuzu with 1/2 cp water and blending to a smooth paste. Add this mixture to the simmering vegetables, stir until all is thick and smooth. Taste for seasonings and add salt if desired.

5. Place cooked noodles in casserole and cover with the vegetable sauce.

6. Bake in 350F oven for 30-40 minutes until browned and bubbling.

7. Garnish with chopped parsley or chives if desired and serve hot.

Comments: Warming & delicious on a cold day.

FRIED RICE WITH TOFU

Serves: 3-4   Time: 00:20

2 CP COOKED BROWN RICE
1 TBL OIL
1 CLOVE GARLIC, CRUSHED
1/2 LB OF TOFU, DICED
1 TBL SHOYU SAUCE
3/4 CP DICED ONIONS
1/2 CP DICED CELERY
3/4 CP FRESH BEAN SPROUTS
EXTRA SHOYU SAUCE IF NEEDED

1. Heat heavy skillet or wok. Add oil and crushed garlic and cook until garlic is light brown and then remove and discard garlic.

2. Add the diced tofu and stir-fry for one minute.

3. Add shoyu sauce and stir in well.

4. Remove tofu from the pan and add onions and celery and stir-fry 2-3 minutes.

5. Add the cooked rice and stir-fry for 1-2 minutes longer.

6. Add the fried tofu and bean sprouts and stir-fry 2 minutes longer.

7. Check for seasoning and add more shoyu sauce if needed.

8. Serve hot topped with chopped green onions.

Comments: Plan ahead to have cooked rice available.

GERMAN STYLE TEMPEH & CABBAGE

Serves: 2-3   Time: 00:30

1 TSP CORN OIL
4 OZ TEMPEH
1/4 HEAD GREEN CABBAGE
1 SMALL ONION
1 CP SAUERKRAUT
1/2 TSP CARAWAY SEED
1/4 CP WATER OR SAUERKRAUT JUICE
1 TSP MELLOW WHITE MISO
1 TBL WATER

1. Heat oil in large skillet.

2. Cube tempeh and add to skillet and cook until golden brown on all sides.

3. Add sliced onion and chopped cabbage.

4. Place sauerkraut on top and sprinkle with caraway seeds. Add water or sauerkraut juice and steam for 10-15 minutes until cabbage is crisply tender.

5. Cream miso with water and add.

6. Simmer gently for a few minutes and serve as a side dish.

Comments: *Goes well with millet mashed potatoes, buckwheat or bulgur.*

LENTIL-WALNUT LOAF

Serves: 3-4   Time: 00:45

1 CP LENTILS, COOKED & DRAINED
1 SMALL ONION, DICED
1 TSP OLIVE OIL
1/4 CP WHEAT GERM
1/4 CP WW BREAD CRUMBS
1/4 CP CHOPPED WALNUTS
1/4 TSP SAGE
1 TBL SOY FLOUR
1/4 CP VEGETABLE BROTH
1 TSP RICE VINEGAR
PINCH SEA SALT

1. Preheat oven to 350F.

2. Saute onion in oil until soft.

3. Mix all ingredients together and place in an oiled loaf pan.

4. Cover tightly and bake for 30 minutes. Remove cover and bake additional 15 minutes or until browned and firm.

5. Serve hot or cold.

Comments: Lentils must be precooked. Recipe can be doubled.

LENTIL PATE LOAF

Serves: 6-8   Time: 00:45

1 1/2 CP LENTILS
3 CP VEGETABLE BROTH/WATER
1 LARGE ONION
1 LARGE CLOVE GARLIC
1 TBL OLIVE OIL
1/4 TSP EACH, DRIED THYME, BASIL & OREGANO
1/2 TO 1 CP DRIED WW BREAD CRUMBS AS NEEDED FOR
CONSISTENCY OF LOAF.
1/2 TSP SEA SALT
1/2 CP CHOPPED PARSLEY
1 TSP UMEBOSHI VINEGAR
1 TSP SHOYU/TAMARI SAUCE

1. Wash lentils, drain and place in 2-3 qt size saucepan. Add stock or water and bring to a boil, reduce heat and simmer, tightly covered for 20 minutes or until very soft.

2. Meanwhile, chop onion and garlic very fine. Heat oil in skillet and saute onion and garlic with herbs over medium heat for about 10 minutes until browned and fragrant. Set aside.

3. Oil a baking loaf tin and preheat oven to 350F.

4. When lentils are done, drain and reserve any extra juice. Mash the cooked lentils with a wooden spoon, add onion mixture, parsley, and bread crumbs as needed to create a smooth texture. Add the vinegar and shoyu sauce. Check for seasonings and adjust as needed.

5. Bake for 30 minutes or until set. Allow to cool to room temperature to serve.

Comments: _Nice for a party. Red lentils create a lighter colored loaf._

LENTIL STEW

Serves: 4-6   Time: 00:50

1 CP GREEN LENTILS
1 3 INCH PIECE KOMBU
1 MED ONION
1 MED CARROT
1 STALK CELERY
1 CLOVE GARLIC (OPTIONAL)
1/2 TSP SEA SALT
1/2 TSP TAMARI

1. Wash lentils and drain.

2. Wipe off kombu with damp cloth and soak in cold water for 10 minutes while you prepare vegetables.

3. Scrub and/or peel vegetables and cut into dice size pieces. Cut kombu in dice size pieces. Layer kombu, vegetables and then lentils in saucepan. Pour spring water down side of pan to just cover all ingredients.

4. Bring mixture to boiling point, cover and simmer for 30 to 45 minutes or until lentils are tender but not mushy.

5. Add salt and tamari and simmer for about 10 minutes longer to blend flavors.

6. Check for seasonings and adjust if needed. Mixture should not be too soupy.

7. Leftovers can be made into a delicious lentil soup by adding vegetable broth and cooking a short while longer.

Comments: _Good hot or cold, carries well for packed lunches._

MACRO MACARONI & CHEESE

Serves: 4   Time: 00:30

1/2 LB WW MACARONI COOKED AND DRAINED

SAUCE
1 LB PKG SILKY OR SOFT TOFU
4 TBL TAHINI BUTTER
3 TBL WHITE MISO
1 TBL FRESH LEMON JUICE
1/4 TO 1/2 CP SPRING WATER OR MORE TO CREATE A THIN
SAUCE.

1. Preheat oven to 350F.

2. Combine all sauce ingredients and blend well. Sauce should be quite thin for baking.

3. Combine macaroni with sauce and place in an oiled casserole.

4. Bake in 350F oven in covered casserole for 20 minutes.

5. Remove cover and bake for 10 to 15 minutes longer to brown top.

6. Serve while still hot.

Comments: Tastes great! You'll never miss the dairy cheese - kids love it.

MARINATED BROILED SNAPPER

Serves: 3-4   Time: 00:20

1 1/2 LBS FRESH FISH

MARINADE:
3 TBL SHOYU SAUCE
1/4 CP SAKE
1 TBL OLIVE OIL
1 TBL LEMON JUICE
1 CLOVE GARLIC, MINCED
1 TSP FRESH GRATED GINGER

LEMON WEDGES AND PARSLEY FOR GARNISH

1. Prepare marinade by combining all ingredients.

2. Rinse fish under cold running water and pat dry. Place in shallow glass dish and pour marinade over. After 2 minutes turn fish over and marinate for 15 minutes, turning often and basting with marinade juices.

3. Preheat broiler and oil baking dish.

4. Remove fish from marinade and place in greased baking dish. Reserve marinade.

5. Broil on first side for 5 minutes, turn and spoon a little reserved marinade over and broil for 3-5 minutes on second side or until fish is no longer transparent and flakes easily.

6. Serve hot with additional marinade poured over the fish, garnish with lemon wedge and parsley.

Comments: Nice with lemon rice pilaf and green veggies.

MEATLESS TOFU BALLS

Serves: 4   Time: 00:30

8 OZ FIRM TOFU
1/4 CP GROUND WALNUTS
1/4 CP WW BREAD CRUMBS OR WHEAT GERM
2 TBL WW FLOUR
1 TBL CHOPPED PARSLEY
1/4 CP MINCED ONION
1/2 TSP BASIL
1/2 TSP OREGANO
2 TSP TAMARI SAUCE OR TO TASTE

1. Mix all ingredients very well, using hands if necessary to obtain a very smooth consistency.

2. Form into 2 inch balls.

3. Bake at 350F until golden brown or deep fry.

4. May be used as a hors d'oeuvre with a dip or covered with a sauce and baked or simmered for an additional 20 minutes and served over pasta, grain, or noodles.

Comments: Use in any manner you would use meat based meatballs.

ORIENTAL FISH STEW

Serves: 4   Time: 00:30

4 DRIED SHIITAKE MUSHROOMS
1 CP SPRING WATER
2 TBL VEGETABLE OIL
1 SMALL ONION THINLY SLICED
1 SMALL CARROT, JULIENNED
1 STALK CELERY THINLY SLICED
1 CP SLICED GREEN CABBAGE
4 CP VEGETABLE STOCK
3/4 LB SCROD OR HADDOCK
2 TBL TAMARI
1 TBL MIRIN OR SAKE
1/4 LB SNOW PEAS
2 SCALLIONS THINLY SLICED

1. Simmer the mushrooms in water for 15 minutes. Drain and reserve the cooking water. Discard the stems and slice and reserve the caps.

2. Saute the onions in a large soup pot until translucent.

3. Add carrots and saute a few minutes, then add celery and cabbage and saute for a few more minutes.

4. Add vegetable stock and reserved cooking water and simmer until vegetables are just tender.

5. Add fish cubes and reserved mushrooms and simmer for 5 to 7 minutes.

6. Combine tamari sauce and mirin and add along with the snow peas and scallions, simmer briefly until peas are a bright green.

7. Check for seasonings and serve hot. For a spicier soup add grated ginger along with the other seasonings.

Comments: Recipe can be doubled, type of fish can be varied.

PASTA WITH GREENS AND BEANS

Serves: 3   Time: 00:30

1/2 LB WW PASTA SPIRALS OR FLATS
3 TSP OLIVE OIL
3 CLOVES OF GARLIC
1 LARGE BUNCH LEAFY GREENS OR BUNCH OF BROCCOLI
1/2 CP WATER
PINCH SEA SALT
1/2 TSP DRIED MARJORAM (OPTIONAL)
1 1/2 CP COOKED CHICKPEAS OR WHITE BEANS, WELL DRAINED

1. Cook pasta al dente, drain and toss while still warm with 1 tsp of olive oil.

2. While pasta is cooking, saute garlic in 2 tsp olive oil using low heat for 1 minute.

3. Add chopped greens or broccoli floret, saute briefly, then add water and seasonings if desired. Cover and cook for 4-5 minutes.

4. Add the beans and simmer gently for 3-5 minutes longer until greens are tender and beans are heated through.

5. Toss the pasta and vegetable bean mixture together.

6. Check for seasonings and serve to 3 hungry people.

Comments: Good way to get those greens and beans into your diet.

QUICHE FOR ALL SEASONS

Serves: 4-6   Time: 00:45

1/2 RECIPE OF SPECIAL PASTRY OR FLAKY PASTRY FILLING
2 TBL OLIVE OIL
2 LG CLOVES GARLIC, MINCED
1/2 CP CHOPPED LEEKS, ONION, SCALLIONS OR SHALLOTS
2 CP STEAMED VEGGIES (CARROT, BROCCOLI, PEAS, GREEN
BEANS, OR CORN)
1 LB SOFT TOFU
2 TBL KUZU DISSOLVED IN
1/4 CP OF COLD WATER
SEA SALT, SHOYU OR MISO AND
UMEBOSHI VINEGAR TO TASTE
THYME & DILL TO TASTE

1. Preheat oven to 350F.

2. If using pastry crust, prepare and set aside.

3. Saute minced garlic and choice of onion until soft. Add your
   choice of vegetables and a small amount of water or vegetable
   stock and steam until just tender.

4. Combine tofu, kuzu mixture, herbs and seasoning in blender or
   food processor and blend until smooth and creamy. Add water,
   vegetable stock or soymilk for a thick creamy consistency.

5. Combine tofu cream and prepared vegetables and pour into crust
   or oiled pan.

6. Bake at 350F for 30-45 minutes or until puffed and set.

7. Cool for 5 minutes before serving.

Comments: Recipe is very adaptable to seasonal veggies. Be sure the mixture is seasoned well for best results. Use the taste test.

ROSY BEAN ROLL

Serves: 6-8   Time: 02:00

2 CP DRY ADUKI BEANS
2 GARLIC CLOVES
2 TBL OLIVE OIL
1 CP DICED ONION
1/2 CP TAHINI
2 TBL LEMON JUICE OR UMEBOSHI VINEGAR
3/4 CP CHOPPED PARSLEY
ROASTED SESAME SEED FOR GARNISH

1. Wash beans and cover with cold water. Soak overnight.

2. Crush garlic cloves and marinate in the oil overnight or for several hours.

3. Drain beans and cover with fresh water. Cook until very tender. Drain beans very well until as dry as possible. Reserve juices for soups.

4. Saute garlic in oil for about 1-2 minutes. Discard garlic and saute diced onion for 1-2 minutes, cover and steam gently until tender.

5. Mash beans, blend 1/2 cp of beans with the onion mixture, tahini, lemon juice or umeboshi vinegar, add remaining beans and parsley, blend all together until smooth and creamy and of consistency which can be formed into rolls.

6. When mixture is very cool form into two rolls. Roll in sesame seeds and refrigerate until ready to slice and serve.

Comments: _Beans must be presoaked. Nice summer dish._

SEITAN STROGANOFF

Serves: 4   Time: 00:60

1 12 OZ JAR SEITAN
2 TBL OLIVE OIL
1 CLOVE CHOPPED GARLIC (OPTIONAL)
2 CP VERY SMALL ONIONS
1/2 LB FRESH MUSHROOMS SLICED 1/4 INCH THICK
2 CP SPRING WATER OR VEGETABLE STOCK
2 TBL WW FLOUR
1/4 LB TOFU BLENDED WITH WATER TO CREAM
CONSISTENCY
2 TSP BARLEY MISO THINNED WITH WATER

1. Drain seitan and reserve liquid.

2. In a large skillet heat olive oil. Saute garlic if using but do not burn. Add peeled small onions and brown lightly. Add sliced mushrooms and saute lightly until they start to loose moisture. Add seitan pieces and water or vegetable stock. Cover and simmer for 30 minutes.

3. Meantime, process tofu in blender until it is a consistency of cream, adding water as needed. Set aside.

4. Blend flour with small amount of water to use as thickener for the gravy. Thin miso with water.

5. When ready to finish the dish, add flour mixture and cook while stirring until thickened. Lower heat and add miso and tofu cream. Cook until all heated thoroughly.

6. Serve over rice or noodles. Garnish with chopped parsley.

Comments: Good company meal. Seitan is wheat gluten which can be purchased or made at home.

SHRIMP FRIED QUINOA

Serves: 4   Time: 00:30

1 TBL OIL
1 TSP FRESH GRATED GINGER
1 FINELY CHOPPED ONION
2 STALKS CELERY & LEAVES, CHOPPED
4 CP COOKED QUINOA
1 CP COOKED SHRIMP, CUT UP
1 CP GREEN PEAS
1-2 TBL TAMARI
1 TBL MIRIN (OPTIONAL)
CAN SUBSTITUTE 1 CP SNOW PEAS SLICED INTO 1/2 INCH
PIECES OR FRESH GREEN BEANS FOR THE GREEN PEAS.

1. Heat a wok or very large skillet. Add oil and ginger, then saute
   onion and celery over medium high heat until partially cooked,
   but still crisp.

2. Add quinoa and tamari, stir to blend ingredients, cover and cook
   for 5 minutes.

3. Add peas, shrimp, and mirin, if desired, and cook for 2-3 minutes
   longer.

4. Serve hot.

Comments: Extends 1 cp of shrimp to serve four people.

SWEET AND TANGY TEMPEH

Serves: 3-4   Time: 00:30

1 6-8 OZ PKG TEMPEH
2 TBL SESAME OIL
2 LARGE ONIONS
2 CP GRATED CARROTS
1-2 TBL TAMARI SAUCE
1-2 TBL UMEBOSHI VINEGAR
TOASTED SESAME SEEDS
CHOPPED SCALLIONS

1. Quarter the tempeh, cut down middle into slices and then cut diagonally into triangles. Boil tempeh in water for 10 minutes. Drain and discard water.

2. Heat oil in skillet, add tempeh, sliced onions and grated carrots. Saute 15-20 minutes, adding water if needed.

3. Add tamari and umeboshi vinegar to taste.

4. Simmer for 5 minutes or more to allow flavors to blend.

5. Garnish with toasted sesame seeds and chopped scallions.

6. Delicious served hot or cold. Tastes even better the next day.

Comments: Thanks to Sal Nietupski for this delicious recipe.

THREE WAY RICE & LENTIL CASSEROLE

Serves: 4   Time: 00:60

3/4 CP LENTILS
1 CP SHORT GRAIN BROWN RICE
1 CP CHOPPED ONION
1 CLOVE GARLIC, MINCED
1 TBL OIL OF CHOICE
1/2 CP COOKED GREEN PEAS
1/2 CP ROASTED SLIVERED ALMONDS

SEASONING CHOICES, CHOOSE ONE GROUP:
1. 2 TSP CURRY POWDER AND
   1/4 TSP DRIED MUSTARD
2. 1 TSP GRATED GINGER
   1/2 TSP DRIED SAGE
3. CHICKEN BOUILLON
   1/2 TSP DRIED SAGE

1. Wash lentils and cook with some of the onion and water to cover until tender.

2. Wash rice and drain well.

3. Heat oil in large saucepan and saute rice, onion and garlic in the oil of your choice. Add 3 cp spring water and/or bullion, if using. Lower heat and simmer for 50 minutes. If using dry seasoning they should be added to the rice at this point.

4. Meanwhile, prepare peas and almonds.

5. Drain lentils and reserve juice. Combine all ingredients and some of the reserve juice if needed.

7. Check for seasonings and serve with garnish of chopped parsley or scallions. Feel free to change the seasonings to your taste and tolerances.

Comments: Your choice of seasonings. Thanks to Joanne Kuricina for this delicious & adaptable recipe.

TOFU-RICE CROQUETTE

Serves: 4   Time: 00:30

16 OZ FIRM TOFU
1/2 PKG PREPARED TOFU-BURGER MIX (FANTASTIC FOODS)
1/2 TSP SEA SALT
8 OZ RAW SUNFLOWER SEEDS
2 TBL TOASTED SESAME SEEDS
1 FINELY GRATED CARROT
1 TO 1 1/2 CP COOKED SHORT-GRAIN BROWN RICE

1. Combine all ingredients.

2. Form into round croquettes and flatten slightly.

3. Pan fry in small amount of sesame oil until brown on both sides.

4. Serve hot. Recipe may be doubled for a crowd. Croquettes may be baked in 350F oven if you need to avoid extra oil. Good with onion-kuzu gravy or mustard and pickles.

Comments: *Our thanks to Margaret Lawson, owner of the Macro Gourmet, Richardson, Tx.*

137

TOFU SWISS STEAK

Serves: 4   Time: 00:30

1 LB FIRM TOFU
6 TBL SHOYU SAUCE
2 TBL RICE VINEGAR
1/2 TSP POULTRY SEASONING
1/4 TSP HERBAMARE *
2 TBL OIL
1 CP SLICED ONION
1/2 CP CHOPPED CARROTS
1/2 CP CHOPPED CELERY
1 CP STOCK (ADD WATER TO RESERVED MARINADE)

* HERBAMARE IS A COMMERCIAL SEASONING AVAILABLE AT
  HEALTH FOOD STORES

1. Freeze the tofu overnight or longer. Thaw, squeeze out as much
   moisture as possible and then slice into equal portions 1/4 inch
   thick.

2. Prepare marinade with shoyu sauce, rice vinegar and seasonings.
   Pour over the tofu slices and marinate for at least 2 hours.

3. Remove slices from marinade and dip in flour and brown well in
   oil in skillet.

4. Add to the pan onions, carrots, celery and stock. Cover and cook
   over low heat for 5 to 10 minutes or until most of moisture has
   been absorbed.

5. Prepare tofu Swiss steak gravy (see recipe). Pour gravy over tofu
   and cook slowly over low heat for about on hour.

Comments: Plan ahead to freeze tofu and to thaw and marinate.

TOFU SWISS STEAK GRAVY

Serves: 4   Time: 00:10

1/4 CP WW FLOUR
1/4 CP OIL
2 TBL SHOYU SAUCE
1 1/2 CP VEGETABLE BROTH OR SPRING WATER

1. In a separate pan, bubble together for two minutes the flour which has first been browned in the oil.

2. Whip in the shoyu and vegetable broth or water and cook until smooth and thick. Pour over the tofu and continue cooking as directed.

TRANSITION TURKEY WITH GRAVY

Serves: 2-4   Time: 00:30

1 8 OZ PACKAGE OF TEMPEH
2 TBL OIL OF CHOICE
1 CP VEGETABLE STOCK OR SPRING WATER
1 TBL CHICK PEA MISO
1/4 TSP SAGE
1/4 TSP SAVORY
1/4 TSP THYME
1 TBL KUZU DISSOLVED IN
2 TBL COLD WATER

1. Cut tempeh into small pieces and saute in oil until golden brown. Drain tempeh and place in saucepan.

2. Prepare gravy by blending together miso and herbs with the stock. Pour over the tempeh and bring to a boil, reduce heat and simmer very gently for 30 minutes.

3. Dissolve kuzu in water and stir into mixture and cook until thickened. Check seasonings and adjust if needed.

4. Serve as a gravy over noodles, mock mashed potatoes, or as a pot pie or hot sandwich. Tempeh pieces can also be removed from sauce before it is thickened and used for sandwiches.

5. Chopped parsley is a nice garnish for this dish.

Comments: _Delicious way to get the taste without serving animal food._

4. SOUP DU JOUR

What is more comforting than a bowl of soup? Soup can make a cold rainy day warm and a bright cheery day even better. Starting the meal with soup prepares the digestive system for the meal to come and is a very good way to slip in those sea vegetables that we all need for our supply of minerals.

STOCKS

BASIC VEGETABLE BROTH
FISH STOCK
HEARTY VEGETABLE STOCK
JIFFY VEGETABLE STOCK
KOMBU STOCK
KOMBU-MUSHROOM

SOUPS

BUTTERNUT SURPRISE
CREAM OF BROCCOLI
CREAMY CARROT W/DILL
CREAMY GARBANZO
CREAMY SPLIT PEA
FRENCH ONION
GINGERED LEEK & LENTIL
GRAIN GREEN AND BEAN SOUP
GREEN SPLIT PEA W/BARLEY
J.A. VICHYSSOISE
KOMBU BOTH W/TOFU & LEMON
LIGHT MISO SOUP WITH
WAKAME
MIDAS ROOT
SPRING GREEN PEA
SUMMER MINESTRONE
SUMMER SQUASH
SUMMERTIME CORN CHOWDER
VEGETABLE BARLEY

HINTS:
Don't forget to save vegetable cooking liquids to add to your stock pot. Good nutrition is going down the drain in most homes today.

BASIC VEGETABLE BROTH

Serves: 8   Time: 00:60

1 LARGE YELLOW ONION
3 STALKS OF CELERY
2 LARGE CARROTS
3 TO 4 SCALLIONS OR 1 SMALL LEEK
1 MEDIUM WHITE TURNIP
1 BAY LEAF
4 SPRIGS OF PARSLEY
6 WHOLE BLACK PEPPERCORNS (OPTIONAL)
2 QT PLUS 1 CP OF WATER

1. Wash and prepare vegetables. It is not necessary to peel, just scrub well. Use the inner layers of onion skin to add color to the broth. Slice or dice the vegetables into small pieces.

2. Place all ingredients in a large stockpot and add the water. Bring to a boil and then reduce to just a simmer. Simmer uncovered for 1 hour adding more water if needed.

3. Strain stock through a fine sieve or cheesecloth-lined colander.

4. Return stock to cleaned pot and cool quickly. Flavor can be adjusted when using by adding tamari sauce, rice vinegar, lemon juice or other seasoning if desired.

FISH STOCK

Serves: 6-8   Time: 00:45

1 LB FISH HEAD & BONES
1 CARROT
1 STALK CELERY
1 MEDIUM ONION
3 INCH PIECE KOMBU
2 QT SPRING WATER
1 CLOVE GARLIC
1 BAY LEAF
1/4 TSP THYME (OPTIONAL)
1 TBL TAMARI SAUCE
1 TSP SEA SALT
1 TSP LEMON JUICE OR RICE VINEGAR

1. Cut vegetables into chunks and combine all ingredients in a large
   stock pot.

2. Bring to boiling point, reduce heat and simmer for 30 minutes.

3. When cool enough to handle, strain through several thicknesses of
   cheese cloth and pour into clean jars.

4. Can be used immediately for soup or sauce. Will keep for 2-3 days
   refrigerated or up to 3 months frozen.

Comments: _Can be used for soups or sauces very good source of calcium._

HEARTY VEGETABLE STOCK

Serves: 6-8   Time: 00:60

1/2 CP WHITE BEANS WASHED AND SOAKED OVERNIGHT
2 TBL OIL
2 LARGE CARROTS
1 LARGE ONION
1 STALK CELERY
1 LARGE LEEK
1 CLOVE GARLIC
2 QT SPRING WATER

SEASONINGS
SMALL HANDFUL OF PARSLEY
1 BAY LEAF
6 BLACK PEPPERCORNS (OPTIONAL)
1 TSP FRESH THYME OR SAVORY (OPTIONAL)
1 TSP BROWN RICE VINEGAR

1. Place beans in a cheesecloth square and tie loosely with string.

2. Place dry seasonings in a cheesecloth square and tie.

3. Heat oil in stockpot and saute chopped vegetables for about 5 minutes.

4. Add water, beans in bag, and seasoning bag. Bring to boil and skim any foam that forms from top of mixture.

5. Cover and simmer for about 1 hour.

6. Remove bean bag and seasoning bag. Strain mixture, add rice vinegar, check for seasoning and adjust as needed.

7. This is a wonderful stock to make french onion soup. Cooked beans can be made into a bean spread.

Comments: Hearty stock for hearty soups and stews.

145

JIFFY VEGETABLE STOCK

Serves: 4   Time: 00:20

1 ONION
1 CARROT
1/2 INCH PIECE OF DAIKON
1 STALK CELERY (OPTIONAL)
2 OR 3 SPRIGS OF PARSLEY
1 1/2 QUARTS SPRING WATER

1. Peel onion and slice. Scrub carrot and slice. Cut daikon radish
   into cubes. Slice celery and chop parsley. Add to water and bring
   to boil. Simmer 15-20 minutes.

2. Strain out vegetables and reserve for other uses.

3. Check for flavor.

*Comments: Can be used immediately for miso soup or refrigerated and used
as desired.*

KOMBU STOCK

Serves: 6   Time: 00:30

1 6 INCH PIECE KOMBU
2 QT COLD WATER

1. Bring water and kombu to a boil. Turn down heat to lowest point
   where still boiling gently and continue cooking for 30 minutes.

2. Reserve liquid as base. Kombu may be used in another dish later
   or may also be diced finely at this point and left in stock.

Comments: Use as base for soups or to cook vegetables or grains.

KOMBU MUSHROOM STOCK

Serves: 6   Time: 00:30

4 DRIED SHIITAKE MUSHROOMS
6 INCH PIECE KOMBU
2 QT SPRING WATER

1. Soak mushrooms in 2 cp water for 5 to 10 minutes.

2. Place kombu in saucepan and add 2 qt of cold water and start on
   high heat. Add mushrooms and their soaking water to the pot.
   Bring to boiling point and then simmer for 10 minutes.

3. Remove kombu and mushrooms and reserve for other uses.
   Kombu can be dried and used again. Mushroom stems should be
   discarded as they are very tough. Mushroom caps can be sliced
   and used in soups.

4. Store stock in refrigerator and used within 5 days.

BUTTERNUT SURPRISE SOUP

Serves: 6   Time: 00:60

2 1/2 TO 3 LB BUTTERNUT SQUASH
1 MEDIUM ONION CHOPPED
2 MEDIUM TART APPLES, PEELED, CORED, AND CHOPPED
3-4 CP VEGETABLE BROTH
PINCH SEA SALT
1/4 TSP DRIED MARJORAM
1/4 TSP NUTMEG
1/4 TSP GINGER OR 1 TSP GRATED FRESH GINGER
1 TSP TAMARI SAUCE OR TO TASTE
1 TBL RICE SYRUP OR TO TASTE

1. Peel and seed the butternut squash, cut into cubes. Place in large saucepan and add the chopped onions and apples.

2. Add 2 to 3 cups of vegetable broth and 1/4 tsp marjoram and simmer gently until the squash is tender.

3. Cool slightly and then blend in small batches to a smooth creamy consistency. Start the blender at low speed and gradually increase to blending speed.

4. When all is blended return to cleaned saucepan and place over low heat.

5. Add additional broth for correct soup texture as needed.

6. Add nutmeg, ginger, tamari, and rice syrup. Check for seasonings.

7. Serve hot with crouton garnish if desired.

Comments: _Wonderful autumn & winter soup._

CREAM OF BROCCOLI SOUP

Serves: 4   Time: 00:30

1 BUNCH OF BROCCOLI
1 LARGE LEEK
1 STALK CELERY WITH LEAVES
1 TBL OLIVE OIL
1 QT VEGETABLE STOCK OR WATER
1 TSP SEA SALT
1/2 CP COOKED BROWN RICE
1 CP SOYMILK

1. Wash broccoli and separate flowerets from stalks. Peel stems if tough and slice into 1/2 inch pieces. Set aside.

2. Prepare leek and celery by cleaning and chopping coarsely.

3. In a 2 qt saucepan saute the leek and celery in the olive oil until tender but not brown.

4. Add broccoli and vegetable stock to the pot and bring to boiling point.

5. Add salt, reduce heat simmer, cover for 10 minutes until broccoli is tender but still bright green.

6. Cool to lukewarm and then process in blender or food processor along with cooked rice and milk.

7. Return to saucepan and heat to serving temperature. Makes 4 generous servings.

Comments: Excellent for spring or fall.

CREAMY CARROT SOUP WITH DILL

Serves: 4   Time: 00:30

1 TBL OIL OF CHOICE
4-5 MEDIUM SIZE CARROTS TO MAKE 2 CUPS SLICED
1 MEDIUM ONION
2 CP VEGETABLE BROTH
1 TBL FRESH DILLWEED OR
1 TSP DRIED DILLWEED
1/2 TSP SEA SALT
1/4 TSP WHITE PEPPER (OPTIONAL)
1/2 CP SOYMILK
CARROT FLOWER & DILL WEED FOR GARNISH

1. Scrub and slice carrots thinly to prepare 2 cups of vegetable. Peel and chop onion.

2. Heat oil in a large saucepan and gently saute the onion until just barely limp (do not brown). Add sliced carrots, vegetable broth and dill and bring to boiling point.

3. Simmer gently for 20-25 minutes or until carrots are very tender.

4. Remove from heat and let cool slightly.

5. Process in batches in blender or food processor until smooth and creamy.

6. Add soy milk, heat again and season to taste with salt and pepper.

7. Serve hot or cover and chill for several hours.

8. When ready to serve garnish with a carrot flower and sprig of fresh dill or sprinkle of dried dill.

Comments: Especially good cold on a hot summer evening.

CREAMY GARBANZO SOUP

Serves: 4-6   Time: 00:45

2 CP COOKED GARBANZO BEANS PREPARED WITH KOMBU
1 TBL OLIVE OIL
1 ONION OR LEEK CHOPPED
1 SMALL CARROT SLICED
1 STALK CELERY
1 CLOVE GARLIC (OPTIONAL)
1-2 CP VEGETABLE BROTH/WATER
SEA SALT & TAMARI TO TASTE OR
HERBAMARE SEASONING TO TASTE

1. Saute onion or leek in oil and add to stockpot with cooked beans, vegetables and stock or water and bring to boiling point. Reduce heat and simmer for 20-30 minutes. Remove cover and let cool to room temperature.

2. Process mixture in small batches in the blender or food processor.

3. Add seasonings and adjust to suit your taste. Reheat and serve with chopped parsley garnish. Great way to use planned over beans.

Comments: Good hearty soup for cold day. Easy with precooked beans.

CREAMY SPLIT PEA SOUP

Serves: 6-8   Time: 01:30

2 CP SPLIT PEAS, SOAKED
2 MEDIUM SIZE LEEKS, CHOPPED
2 LARGE STALKS CELERY, CHOPPED
2 LARGE CARROTS, CHOPPED
1 CLOVE GARLIC, MINCED
1/2 CP DULSE
2 SHIITAKE MUSHROOMS (OPTIONAL)
5-6 CP VEGETABLE STOCK OR SPRING WATER
1 TSP SEA SALT
1 TBL SHOYU/TAMARI SAUCE

1. Soak the split peas and shiitake mushrooms for several hours before preparing the rest of vegetables for the soup.

2. Mince the garlic, chop leeks including some of the green portion and place in large soup kettle.

3. Chop celery and layer over the leeks. Chop carrots and layer over the celery. Drain split peas and mushrooms and layer over the vegetables.

4. Rinse and chop dulse and add to the other ingredients.

5. Pour the vegetable broth or water down the side of the pot until 2 inches over the top of the ingredients. Bring to a boil over a medium heat and then simmer for 1-2 hours until peas are soft. Add more liquid if needed.

6. Add salt and tamari and check for seasoning.

7. Force through a food mill into a clean pan and reheat gently before serving.

8. Garnish with chopped parsley or chives.

Comments: _Good on a cold rainy day, very hearty and filling._

FRENCH ONION SOUP

Serves: 4   Time: 00:60

2-3 SPANISH ONIONS (APPROX. 2 LB.)
2 TBL OLIVE OR SESAME OIL
1 CLOVE GARLIC, CHOPPED FINE
2 TBL WW FLOUR
4 CP VEGETABLE STOCK/WATER
1/4 TSP THYME
1 BAY LEAF
1 TBL TAMARI SAUCE OR TO TASTE
2 TSP LEMON JUICE
1 TBL BARLEY MISO DILUTED IN
1/4 CP SPRING WATER

1. Peel onions and trim ends. Cut onions in half lengthwise, then cut crosswise into thin slices.

2. Heat oil in a large heavy-bottomed kettle or Dutch oven. Add sliced onions and stir well to coat with oil. Cover and cook at medium-low temperature until onions are very limp and just beginning to color, about 20 minutes. Stir in chopped garlic.

3. Increase heat to medium and cook uncovered, stirring frequently until onions are amber or caramel colored, about 30 minutes.

4. Sprinkle flour into onion and stir thoroughly. Cook over medium heat for 2-3 minutes.

5. Stir in 1 cp of broth and stir well, scraping up browned bits from bottom of the pan. Add remaining broth and simmer partially covered for 20-30 minutes.

6. Remove bay leaf and add tamari sauce and dilute miso. Simmer gently for a minute and check seasonings. Serve hot with croutons.

Comments: *Serve with WW croutons and grated soy cheese if desired.*

153

GINGERED LEEK AND LENTIL SOUP

Serves: 4-6   Time: 00:30

1/2 LB LENTILS
8 CP VEGETABLE BROTH
2 TBL OLIVE OIL (OPTIONAL)
2 CP CHOPPED LEEKS
1 TBL MINCED GARLIC
1 TBL MINCED FRESH GINGER
1 TSP TAMARI SAUCE

1. Add washed lentils to the 8 cups of hot vegetable broth and let set for 15 minutes.

2. While soaking lentils, saute the leeks in oil for 3-4 minutes until softened. Add garlic and ginger and saute for 2-3 minutes longer.

3. Combine with lentils and broth and simmer until lentils are tender but not mushy, about 25 minutes.

4. Remove from heat and stir in tamari sauce. Check for seasonings and serve hot.

Comments: Reheats well.

GRAIN, GREEN AND BEAN SOUP

Serves: 4   Time: 00:20

1 TBL OLIVE OIL
1 LARGE CARROT, CHOPPED
1 CELERY STALK, CHOPPED
1 SMALL ONION, CHOPPED
3 CP VEGETABLE STOCK
1 CP SLICED, PACKED GREENS (KALE OR BOK CHOY ARE
GOOD)
1 CP COOKED GARBANZO BEANS
1 CP COOKED SHELL MACARONI
SEA SALT TO TASTE
SHOYU TO TASTE

1. In large saucepan, heat olive oil and saute carrot, celery, and onion
   for 5 minutes over medium heat until limp. Do not brown or burn.

2. Add vegetable broth and chopped greens. Cover and simmer for
   10 minutes.

3. Add cooked beans and pasta, simmer until heated through.

4. Season to taste with sea salt and shoyu and serve with garnish of
   chopped parsley or green scallions.

Comments: Easy to make and delicious to eat.

GREEN SPLIT PEA/BARLEY SOUP

Serves: 12   Time: 00:60

2 CP GREEN SPLIT PEAS
1/4 CP BARLEY
10 CP SPRING WATER
1 BAY LEAF
2 ONIONS, CHOPPED & SAUTEED
2 CARROTS, GRATED
3 CLOVES GARLIC, MINCED
1 TSP DRIED THYME
2 TSP SEA SALT
1 TBL BROWN RICE MISO

GARNISH
FINELY CHOPPED SCALLIONS

1. Bring first 4 ingredients to a boil, reduce heat and simmer about 40 to 50 minutes.

2. Add the sauteed onion, carrot, garlic and thyme to the soup pot.

3. Season with sea salt and brown rice miso. Simmer an additional 15 minutes.

4. Serve with finely chopped scallions.

Comments: Our thanks to Margaret Lawson, owner of the Macro Gourmet, Richardson, TX.

J.A. VICHYSSOISE

Serves: 4-6   Time: 00:30

1 LB JERUSALEM ARTICHOKES
1 MEDIUM SIZE ONION
1 CP SPRING WATER
1 CP SOY MILK
PINCH SEA SALT
HERBAMARE SEASONING TO TASTE
ADDITIONAL SOY MILK AS NEEDED FOR PROPER
CONSISTENCY

1. Scrub and scrape the artichokes.

2. Combine artichokes, water, soy milk, and sea salt in a 3 qt saucepan and bring to a boil. Reduce heat and simmer until artichokes are very tender, about 10-12 minutes.

3. Remove from heat and cool slightly.

4. Force mixture through a foley food mill or place in a electric blender to liquify. Return to saucepan and add Herbamare seasoning and additional soymilk as needed to obtain the proper texture.

5. Serve with freshly snipped chives. Can be served hot or cool.

Comments: _Nice beginning to a special dinner._

KOMBU BROTH WITH TOFU & LEMON

Serves: 4-6   Time: 00:30

4 CP COLD VEGETABLE BROTH
6 INCH PIECE OF KOMBU
1/2 LB FIRM TOFU
4 GREEN SCALLIONS
1 LEMON
1 TBL SHOYU OR TO TASTE

1. Wipe kombu piece with a damp cloth. Place in 2 qt pot and add the vegetable broth. Bring to boil, reduce heat and simmer for 5 minutes.

2. Remove kombu and reserve for use another time.

3. Cut tofu into 1/4 inch squares and slice scallions into thin rounds. Add to soup and simmer gently for 10 minutes.

4. Cut lemon in half. Juice one half and add juice to soup. Add shoyu sauce and check for seasonings.

5. Slice other half into very thin slices and float one slice on top of each bowl of soup.

6. Serve hot.

Comments: _Nice light soup for summer or before a heavy meal._

LIGHT MISO SOUP WITH WAKAME

Serves: 4   Time: 00:20

3 INCH PIECE OF WAKAME
3 INCH PIECE OF DAIKON RADISH OR
4 RED RADISHES
3 GREEN SCALLIONS
2 1/2 CP VEGETABLE BROTH OR SPRING WATER
1 TBL MELLOW WHITE MISO OR CHICK PEA MISO

1. Cut or break wakame into small pieces.

2. Bring vegetable broth or water to a boil and add wakame, sliced radishes and white portion of green onion and simmer for 10-15 minutes.

3. While soup is simmering, chop green portion of scallions very finely for garnish.

4. Dissolve miso in 2 tbl water. Remove soup from heat and add miso and let sit for several minutes before serving.

5. Garnish with chopped green portion of scallions.

Comments: *Nice beginning for a heavy meal or for breakfast.*

MIDAS ROOT SOUP

Serves: 4-5   Time: 00:30

4 LARGE CARROTS
4 LARGE PARSNIPS
1 LARGE ONION
4-5 CP VEGETABLE STOCK OR SPRING WATER
1 TBL TAMARI
1 TBL MELLOW WHITE MISO
CHOPPED PARSLEY OR SCALLIONS FOR GARNISH

1. Cut vegetables into large chunks. Combine with stock or water in pressure cooker and pressure cook for 20 minutes.

2. Let cool to room temperature and then process in blender for creamy consistency. Add more stock or water if too thick.

3. Return to clean saucepan. Heat gently and add tamari.

4. Dilute miso with water and add just before serving. Allow to simmer for 2-3 minutes.

5. Garnish with chopped parsley or scallions and serve.

Comments: _Easy to make, very delicious and good for the sweet tooth._

SPRING GREEN PEA SOUP

Serves: 6   Time: 00:30

1 LB FRESH GREEN PEAS OR
1 10 OZ PACKAGE FROZEN PEAS
1/2 CP PACKED ROMAINE LEAVES
1 TBL OLIVE OIL
2 CP WATER OR STOCK
4 OZ SOFT TOFU
1 CP SOYMILK
SEA SALT TO TASTE OR
HERBAMARE OR TAMARI
1 TBL MIRIN (OPTIONAL)

1. In large saucepan, saute peas and Romaine in the olive oil for 3-4 minutes.

2. Add water or broth and simmer for 15 minutes.

3. Cool to room temperature. Blend in batches with the tofu until very smooth.

4. Force through strainer to remove fiber if desired.

5. Add soy milk to the puree and heat to desired temperature. Do not boil.

6. Season to taste.

Comments: *May be served hot or cold. Garnish with chopped fresh chive if desired.*

SUMMER MINESTRONE

Serves: 6-8   Time: 00:60

1 QT VEGETABLE STOCK
1/2 CP SPLIT PEAS WASHED AND DRAINED
1 CARROT, THINLY SLICED
1 ONION, THINLY SLICED
1 BAY LEAF
1 CP WW MACARONI
1/2 CP COOKED GARBANZO BEANS
1 SMALL SUMMER SQUASH
2 CELERY STALKS, CHOPPED
1/2 CP CUT GREEN BEANS
1/2 TSP SEA SALT OR TAMARI
1 CP SHREDDED ESCAROLE
1/4 CP CHOPPED BASIL
2 TBL FRESH LEMON JUICE

1. Bring stock to boil with the split peas, carrot, onion and bay leaf. Reduce heat and simmer for about 45 minutes or until peas are tender.

2. Meanwhile, cook macaroni and chop other vegetables. When peas are tender, add the squash, celery, beans, macaroni, and salt. Simmer for 5 minutes.

3. Add escarole and basil, simmer for 5 minutes more.

4. Add lemon juice and adjust seasonings. Serve hot.

Comments: *Nice beginning for a summer meal, or a soup and sandwich lunch. Good way to use up all those wonderful fresh vegetables.*

SUMMER SQUASH SOUP

Serves: 2-4   Time: 00:30

1 TBL OLIVE OIL
1 MED SIZE YELLOW SQUASH
1 MED SIZE ZUCCHINI SQUASH
3/4 CP CELERY LEAVES, PACKED
3 CP CHICKEN BROTH OR VEGETABLE BROTH
1/4 CP FRESH BASIL
1/2 TSP SEA SALT
1/4 TSP WHITE PEPPER
CHOPPED CHIVES OR PARSLEY FOR GARNISH

1. In large saucepan saute onion in oil until limp. Dice squashes and add to mixture along with celery leaves and fresh basil. Add 1 cp of broth and simmer gently until vegetables are tender.

2. Cool to room temperature and then blend in batches to a smooth thick consistency, adding more broth as needed.

3. Return to saucepan and add seasonings. Taste and adjust to taste.

4. Heat again to serve hot or refrigerate to serve cold.

5. Soup should be rich and creamy, not watery. Garnish with chopped chives or parsley before serving.

Comments: Wonderful as a first course either hot or cold.

SUMMERTIME CORN SOUP

Serves: 6   Time: 00:45

1 TBL COLD PRESSED OIL
1 MEDIUM ONION, MINCED
1/2 TSP GRATED FRESH GINGER
KERNELS FROM 5 EARS OF CORN (ABOUT 2 CP)
5 CP VEGETABLE STOCK OR SPRING WATER
3 INCH PIECE OF KOMBU
1 TSP SEA SALT
1/2 CP OATMEAL
1/2 CP WATER
1 TBL SHOYU OR TAMARI
INNER LEAVES OF SWEET CORN MAKE EXCELLENT SWEET
VEGETABLE BROTH

1. Heat oil in a large saucepan, saute onion and ginger in the oil for 4-
   5 minutes, until soft. Add corn, vegetable broth or water, kombu,
   and salt to the saucepan. Bring to boil, reduce heat and simmer for
   15 to 20 minutes.

2. Combine oats and water and blend together. Add to soup mixture
   and simmer for 15 minutes longer.

3. Add shoyu at end of cooking period.

4. Remove kombu, cut into small pieces and return to the soup.

5. Check seasonings and serve.

Comments: *Easy to make and a delicious way to use leftover sweet corn.*

VEGETABLE-BARLEY SOUP

Serves: 4   Time: 00:60

4 CP VEGETABLE STOCK/WATER
1 4 INCH PIECE OF KOMBU
2 CELERY STALKS
2 CARROTS
2 LEEKS
1/4 CP CHOPPED PARSLEY
2 SMALL BAY LEAVES
1/4 CP UNCOOKED BARLEY
1 CLOVE GARLIC (OPTIONAL)
1/2 TSP DARK SESAME OIL
SHOYU SAUCE TO TASTE

1. Bring vegetable stock or water and kombu to a boil in a large soup kettle.

2. Slice celery, carrots, and leeks on the diagonal. Chop parsley. Add vegetables and uncooked barley to the stock. If you are using the garlic, mince finely and add to the pot. Add sesame oil and simmer gently for 1 hour. Check near end of cooking time and add additional stock or water if too thick.

3. When cooking time is up remove the bay leaves and discard. Remove the kombu, slice into small thin slices and return to the soup.

4. Check for seasonings and add shoyu sauce and salt to taste. Serve hot. Soup prepared with vegetable stock is much more flavorful than that made with water. Garnish with more chopped parsley or a mix of chopped parsley and chopped scallions.

Comments: Barley is a natural thickener for the soup.

5. LIGHTEN UP: SALADS & PICKLES

America has an obsession with salads. We really don't need a salad with every meal. Following the seasonal way of eating it is best to use more raw salads in the spring and summer and blanched, pressed, pickled and root salads in the fall and winter. Salads can range from a light mixed green, to hearty root vegetable salads, to main dish grain and bean salads. Salads can be made from vegetables, beans, grains and fruits and sea vegetables. TRY THEM ALL!!

SALADS

BEAN SALAD W/SPRING VEGGIES
BARLEY NUT SALAD
CELEBRATION SALAD
CHINESE CABBAGE PRESSED SALAD
COLESLAW WITH CELERY SEED
DRESSING
COUSCOUS VINAIGRETTE
HIJIKI W/CREAMY DRESSING
MOLDED CRANBERRY
PERFECTION
RAW PRESSED SALAD
ROSY SALAD
SUNSHINE SALAD
SUMMER GREEN BEAN SALAD
TABOULI
WATERCRESS WINTER SALAD
WINTER ROOT SALAD
WHOLE MEAL SALAD

PICKLES

FRESH CUCUMBER
KOSHER DILLS
PICKLED VEGETABLES W/DULSE
RUSSIAN PICKLE RELISH
SPICED CRANBERRY RELISH
UMEBOSHI VEGETABLE PICKLES

166

HINTS:
One bar of kanten equals 3 tbl agar-agar flakes. One bar or 3 tbl of agar-agar thickens 3 cups of liquid.

BEAN SALAD WITH SPRING VEGGIES

Serves: 4   Time: 00:30

2 CP WELL DRAINED COOKED PINTO BEANS
1 STALK CELERY
6 RED RADISHES
1 CP SNOW PEAS

1. Cut vegetables into bite-sized pieces and blanch for 30-60 seconds in 2 cp of boiling water until they turn a bright color.

2. Drain and cool quickly. Save blanching liquid for soup stock.

3. Combine beans and vegetables.

4. Prepare dill dressing (see recipe).

5. Pour dressing over salad ingredients and mix well.

6. Marinate for several hours before serving. Garnish with chopped parsley, chives, or scallions.

Comments: _Can use other types of beans._

BARLEY NUT SALAD

Serves: 3-4   Time: 00:60

1 CP UNCOOKED BARLEY
1/3 CP WHEAT BERRIES
2 2/3 CP SPRING WATER
1/2 CP FRESH LEMON JUICE
1/3 CP OLIVE OIL
1/2 TSP SEA SALT
2 STALKS CELERY, CHOPPED
1 CARROT, FINELY CHOPPED
1 MEDIUM ONION, FINELY CHOPPED
1/2 CP MINCED FRESH PARSLEY
1/2 CP ROASTED NUTS (ALMONDS, WALNUTS, OR
HAZELNUTS)

1. Wash barley and wheat berries thoroughly.

2. Combine with water in a 1 1/2 - 2 qt saucepan and bring to a boil.
   Cover and simmer until all water is absorbed and the grains are
   tender (50-60).

3. Allow to cool while preparing the dressing and vegetables.

4. Wash and chop the celery, onion, and carrot. Mince parsley and
   chop nuts. Combine lemon, oil and salt.

5. Combine all ingredients and mix thoroughly. Check for seasoning
   and adjust if needed.

6. Refrigerate for several hours before serving to blend flavors.

7. Can be served as is, on a bed of salad greens, or as filling for pita
   bread sandwich with sprouts.

CELEBRATION SALAD

Serves: 4-6   Time: 00:30

4 CP COOKED BROWN RICE OR OTHER GRAIN OF CHOICE
2 CP VEGETABLES, SLICED (ANY COMBINATION OF ONIONS,
BROCCOLI, BEANS, RADISHES, PARSNIPS, ETC.)
1 1/2 CP CHOPPED KALE OR COLLARDS
1 CP TOASTED SEED (SESAME, SUNFLOWER OR PUMPKIN)
1 DILL PICKLE, DICED
SALAD DRESSING OF CHOICE

1. Boil vegetable slices 1-3 minutes in boiling water. Drain and save water for soup stock.

2. Boil greens in fresh water for 3-6 minutes. Drain.

3. Toss all ingredients together, add dressing and mix well.

4. Garnish with more seeds, sprigs of watercress, parsley or chopped scallions.

5. Serve chilled in warm weather, serve warm in cold weather.

6. To boost protein level, add cooked beans or 1 Lb of cubed tofu which has been lightly boiled.

7. To boost nutrient levels, add wakame, kombu or dulse (finely cut) and cooked with the grain.

8. Your choice of dressings or try either of these: 1/2 cp tahini with 1/2 cp umeboshi paste. Blend well. OR 1/2 cp tahini with 3/4 - 1 cp umeboshi vinegar. Blend well.

Comments: Great for traveling. Thanks to P. J. Tetreault for this great recipe.

CHINESE CABBAGE PRESSED SALAD

Serves: 4   Time: 00:15

1/2 HEAD CHINESE CABBAGE, THINLY SLICED (ABOUT 5 CP TIGHTLY PACKED)
5 THINLY SLICED RED RADISHES
1 SMALL CARROT, SLIVERED
1 SMALL ONION, FINELY SLICED
1 SMALL ZUCCHINI SQUASH OR
1 SMALL CUCUMBER
1 TSP UMEBOSHI VINEGAR
1/2 TSP SEA SALT

1. Cut all vegetables very finely and place in a salad press or place in a bowl which a plate will fit into so you can place a weight on it to create 5-10 Lbs pressure. A large jar filled with water will do with a 5 Lb bag of flour balanced on top.

2. Sprinkle the umeboshi vinegar and salt over the salad ingredients and put under pressure for a minimum of 1-2 hours.

3. Gently squeeze juice from the vegetables.   Taste to check for seasonings.

4. If too salty, rinse under cold water and squeeze out again before serving.

171

COLESLAW WITH CELERY SEED

Serves: 4-6   Time: 00:20

1/2 HEAD CABBAGE, SHREDDED
1 STALK CELERY, FINELY SLICED
3-4 SCALLION, FINELY SLICED (USE GREEN PORTION TOO)
3-4 RED RADISHES, THINLY SLICED

DRESSING:
1/2 CP TOFU MAYONNAISE
1 TSP UMEBOSHI VINEGAR
DASH SEA SALT
1/2 TSP CELERY SEEDS

1. Prepare vegetables and set aside while you prepare the dressing.

2. Combine all dressing ingredients and stir until smooth. Check for seasonings.

3. When ready to serve combine vegetables and dressing until well mixed.

COUSCOUS VINAIGRETTE

Serves: 4   Time: 00:15

1 CP COUSCOUS
2 CP BOILING SPRING WATER
3 TBL OLIVE OIL
1 1/2 TBL RICE VINEGAR
3 TBL MINCED PARSLEY
1/4 - 1/2 TSP SEA SALT
DASH WHITE PEPPER (OPTIONAL)
DASH HERBAMARE SEASONING (OPTIONAL)

1. Place couscous in large mixing bowl and pour in boiling water.

2. Cover bowl with plate and let stand for 10 minutes or until the couscous has absorbed all the water.

3. Wisk together the remaining ingredients in a small bowl.

4. Add vinaigrette to the couscous and stir with a fork.

5. Serve warm or at room temperature with garnish of chopped scallion or more minced parsley.

Comments: _Very easy, very fast, and very delicious._

HIJIKI WITH CREAMY DRESSING

Serves: 3-4   Time: 00:60

1/2 OZ HIJIKI
1 TBL DARK SESAME OIL
1 TBL SHOYU SAUCE
2 TBL WHITE MISO
1/2 LB TOFU, SOFT VARIETY
2 TBL RICE VINEGAR
1 TBL TAHINI
1 TSP RICE SYRUP
1 CLOVE GARLIC

GARNISH FOR SALAD:
LETTUCE LEAVES
TOASTED SESAME SEEDS

1. Wash hijiki in cold water. Cover with water and soak overnight or at least 12 hours. Drain and discard soaking water. Chop into 1 inch lengths.

2. Saute in a heavy skillet with the sesame and shoyu for 2 to 3 minutes. Add water to cover halfway and simmer gently for 1 hour, covered.

3. Meanwhile, prepare sauce. Blanch tofu for 2 minutes in boiling water. Drain well and place in blender or food processor with the white miso, rice vinegar, tahini, garlic and rice syrup.

4. Blend until very smooth and creamy.

5. Drain hijiki and mix gently with the sauce.

6. Serve as side dish or place on dark romaine leaf and garnish with sliced red radish, chopped scallions, and carrot curls.

Comments: *Must presoak hijiki for 12 hours. Can be served as a salad.*

MOLDED CRANBERRY SALAD

Serves: 6-8   Time: 00:30

2 CP FRESH CRANBERRIES
2 CP RED COOKING APPLES, CHOPPED
2 TBL AGAR-AGAR
1 1/2 CP SWEET CIDER
1/4 CP MAPLE SYRUP
1 CINNAMON STICK
GRATED RIND OF A LEMON

1. Wash and pick over the cranberries.

2. Wash, peel and chop apples.

3. Combine agar-agar, apple cider, maple syrup, and cinnamon stick in a saucepan.

4. Cook over medium heat until the agar-agar is dissolved. Add cranberries and apples and cook until the cranberries start popping, about 10 minutes.

5. Remove from heat, mix thoroughly, remove cinnamon stick and add lemon rind.

6. Pour into 1 1/2 qt ring mold, or mold in flat dish. Chill for 2 hours or more before serving.

7. Nice served on dark green romaine with tofu sour cream as a dressing. Also very nice just plain.

Comments: _Lovely salad for autumn and winter holidays._

PERFECTION SALAD

Serves: 4   Time: 00:20

3 TBL AGAR-AGAR
3 CP SPRING WATER
1 TSP LEMON JUICE
1/4 TSP KELP POWDER
2 CP GRATED CARROTS
1/2 CP FINELY CHOPPED CABBAGE
1/2 CP FINELY CHOPPED CELERY
1 TBL GRATED ONION
1/3 CP SUNFLOWER SEEDS (OPTIONAL)

1. Soak agar-agar in the water for 5 minutes. Bring to a boil and simmer for 5 minutes or until completely dissolved.

2. Add lemon juice and kelp, remove from heat and allow to cool slightly.

3. Stir prepared vegetables and sunflower seeds, if using, into the mixture.

4. Place in mold and allow to firm at room temperature or chill in refrigerator.

5. Serve with either soy mayonnaise or tofu sour cream as a dressing if desired.

Comments: _Much like mother used to make._

RAW PRESSED SALAD

Serves: 4   Time: 00:20

1 CP FINELY SLICED OR SLIVERED ROOT VEGETABLES
1 CP FINELY CHOPPED GREENS
1/2 TSP SEA SALT
VEGETABLES SHOULD BE VARIED AND SEASONAL
FOR DIFFERENT FLAVORS

1. Prepare vegetables and place in a large bowl or a salad press.
   Sprinkle with salt. Cover with a flat plate if using the bowl. Put a
   weight on top (such as a quart jar filled with water).

2. Press for 30 minutes or longer. Pour off the liquid as it is
   expressed.

3. When ready to serve, check for saltiness. If too salty, rinse quickly
   in fresh water and drain well before serving.

4. Serving size is about 1/4 cp per person.

Comments: Quick to prepare but needs to sit for minimum of 30 minutes.

ROSY SALAD

Serves: 4-5   Time: 00:15

2 RED ONIONS, THINLY SLICED
6 RED RADISHES, THINLY SLICED
1 CP DRY DULSE
1/2 TBL RICE VINEGAR
1/2 TBL UMEBOSHI VINEGAR
DASH OF SEA SALT

1. Wash dulce and soak in cool water.

2. Slice red onion and radishes and combine in bowl.

3. Drain dulse and squeeze out excess liquid. Add to onion and radishes.

4. Mix well and add vinegars and sea salt.

5. Let mixture sit at room temperature for a minimum of 2 hours before serving.

6. Nice served on green lettuce leaves.

Comments: *Very pretty as well as good to eat. Leftovers will keep well for a day or so.*

SUMMER GREEN BEAN SALAD

Serves: 4   Time: 00:20

3 CP WHOLE GREEN BEANS
1/2 CP TOFU MAYONNAISE
FRESH GREENS
2 FINELY SLICED SCALLIONS
4 TSP MINCED SUMMER SAVORY, CHERVIL OR CHIVES

1. Blanch green beans until they turn a very bright green color. Cool quickly and drain.

2. Arrange greens on separate salad plates and place beans and sliced scallions over greens.

3. Dress with tofu mayonnaise or dressing of your choice.

4. Sprinkle with chives and/or herbs of your choice.

Comments: Gardeners delight: Fresh herbs and vegetables from your garden.

SUNSHINE SALAD

Serves: 4   Time: 00:15

3 MED CARROTS, GRATED
1/4 CP RAISINS
1/4 CP SUNFLOWER SEED (OPTIONAL)

DRESSING:
1/8 LB TOFU
1 TBL OIL
1 TSP RICE VINEGAR
1 TSP RICE SYRUP
PINCH SEA SALT
1 TBL TAHINI
1-3 TBL WATER

1. Prepare dressing by boiling tofu for 1 minute, remove from water
   and blend with oil, vinegar, rice syrup, tahini, and water as needed
   to create proper consistency.   You can use a blender, food
   processor, or a suribachi.

2. Grate carrots, add raisins and seeds if using.

3. Combine carrot mixture with the dressing and refrigerate for at
   least one hour before serving.

Comments: Will remind you of the carrot salad mother used to make.

TABOULI

Serves: 4   Time: 00:30

1 CP BULGUR WHEAT
1 CP BOILING SPRING WATER
1 CP CHOPPED PARSLEY
1/2 CP CHOPPED SCALLIONS
1 DICED TOMATO (OPTIONAL)
2 TBL FRESH LEMON JUICE
1/4 CP OLIVE OIL
1/4 TSP SEA SALT
1 TBL FRESH MINT, CHOPPED OR
1/2 TSP DRIED MINT

1. Bring water to a boil, add bulgur and salt.

2. Remove from heat and let sit for 30 minutes to cook the grain while you prepare the rest of the ingredients.

3. Toss the vegetables and seasoning with the grain and chill until ready to serve.

4. Nice served on fresh greens.

Comments: _Good summer salad, very filling and satisfying._

WATERCRESS WINTER SALAD

Serves: 4   Time: 00:20

2 CP WATERCRESS
1 CP SLICED CABBAGE
1/2 CP DULSE
1/2 TO 1 TSP SALT
1/2 CP ROASTED SUNFLOWER

1. Break watercress into bite sized pieces. Slice cabbage very thinly. Break dulse into bite sized pieces. Add salt and mix well.

2. Place in large bowl or salad press. If using bowl, cover with a plate and heavy weight on top to press the salad. If using a salad press tighten down.

3. Allow to set for 2-3 hours.

4. Roast the sunflower seeds and set aside.

5. When ready to serve, drain the vegetables. Check for salt and rinse in cold water and drain again if too salty.

6. Mix in seeds and serve on lettuce leaf with additional seed garnish or red radish slice garnish.

Comments: _Preparation is easy, but must be made 2-3 hours before serving._

WHOLE MEAL SALAD

Serves: 4   Time: 00:20

DRESSING:
1 TBL LIGHT MISO
1 TBL SHOYU SAUCE
1 TBL BROWN RICE VINEGAR
1 TSP SESAME OIL

2 CP COOKED BROWN RICE
1 1/2 CP COOKED ADUKI BEANS
1 SMALL ZUCCHINI DICED AND BLANCHED
1/2 CP CHOPPED SCALLIONS
CHOPPED PARSLEY FOR GARNISH

1. Combine dressing ingredients in a screw top jar and shake until well blended. Set aside.

2. Blanch the zucchini in boiling water for 1 minute.

3. Combine all salad ingredients and pour dressing over and toss until all ingredients are blended.

4. Serve on fresh greens with chopped parsley garnish.

5. Is even better if allowed to marinate for a few hours.

Comments: *Nice summer salad - plan ahead to have cooked rice & beans.*

WINTER ROOT SALAD

Serves: 6   Time: 00:15

1/2 LB PURPLE TOP TURNIPS
1/2 LB CARROTS
2 TBL OLIVE OIL
1 TBL RICE VINEGAR
1 TSP NATURAL PREPARED MUSTARD
1/2 CP THINLY SLICED RADISH
2 TBL CHOPPED PARSLEY
1 TBL CHOPPED CHIVES OR SCALLIONS

1. Scrub and shred the turnips and carrots.

2. Combine prepared vegetables, oil, vinegar, and mustard in a bowl. Cover tightly and refrigerate for 2 hours.

3. To serve, place a mound of turnip mixture on a lettuce leaf on individual plates. Spread radishes around outside of mound and sprinkle the parsley and chives over the top.

4. Leftovers keep well in the refrigerator.

Comments: Prepare at least 2 hours before serving.

FRESH CUCUMBER PICKLES

Serves: 4-6   Time: 00:15

2-3 MEDIUM SIZE CUCUMBERS
1/2 CP RICE VINEGAR
1/2 CP SPRING WATER
1/2 TSP SEA SALT

1. You will need a quart size glass jar with a tight fitting cover for the pickles.

2. Scrub the cucumbers and score with the tines of a fork, lengthwise on the skin.

3. Slice thinly and set aside while you prepare the marinade.

4. Combine the rice vinegar, water and sea salt. Taste to be sure it is not too weak or strong.

5. Add cucumber slices and marinate for 2-3 hours minimum and as much as a week or more.

6. This same solution can be reused by adding more cucumbers, vinegar, water, and salt as needed. Store in the refrigerator.

Comments: Very easy and tasty pickle for all summer.

KOSHER DILL PICKLES

Serves: 1 quart   Time: 00:15

PICKLE-SIZE CUCUMBERS
2 CP BOILING WATER
1 TBL SEA SALT
1 WHOLE CLOVE GARLIC
1 BAY LEAF
2 SPRIGS FRESH DILL OR
1 TBL DILL SEEDS

1. Sterilize quart jar and new lid.

2. Scrub cucumbers.

3. Place spices in bottom of jar and pack cucumbers in tightly.

4. Bring water and salt to a boil and pour over ingredients in the jar, up to one inch of top.

5. Seal and store for at least 2 weeks before using. Extra quarts will keep well in a cool area.

Comments: _Can be made one quart at a time or in quantity for the year._

PICKLED VEGETABLES WITH DULSE

Serves: 8   Time: 00:20

MARINADE:
1/2 CP RICE VINEGAR
1/2 TSP OLIVE OIL
1 BAY LEAF
1/2 TSP BASIL (OPTIONAL)
1/2 TSP KELP POWDER

2 CP OF DICED VEGETABLES CHOICE OF CELERY, CARROT, CABBAGE, CUCUMBER, DAIKON, PEARL ONIONS, YELLOW SQUASH
3/4 CP DULSE
4 CP BOILING WATER

1. Prepare marinade and set aside.

2. Clean and prepare vegetables and drop into boiling water. Remove from heat, cover and let sit for 3-4 minutes.

3. Drain vegetables and combine in layers with dulse in a sterilized jar. Pour marinade over. It should cover the vegetables.

4. Seal jar and refrigerate.

5. Keeps for several weeks and flavor improves as it marinates. Serve as a condiment with any meal.

Comments: Quick to prepare, but best after marinating for several days.

RUSSIAN PICKLE RELISH

Serves: 4-6   Time: 00:15

1 CP SAUERKRAUT
1/2 CP GRATED CARROT
1/2 CP THIN SLICED SCALLIONS
1 TBL LIGHT OIL

1. Drain sauerkraut and press lightly to remove as much juice as possible.

2. Grate carrot and thinly sliced scallions, using both white and green portions.

3. Combine all ingredients with the oil and mix gently until well combined.

4. Cover and let sit to blend flavors.

5. Serve as a small side dish or relish.

Comments: _Use small servings, as it is quite salty._

SPICED CRANBERRY RELISH

Serves: 3 pints   Time: 00:15

1 LB FRESH CRANBERRIES
2 CP CHOPPED DRIED APRICOTS
1 CP RAISINS
1 TBL GRATED ORANGE RIND
1/4 TSP GINGER
1/8 TSP CLOVES
1/8 TSP ALLSPICE
2 CP APPLE JUICE

1. Combine all ingredients in saucepan and bring to a boil. Lower heat and simmer 10 minutes.

2. Remove from heat and stir while cooling.

3. Cool and pack into pint jars, cover and refrigerate.

4. Filled jars can be processed in water bath and will keep on your pantry shelf.

Comments: Nice condiment with a holiday dinner. Nice holiday gift.

UMEBOSHI VEGETABLE PICKLES

Serves: 12   Time: 00:20

1 PINT SPRING WATER
2 UMEBOSHI PICKLES
SLICED FRESH VEGETABLES: CARROTS, RADISH, ONION,
CABBAGE, SUMMER SQUASH OR CUCUMBER ARE A GOOD
MIX OR USE ANY DESIRED

1. Mash umeboshi plums and place in bottom of jar.

2. Prepare vegetables and place in jar. Pour water over to cover
   vegetables.

3. Cover jar and place in refrigerator for 4 to 5 days before serving.

4. Vegetables will have a pink tint and will be quite salty. These are
   salt pickled and usually safe for those who cannot tolerate
   ferments.

Comments: Quick to prepare, but must set 4 to 6 days before serving.

6. GIVE US OUR DAILY BREAD

Do you remember the wonderful aroma of freshly baked bread or hot muffins as they came from the oven? Most people today don't take time to bake bread at home and perhaps you won't want to either, but if you decide to try, here are a few recipes to start with. Muffins are quick and easy for starters. Good alternatives to home made are available, such as Essene bread and natural whole grain unyeasted breads available at health food stores, usually found in the freezer case. Of course there are always good old rice cakes as a vehicle for spreads. People on a transition diet could use pita breads and corn tortillas also. Flour is not a whole grain and baked products should be used in moderation, including pasta products.

BREADS

SOURDOUGH BREAD
WHOLE GRAIN RICE BREAD
WHOLE WHEAT HERB BREAD

MUFFINS

BASIC OAT BRAN
CORN BREAD
SWEET POTATO
WHEAT FREE

STUFFINGS

HARVEST STUFFING

SOURDOUGH BREAD

Serves: 1-2   Time: 05:30

1 CP SOURDOUGH STARTER AT ROOM TEMPERATURE (SEE RECIPE)
9 CP WW BREAD FLOUR
1/2 TSP SEA SALT
3 CP SPRING WATER

1. Pour starter into a large mixing bowl, add the water and mix well. Add salt to liquid mixture and stir well.

2. Add flour, 1 cup at a time, reserving the final cup for kneading.

3. Beat the flour into the mixture with a large spoon. When dough becomes too heavy to stir, transfer to a floured surface and knead the remaining flour in by hand.

4. Return to bowl. Cover with a clean kitchen towel and set in a draft free, warm place to rise. This will take 1-4 hours depending on temperature and leavening effect.

5. When dough has doubled, punch down and form into loaves. Place in bread pans, cover and let rise again.

6. Place in cold oven with pan of water on bottom shelve.

7. Bake at 425F for 15 minutes, lower heat to 350F and continue baking until golden brown, about 45 minutes.

8. Remove from pans to cool. Yield 2 small loaves.

Comments: _Plan ahead to have the starter ready._

SOURDOUGH STARTER

Serves: 1   Time: 72:00

1 TBL MELLOW WHITE MISO
2 CP LUKEWARM WATER
2 CP WW FLOUR

1. Dissolve the miso in water, add flour and stir thoroughly.

2. Place in glass jar, cover loosely, and keep at room temperature for 3 days, stirring occasionally, until bubbly and yeasty smelling.

3. Set aside 1 cup of starter and refrigerate.

4. When you want starter again, remove from refrigerator and add 2 cups water and 2 cups of flour to the starter, leave at room temperature for 8 to 24 hours until bubbly.

5. If you do not plan to use weekly it must be freshened by adding flour and water to feed it and keep it alive.

6. Starter can also be frozen for 4 to 6 months. The remaining starter will do your first loaves.

Comments: This is the leavening for sourdough bread.

WHOLE GRAIN RICE BREAD

Serves: 8   Time: 72:00

1 CP BROWN RICE
2 CP SPRING WATER
1-2 TSP SEA SALT
2-4 CP WW FLOUR
IF YOU ARE NOT SURE THE RICE IS FERMENTED ENOUGH, ADD 1 TBL OF MELLOW WHITE MISO TO HELP THE DOUGH TO RISE.

1. Cook the rice in spring water.

2. Remove from pot to a wooden bowl or flat dish. Lightly sprinkle with about 1/4 cup of water. Cover dish with a bamboo mat or kitchen towel and set in a warm spot for 3 days or until it gives off a slightly fermented odor.

3. Mix rice with salt and equal amount of flour to form a sticky dough.

4. Turn out onto a floured surface and knead for about 5 minutes until the dough becomes elastic and gluten is formed. Do not add too much flour. Dough should be quite sticky.

5. Oil bread pans and fill about 3/4 full with dough. Set aside to rise in a very warm place, such as an oven with pilot light. Temperature should be about 100F if possible.

6. Bake for about 1 hour at 325F.

7. Remove from pans and cool. Wrap in clean towels. No need to refrigerate.

Comments: *Have to plan ahead, delicious, nutritious and very safe.*

WHOLE WHEAT HERB BREAD

Serves: 10   Time: 02:00

1/2 CP LUKEWARM WATER
2 TBL ACTIVE DRY YEAST
3 CP LUKEWARM WATER
1 TSP SEA SALT
1/4 CP OIL
1/4 CP BARLEY MALT SYRUP
1/4 CP SOFT TOFU
1 TBL DRIED DILL WEED
1 TBL DRIED PARSLEY
1 TBL DRIED SAGE
6-7 CP WW BREAD FLOUR

1. Dissolve yeast in 1/2 cup lukewarm water.

2. Combine water, salt, oil, and barley malt in a saucepan and heat until combined.

3. Pour into a large mixing bowl and cool to lukewarm.

4. Stir in yeast mixture, tofu and herbs. Stir in 3 cups of flour and beat well to develop gluten. Add remaining flour and turn out onto a floured board and knead thoroughly.

5. Divide dough into 2 parts, form into loaves and place in oiled bread tins or Pyrex glass casseroles.

6. Let rise in warm place, covered with clean towel for 40 minutes or until bread is above the tops of the pans.

7. Bake 45 minutes at 375F.

8. Run knife around edges of loaves before removing from pans.

9. Great served hot with soup. Also good cold with a spread.

Comments: Yeast raised, wonderful with home made soup.

BASIC OAT BRAN MUFFINS

Serves: 6   Time: 00:25

1 CP OAT BRAN
1 CP WW PASTRY FLOUR
3 TSP BAKING POWDER
1/2 TSP CINNAMON
1/4 CP VEGETABLE OIL
1/4 CP HONEY, MAPLE SYRUP, RICE SYRUP OR BARLEY MALT
SWEETENER
1 CP SOYMILK OR APPLE JUICE

1. Preheat oven to 350F.

2. Combine all dry ingredients in a large mixing bowl.

3. Combine all liquid ingredients in a 2 cup measure.

4. Prepare muffin tins.

5. Combine wet ingredients with dry ingredients and stir just until
   moistened. Do not beat.

6. Divide batter between the 12 muffin cups.

7. Bake at 350F for 15 minutes.

*Comments: Up to 1/2 cup of nuts, raisins, blueberries or chopped fresh
apples can be added if desired.*

CORN MUFFINS

Serves: 12   Time: 00:45

2 CP CORN MEAL
1 CP WW PASTRY FLOUR
2/3 CP SOFT TOFU
3 CP SPRING WATER
1/2 TSP SEA SALT

1. Preheat oven to 400F and prepare muffin pans.

2. Combine cornmeal, WW flour, and salt together in a large bowl.

3. Crumble tofu into a blender. Bring water to a boil and add to the tofu in blender. Blend until smooth and creamy, immediately add to the flour mixture and mix well.

4. Spoon into prepared muffin tins and bake for 30 minutes. Cool slightly before serving.

Comments: _Good anytime._

WHEAT FREE MUFFINS

Serves: 12   Time: 00:30

1 CP ROLLED OATS
1 1/2 CP OAT BRAN
1/2 CP CHOPPED WALNUTS
1 TBL BAKING POWDER
DASH OF SEA SALT
1/2 CP APPLESAUCE
1/3 CP FLAXSEED MIXTURE (EGG SUBSTITUTE, SEE RECIPE)
3 TBL OIL
2 TBL HONEY OR BARLEY MALT
3/4 CP APPLE JUICE OR SOY MILK
1/2 TSP VANILLA (OPTIONAL)
1/2 TSP CINNAMON

1. Preheat oven to 400F.

2. Combine all dry ingredients in a large bowl.

3. Combine wet ingredients in a 2 cup measure.

4. Combine dry and liquid ingredients and stir just until all moistened. Do not beat.

5. Divide mixture between the 12 muffin cups (they will appear to be very full, but it is O.K. They do all their rising in the mixing).

6. Bake at 400F for 20 minutes.

Comments: _You can substitute fruit and liquids for variety as long as you keep proportions the same. Use your imagination, it is a very forgiving recipe._

SWEET POTATO MUFFINS

Serves: 12   Time: 00:30

1 CP WW PASTRY FLOUR
1 CP UNBLEACHED WHITE FLOUR
1/2 TSP BAKING SODA
1/2 TSP SEA SALT
2 TSP BAKING POWDER
1/2 TSP CINNAMON
1/4 TSP NUTMEG (OPTIONAL)
1/2 CP COOKED PUREED SWEET POTATOES
1/3 CP CORN OR WALNUT OIL
1 CUP SOY MILK OR NUT MILK
1/2 CP CHOPPED WALNUTS (OPTIONAL)

1. Preheat oven to 400F.

2. Combine dry ingredients in a large mixing bowl and set aside.

3. Combine sweet potato with rest of liquid ingredients.

4. Chop walnuts if using.

5. Combine wet ingredients with dry ingredients and mix just enough to moisten. Add nuts if using.

6. Spoon into prepared muffin tins and bake for about 25 minutes.

7. Serve hot with apple butter or other spread of your choice.

HARVEST STUFFING

Serves: 4-6   Time: 00:30

1 CP SHREDDED CARROT
1 CP CHOPPED CELERY
1 MED ONION CHOPPED
8 CP DRY WW BREAD CUBES OR CRUMBS
2 CP FINELY CHOPPED APPLES
1/2 CP CHOPPED WALNUTS
1/4 CP WHEAT GERM (OPTIONAL)
1 TBL OIL
1 TSP SAGE
1/4 TSP SAVORY
1/4 TSP THYME
1/4 TSP CINNAMON
1/2 TSP SALT
1/2 - 3/4 CP HOT WATER OR STOCK TO MOISTEN

1. In skillet saute carrot, celery and onion in oil. Stir in seasonings.

2. In a large mixing bowl, combine bread cubes, apples, nuts, and wheat germ.

3. Add cooked vegetable mixture and gradually add hot water or cooking broth to consistency desired.

4. Stuff poultry or squash lightly and bake. Extra stuffing can be baked in a lightly oiled covered casserole. Bake at 325-350F.

Comments: Holiday or any day, delicious and great for filling a turkey or a squash.

7. SMALL PLEASURES

The little touches that make a meal memorable. Condiments, dips, sauces, gravies, salad dressings, butters, and spreads are the way to add variety and flavor to the grains, vegetables and beans which are the basis of the diet. ENJOY THEM EVERY DAY! No dull meals at your house.

COOKING INGREDIENTS

CORN FREE BAKING POWDER
FLAXSEED EGG SUBSTITUTE
SOY YOGURT
TOFU CHEESE
TOFU RICOTTA CHEESE
TOFU MAYONNAISE
TOFU SOUR CREAM

SAUCES

BECHAMEL
GINGER
GINGER MISO
ITALIANO STYLE RED SAUCE
ITALIANO STYLE WHITE SAUCE
LEMON SAUCE W/DILL
LEMON DESSERT SAUCE
NUT SAUCE
SWEET DESSERT TOPPING
SWEET-SOUR

CONDIMENTS

GRATED DAIKON RADISH
NORI PUMPKIN SEED TREATS
SESAME SALT (GOMASHIO)
SUNNY CONDIMENT

DIPS

ALMOND DIP
CURRY DIP
OLIVE-WALNUT DIP
SPRING CHIVE DIP

SPREADS

GINGER PUMPKIN BUTTER
HUMMUS
SWEET VEGETABLE BUTTER
TOFU-VEGGIE
TUNA STYLE TEMPEH
WALNUT BUTTER

GRAVIES

HEARTY MISO
ONION
ONION-MUSHROOM
TAHINI

SALAD DRESSING

CREAMY GINGER MISO
DILL
GREEN GODDESS
LEMON-OIL-HERB VINAIGRETTE
MUSTARD
WALNUT OIL VINAIGRETTE

CORN FREE BAKING POWDER

Time: 00:10

1 TBL CREAM OF TARTAR
1 TBL ARROWROOT
1 1/2 TSP BAKING SODA

1. Have ready a clean dry glass jar.

2. Combine all ingredients and mix well.

3. Place in glass jar with a tight screw on cover.

4. Use in same proportions as regular baking powder.

5. Make in small amounts and use up quickly so it stays fresh.

Comments: *For people who can not use corn. Keep in tightly sealed jar.*

FLAXSEED EGG SUBSTITUTE

Time: 00:10

1/3 CP FLAXSEED
1 CP SPRING WATER

1. Grind flaxseed in blender, add water and blend again until thick.

2. Three tablespoons of mixture equals 1 egg for baking purposes.

3. Mixture will keep in refrigerator for one week or can be frozen in one egg portions for future use.

Comments: *For baking uses only. Good binder for cookies, muffins, etc.*

SOY YOGURT

Serves: 2-4   Time: 4-8 hrs

2 CP SOYMILK
1 TBL MAPLE SYRUP
1 1/2 TSP OF YOGURT OR LACTOBACILLUS STARTER

1. Heat soy milk and maple syrup to 112F. Use thermometer to be sure temperature is correct.

2. Remove thin film which will form on top surface of the milk and reserve. (Film is called yuba and is good to eat with a little tamari garnish.)

3. Stir starter into the mixture and pour into very clean hot jars and cover. Incubate at 105F for 4-8 hours. A commercial yogurt maker or a gas oven with a pilot light will give proper temperature.

4. Check for consistency after 4 hours.

5. Yogurt can also be incubated at room temperature (70 degrees or above) for 14-18 hours.

6. For a creamier yogurt, heat 2 1/4 tsp of agar flakes in a little water until dissolved and add to soy milk mixture before incubating to act as a stabilizer.

7. Save several spoonfuls as starter for next batch.

Comments: _Great substitute for dairy use in same way as dairy yogurt._

TOFU CHEESE

Serves: 4-6   Time: 24:00

1/2 LB FIRM TOFU
1/2 CP MISO OF YOUR CHOICE

1. Drop tofu into boiling water, remove from heat and let set for 5 minutes. Remove from water and pat dry.

2. When partially cool, spread miso on all sides of the block of tofu. Cover tightly and let cure at room temperature for 24 hours.

3. When ready to serve scrape excess miso from block and serve as is with crackers or use for cooking purposes.

4. The type of miso that you use determines the flavor of the cheese. Can also be blended with other ingredients such as chives, parsley, nuts or other ingredients to make a cheese spread or cheese ball.

Comments: Great when you have old dairy cheese cravings.

TOFU RICOTTA CHEESE

Serves: 4-6   Time: 00:15

1 LB FIRM TOFU
3 TBL MELLOW WHITE MISO
2 TBL TAHINI BUTTER
1 CLOVE MINCED GARLIC
2 TSP LEMON JUICE

1. Drop tofu into a pan of boiling water, remove from heat and let sit for 5 minutes.

2. Remove tofu and let cool to room temperature. Squeeze out any excess water and crumble into a bowl.

3. Add remaining ingredients and mix well.

Comments: Use in any recipe calling for ricotta cheese.

TOFU MAYONNAISE

Serves: 4-5   Time: 00:15

1/2 CAKE SOFT TOFU
1/2 CP SPRING WATER
1 TBL BROWN RICE VINEGAR OR UMEBOSHI VINEGAR
1 TBL FRESH LEMON JUICE
1 TBL OLIVE OIL
1/4 TSP DRIED MUSTARD
1/2 TSP SEA SALT OR TO TASTE

1. Combine all ingredients and blend until thick and creamy.

2. Can be refrigerated for several days. If mixture separates, stir well before using.

Comments: Use as you would any mayonnaise, can be refrigerated several days.

TOFU SOUR CREAM

Serves: 4-6   Time: 00:20

1/2 LB FIRM FRESH TOFU
1 TBL LIGHT OIL
2 TSP FRESH LEMON JUICE
DASH SEA SALT
1/2 TSP UMEBOSHI VINEGAR
1/2 TSP UMEBOSHI PASTE
SPRING WATER AS NEED TO OBTAIN CREAM CONSISTENCY
RECIPE WILL MAKE 1 CP SOUR CREAM. RECIPE CAN BE
DOUBLED.

1. Place tofu chunk in fresh water to cover, bring to a boil and
   simmer for 5 minutes.

2. Drain and cool.

3. Blend with remaining ingredients until smooth creamy texture,
   add water only if needed for proper consistency.

4. Use immediately or refrigerate until needed.   If ingredients
   separate, stir well before serving.

Comments: _Use as a cooking ingredient to replace dairy sour cream._

BECHAMEL SAUCE

Serves: 4   Time: 00:10

1 TBL OIL
1 TBL UNBLEACHED FLOUR
1 CP WARM SPRING WATER
1/2 TSP SEA SALT
NUTMEG OR GINGER (OPTIONAL)

1. Heat oil in small saucepan.

2. Add flour and keep stirring until it is a light brown color.

3. Add 1 cup lukewarm water gradually while stirring until thickened.

4. Season to taste. Use nutmeg for vegetable sauce and ginger for fish sauce.

Comments: _Basic white sauce._

GINGER SAUCE

Serves: 4   Time: 00:10

2 FINELY CHOPPED SCALLIONS
1/2 TBL CORN OR OLIVE OIL
1 TBL TAHINI
1 TBL TAMARI SAUCE
1 CP SPRING WATER
1/2 TBL KUZU
1 TSP FRESHLY GRATED GINGER OR MORE TO TASTE

1. Saute finely chopped scallions in oil until limp.

2. Add tahini, tamari, and water, heat to boiling point.

3. Dissolve kuzu in 1/4 cup water. Add kuzu mixture and freshly grated ginger to the mixture and simmer until thickened.

4. Check seasonings and adjust if needed.

Comments: _Excellent sauce for noodles or buckwheat grain dish._

GINGER MISO SAUCE

Serves: 4   Time: 00:15

2 TSP SESAME OIL
1 MED CHOPPED ONION
1/2 CP CHOPPED PARSLEY
1 3/4 CP BOILING WATER
1/2 TSP GRATED GINGER
2 TBL BARLEY MISO
2 TBL KUZU DISSOLVED IN
1/4 CP COLD WATER

1. Saute onion in oil until translucent.

2. Add parsley and saute for one more minute or so.

3. Add boiling water and simmer for 5 minutes.

4. Blend miso, ginger and 1/4 cup of the broth in a small bowl. Add to vegetables and rest of broth.

5. Stir dissolved kuzu into mixture and bring to boiling point. Simmer gently until gravy consistency.

6. Pour into serving bowl and serve. Makes 2 1/2 cups of sauce.

Comments: _Serve with grain or noodles. Great with Golden Loaf._

ITALIANO RED SAUCE

Serves: 4-6   Time: 00:45

1 LB CARROTS
1 SMALL BEET
1 LARGE ONION
1 STALK CELERY
1 BAY LEAF
1 CP SPRING WATER
3 CLOVES GARLIC (OPTIONAL)
1 TBL OLIVE OIL
1 TSP BASIL
1 TSP OREGANO
1/2 CP CHOPPED PARSLEY
1 CP SLICED MUSHROOMS (OPTIONAL)

1. Scrub and slice the carrots and beet, peel the onion and slice. Place all in saucepan and add bay leaf and 1 cup water. Bring to boil and simmer until very soft.

2. Remove bay leaf and puree the vegetables in a food mill or blender.

3. Heat oil in a small skillet and saute the chopped garlic.

4. Add the seasonings and saute gently. If using the mushrooms, add and saute until limp.

5. Combine vegetable ingredients and seasonings and adjust texture by adding more water if needed.

6. Check for seasonings and add sea salt and or shoyu/tamari. If sauce is too thin it can be thickened with kuzu. For Tex-Mex sauce alter the seasoning to cumin and coriander and add hot pepper sauce.

Comments: *Variations of seasonings make it Italian or Tex-Mex sauce.*

ITALIANO STYLE WHITE SAUCE

Serves: 4   Time: 00:30

1 LB FIRM TOFU
2 MED ONIONS, FINELY CHOPPED
3 GARLIC CLOVES, MINCED
2 TBL TAHINI
1/2 CP SPRING WATER
PINCH OF SEA SALT
1 TBL OLIVE OIL
1/2 TSP BASIL
1/2 TSP OREGANO
1 TBL CHOPPED PARSLEY
1 7 OZ CAN OF CHOPPED CLAMS (OPTIONAL)

1. Drain the tofu and press to remove extra water. Dice the tofu into small squares.

2. Saute onions and garlic in the olive oil until soft but not browned.

3. Add diced tofu and the tahini, water and herbs and simmer for 15 minutes.

4. Let cool to lukewarm and then puree in blender for a smooth sauce.

5. Reheat gently and serve over pasta.

6. Almost Noodles Alfredo? For a clam sauce, add 1 can well drained chopped clams.

Comments: *Serve with whole wheat or sesame rice pasta.*

LEMON SAUCE WITH DILL

Serves: 4-6   Time: 00:15

1 1/4 CP SPRING WATER OR
FISH STOCK OR SOY MILK
1/2 CP FRESH SQUEEZED LEMON JUICE
2 TBL CHOPPED FRESH DILL OR
1 TSP DRIED DILL
1/2 TSP SEA SALT
1/4 TSP TURMERIC
2 TBL KUZU DISSOLVED IN
2 TBL COLD WATER
DASH OF UMEBOSHI VINEGAR (OPTIONAL BUT ADDS NICE
FLAVOR)

1. Combine all ingredients except for the kuzu and bring to boiling
   point.

2. Dissolve kuzu in water and add to hot liquid. Simmer until sauce
   thickens.

3. Serve hot or cold. The fish stock or water will make a clear sauce.
   The soy milk will make a creamy sauce which is especially nice on
   cold fish.

Comments: Tasty sauce to use with fish or vegetable dishes.

LEMON DESSERT SAUCE

Serves: 4-6   Time: 00:20

1 CP SOY MILK
1 CP APPLE JUICE
PINCH SEA SALT
1 TSP GRATED LEMON PEEL
1 TBL RICE SYRUP
1 1/2 TBL KUZU
JUICE OF ONE LEMON

1. Combine first 5 ingredients in a small saucepan. Bring to boil, reduce heat and simmer for 5 minutes.

2. Dissolve kuzu in lemon juice and add to hot mixture. Cook and stir until sauce thickens slightly.

3. Taste for sweetness and add more rice syrup if too tart.

4. Can be served hot or cool. Can be reheated.

Comments: *Special dessert sauce. Great on berries or over gingerbread cake.*

NUT SAUCE

Serves: 4   Time: 00:10

1 CP WALNUTS OR PECANS
1 CP SPRING WATER
3 TBL MELLOW WHITE MISO
1 TBL MIRIN (OPTIONAL)

1. Roast the nuts in a dry skillet over medium heat, stirring constantly until crisp and fragrant.

2. Combine all ingredients in a blender and blend until smooth. Makes 1 1/2 cups.

Comments: Good over steamed vegetables or noodles.

SWEET DESSERT TOPPING

Serves: 6   Time: 00:15

1/2 LB SOFT TOFU
2 TBL COLD PRESSED OIL
1/4 CP RICE SYRUP
1/2 TSP LEMON JUICE
DASH SALT
1 TSP VANILLA

1. Blend all together in blender until very smooth and creamy.

2. Chill and serve as you would whipped cream.

SWEET SOUR SAUCE

Serves: 4   Time: 00:10

1 CP WATER OR STOCK
1/4 CP HONEY
1/4 CP RICE VINEGAR
1 TBL KUZU DISSOLVED IN
1/4 CP WATER
TAMARI OR SEA SALT TO TASTE

1. Combine stock, vinegar, honey, tamari and mirin in a small saucepan. Bring to a simmering point.

2. Dissolve the kuzu in equal amount of cold water and add to the simmering mixture.

3. Stir in well and continue stirring until mixture is hot and thickened.

4. Serve hot. Makes approximately 1 cup of sauce.

Comments: Many uses as sauce for flavor.

217

GRATED DAIKON RADISH CONDIMENT

Serves: 4   Time: 00:15

1 CP GRATED DAIKON RADISH
1 TSP GRATED GINGER ROOT (OPTIONAL)
1/2 TSP TAMARI SAUCE (OPTIONAL)

1. Grate daikon radish and add desired seasonings.

2. Serve in small portions as a condiment with fried or greasy foods to aid digestion.

NORI-PUMPKIN SEED (HERB WALLEY)

Serves: 16   Time: 00:15

1 CP ROASTED PUMPKIN SEEDS
4 SHEETS OF NORI

1. Roast pumpkin seeds, cool and store in a glass jar.

2. Lightly toast nori sheets over a flame or hot burner.

3. Tear nori sheets into quarters.

4. When ready to eat, roll quarter sheet piece of nori into a cornucopia and fill with roasted pumpkin seeds. Fold over top and eat. DELICIOUS!!!

Comments: Both pumpkin seeds and nori can be prepared ahead. They both keep well at room temperature when stored in covered containers. Many thanks to Mr. Herb Wally for this invention which sweetens the nori.

SESAME SALT (GOMASHIO)

Serves: 16   Time: 00:15

1 CP UNHULLED SESAME SEEDS
1/2 TBL SEA SALT

1. Wash seeds. Drain well.

2. Dry roast salt in a heated skillet over medium heat. Remove to suribachi or a dish.

3. Do the same procedure for the washed seeds, stirring constantly until they give off a nutty aroma and start to turn a golden brown color and begin to pop. Remove from skillet immediately so they do not burn.

3. Grind with a suribachi (mortar) and pestle or in a blender at slow speed until each seed is half-crushed.

4. Store in a glass jar with tight cover.

5. Use in place of salt for flavor. Sprinkle on grains and cereals. Good source of calcium, iron, and vitamins A and B.

Comments: Aids digestion, adds minerals and vitamins to a meal.

219

SUNNY CONDIMENT

Serves: 12   Time: 00:20

1/2 CP SUNFLOWER SEEDS
1/2 OZ SEA PALM (DRIED)

1. Place sunflower seeds and sea palm in separate flat baking dishes and place in oven. Sea palm will be ready in about 10 minutes. Watch closely so it doesn't burn. Sunflower seeds will take a little longer.

2. Remove from oven when golden brown and fragrant.

3. Let cool at room temperature and then grind the seeds at low speed in the blender for 30 seconds.

4. Add sea palm and blend briefly.

5. Texture should be similar to sesame salt. Store in refrigerator in glass jar.

Comments: *Use the same way as sesame salt for flavor and sea vegetable nutrition.*

ALMOND DIP

Serves: 6   Time: 00:15

1/2 LB TOFU, MASHED
3 TBL LEMON JUICE
2 TBL OIL
2 TSP RICE SYRUP
1/2 TSP SEA SALT OR TO TASTE
1/4 CP ROASTED CHOPPED ALMONDS

1. Blend the first five ingredients in blender until smooth and creamy.

2. Pour into a bowl and fold in the chopped almonds.

3. Chill briefly before serving.

Comments: Nice served with plain rice crackers.

CURRY DIP

Serves: 6   Time: 00:15

1/2 LB TOFU, CRUMBLED
2 TBL OIL
2 TBL RICE VINEGAR
1/2 TSP SEA SALT
1 TSP CURRY POWDER (OR TO TASTE)
1/2 TSP RICE SYRUP
JUICE FROM 1 CLOVE GARLIC, CRUSHED

1. Blend all in blender until smooth and creamy.

2. Chill briefly before serving with assorted raw veggies.

OLIVE-WALNUT DIP

Serves: 6   Time: 00:15

1/2 LB TOFU, MASHED
2 TBL OIL
2 TSP RICE SYRUP
3 TBL LEMON JUICE
1/2 TSP SEA SALT
2 TBL FINELY CHOPPED WALNUTS
1 TBL CHOPPED OLIVES

1. Blend in a blender until smooth and creamy the first 5 ingredients.

2. Fold in the chopped walnuts and olives.

3. Check for seasonings and adjust as needed.

4. Chill briefly before serving.

Comments: *Serve with raw vegetables, pita bread or macro crackers.*

SPRING CHIVE DIP

Serves: 8   Time: 00:15

1/2 LB TOFU, CRUMBLED
2 TBL OIL
1 1/2 TSP RICE VINEGAR
1 TSP SHOYU SAUCE
1 SMALL CLOVE GARLIC, CRUSHED
1/4 CP FRESH CHIVES, CHOPPED

1. Blend the first five ingredients in blender until smooth and creamy, pour into a bowl and fold in the chopped chives.

2. Chill briefly and serve with fresh veggies.

GINGER PUMPKIN BUTTER

Serves: 4-6   Time: 00:30

2 CP PUREED PUMPKIN (CAN SUBSTITUTE SQUASH)
1/2 CP RICE SYRUP
1 TSP GRATED LEMON RIND
1 TBL FRESH LEMON JUICE
DASH SEA SALT
JUICE FROM 1 TBL GRATED GINGER
DASH OF CINNAMON (OPTIONAL)

1. Combine all ingredients and stir well.

2. Place over low heat and simmer for approximately 30 minutes, stirring frequently until quite thick.

3. When it is a thick spreadable consistency, pour into jars and refrigerate until ready to use.

Comments: _Delicious as spread on toast, muffins or pancakes._

HUMMUS (GARBANZO DIP & SPREAD)

Serves: 6   Time: 00:15

2 CP COOKED GARBANZO BEANS
1/4 CP COOKING LIQUID
1/4 CP TAHINI
2 TBL OLIVE OIL
2 TBL LEMON JUICE
1 TSP MINCED GARLIC
1/2 TSP SEA SALT

1. Combine in food processor or blender cooked garbanzo beans, 2 tbl of reserved cooking liquid, lemon juice, and olive oil.

2. Blend until well mashed adding more cooking liquid if needed.

3. Blend in the tahini, garlic and seasonings. Do not overblend. The texture should be creamy and rough at the same time. If using a blender, it may be necessary to process in several smaller batches.

4. Cover and refrigerate until ready to serve.

5. Serve with raw vegetable dippers or as a spread for pita bread. Will keep several days refrigerated. Freezes very well.

Comments: *Beans must be cooked ahead.*

MOCK EGG & OLIVE SALAD

Serves: 4   Time: 00:15

8 OZ FIRM TOFU
2 TBL SOY MAYONNAISE
1/2 TBL RICE VINEGAR
1 TSP NATURAL MUSTARD
DASH OF SEA SALT
1/4 TSP TURMERIC (OPTIONAL)
2 TBL CHOPPED GREEN OLIVES
1 TBL FINELY CHOPPED ONION OR SCALLION

1. Drain the tofu well and then chop coursely.

2. Stir together the mayonnaise, vinegar, mustard and seasonings.

3. Fold in the chopped olives and onion.

4. Check for seasonings and adjust if needed.

5. Refrigerate to blend flavors.

Comments: Use as a sandwich spread or as a salad served on fresh greens.

TOFU-VEGGIE SANDWICH SPREAD

Serves: 4   Time: 00:15

8 OZ FIRM TOFU
1 SMALL CARROT
2 GREEN SCALLIONS
1 SMALL STALK CELERY
1 LARGE RADISH
FRESH OR DRIED DILLWEED
1 TBL CHOPPED GREEN OLIVES (OPTIONAL)
1 TBL TOFU MAYONNAISE

1. Chop vegetables very fine using food processor if available.

2. Crumble tofu and combine with veggies.

3. Slice olives and combine along with dill weed to taste.

4. Blend in tofu mayonnaise and season to taste with sea salt. A dash of tamari and umeboshi vinegar will also give more flavor.

5. Can be used immediately for sandwich filling or on greens as a main course salad. Recipe can be doubled easily.

Comments: _Very easy to prepare, and great in pita bread for lunch._

TUNA STYLE TEMPEH SPREAD

Serves: 4   Time: 00:20

8 OZ TEMPEH
1 TBL WATER
1/4 CP SOY MAYONNAISE
2 MINCED SCALLIONS
2 TBL MINCED CELERY
1/4 TSP TAMARI SAUCE OR
1/4 TSP SEA SALT (OPTIONAL)

1. Steam tempeh for approximately 20 minutes.

2. Add 1 tbl water and mash.

3. Allow to cool to room temperature.

4. Add 1/4 cup soy mayonnaise and the chopped onion and celery.

5. Season to taste with the tamari sauce or sea salt.

6. Serve as sandwich filling, salad or spread for crackers.

SWEET VEGETABLE BUTTER

Serves: 4-6   Time: 00:20

2 CP SLICED CARROTS
2 CP SLICED PARSNIPS
3/4 CP SPRING WATER
DASH SEA SALT
2 TBL SESAME TAHINI
1/2 TSP SHOYU (OPTIONAL)

1. Scrub vegetables and slice. Place in steamer basket and add water. Bring to a boil, lower heat and steam until very tender (about 10-15 minutes).

2. Drain vegetables thoroughly and reserve cooking liquid.

3. Puree vegetables in blender or food processor, adding only enough cooking liquid to obtain butter consistency.

4. Add tahini and shoyu if using and blend again. Add more cooking liquid if needed to obtain butter texture. Check for seasonings.

5. Place in bowl or jar and refrigerate. Bring to room temperature before serving for best flavor.

6. Can also be thinned to make a vegetable sauce for grains. Save any extra cooking liquid for soups.

WALNUT BUTTER

Serves: 1 cup   Time: 00:15

2 CP LIGHTLY ROASTED WALNUTS
2 TBL WALNUT OIL
1 TBL SPRING WATER

1. Grind 1 cup of walnuts at a time in the electric blender until you have a powder.

2. Then add oil and water and blend again until the mixture forms a butter consistency.

3. For a chunky butter, grind for a shorter time.

4. Store in covered container in refrigerator. If oil separates stir before serving.

Comments: Delicious spread, but full of fat so use carefully.

HEARTY MISO GRAVY

Serves: 4-6   Time: 00:15

1 TBL OIL
1 MED ONION, CHOPPED
3 TBL WW FLOUR
1 1/2 CP SPRING WATER
3 TBL BARLEY MISO DISSOLVED IN
1/2 CP SPRING WATER
1 TBL MIRIN (OPTIONAL)
MINCED PARSLEY FOR GARNISH

1. In small saucepan saute the onion in oil until limp but not browned.

2. Reduce heat and stir in whole wheat flour. Cook gently for about a minute.

3. Gradually add the 1 1/2 cups water and cook gently until the mixture thickens.

4. Dilute the miso with 1/2 cup water and add to the gravy mixture and simmer for 5-10 minutes.

5. Add mirin and check for seasoning. Add minced parsley if desired.

6. Serve and enjoy.

Comments: *For variety on basic recipe, add garlic sauteed with onion or change type of miso used for flavor. Delicious over hearty grains, warming and satisfying.*

ONION GRAVY

Serves: 4   Time: 00:25

2 LARGE ONIONS, SLICED THINLY
1 TSP OIL
2 CP SPRING WATER
2 TSP TAMARI OR TO TASTE
1 1/2 TBL KUZU
DASH OF SEA SALT, IF DESIRED

1. Slice onions thinly and saute in skillet with the oil. Cook at very low temperature until onions become very brown and bottom of pan is well browned.

2. Add water and simmer for 10 to 15 minutes.

3. Combine tamari and kuzu with enough cold water to dissolve.

4. Add to onion and water mixture, stir over medium heat until thick and clear.

5. Taste and adjust seasonings.

Comments: Serve over millet mashed potatoes or any grain burger or croquette.

ONION-MUSHROOM GRAVY

Serves: 4   Time: 00:15

1 TBL SESAME OIL
1 CLOVE GARLIC (OPTIONAL)
1 MED ONION, THINLY SLICED
1 CP MUSHROOMS, SLICED
2 CP WATER OR KOMBU BROTH
1 HEAPING TBL KUZU DISSOLVED IN 2 TBL WATER
TAMARI SAUCE TO TASTE
SEA SALT TO TASTE

1. Heat oil in skillet.

2. Add garlic, onions and mushrooms and saute until limp and lightly browned.

3. Add kombu broth or water and simmer for 5 to 10 minutes.

4. Dissolve kuzu in cold water and add to mixture gradually stirring well until it thickens.

5. Add tamari or sea salt and let simmer for 5 minutes.

6. Ready to serve over dish of your choice.

Comments: Good over grains or grain burgers and no-meat loaves

TAHINI GRAVY

Serves: 3-4   Time: 00:15

1/4 CP TAHINI BUTTER
1 CP SPRING WATER
1 TBL KUZU
DASH SEA SALT
2 TSP TAMARI OR TO TASTE

1. Place tahini butter in a small saucepan.

2. Dissolve kuzu in the cup of water.

3. Slowly add kuzu mixture to the tahini, stirring well to combine the tahini.

4. Bring to boiling point, reduce heat and stir until the mixture thickens.

5. Add sea salt and tamari to taste.

6. Serve over grain or burgers. Light and tasty gravy.

Comments: *Good gravy for buckwheat or burgers.*

CREAMY GINGER-MISO DRESSING

Serves: 4   Time: 00:15

2 TBL MELLOW WHITE MISO
1 TBL GRATED GINGER ROOT
2 TBL RICE VINEGAR OR LEMON JUICE
1 TBL DARK SESAME OIL
1/2 CP LIGHT SESAME OIL
1/4 CP SPRING WATER

1. In blender at low speed, combine the miso, ginger, vinegar or lemon juice, and dark sesame oil.

2. Gradually add the light sesame oil in a thin, steady stream until well mixed. Then very slowly add the water until dressing is creamy and thick.

3. Check for seasonings and adjust if needed.

4. If dressing separates before serving, it may be reblended.

Comments: Keeps very well if refrigerated. Excellent on dark greens.

DILL DRESSING

Serves 4   Time: 00:10

2 TBL OLIVE OIL
1/4 CP RICE VINEGAR
1 TBL UMEBOSHI VINEGAR
1 TBL SPRING WATER
1/8 TSP WHITE PEPPER
1 TSP DRIED DILL WEED OR
1 TBL FRESH DILL

1. Combine all ingredients in a screw-top jar and shake well.

2. Pour over beans and veggies and stir well.

3. Refrigerate for a least one hour to develop flavor.

4. Serve salad on fresh lettuce or romaine leaves.

Comments: Serve with bean salad with spring veggies.

GREEN GODDESS DRESSING

Serves: 4   Time: 00:15

4 OZ TOFU CRUMBLED
3 FRESH SPINACH LEAVES
1 FINELY CHOPPED SCALLION
1 1/2 TBL FRESH BASIL OR
1/2 TSP DRIED BASIL
1 1/2 TBL RICE VINEGAR
1/4 TSP SEA SALT
1/8 TSP WHITE PEPPER
1/4 CP SPRING WATER
1/2 CP OIL OF CHOICE

1. Place all ingredients except for oil in a blender and process until liquefied.

2. With blender at low speed, slowly add oil in a steady stream until the dressing is thick and creamy.

3. Cover and refrigerate until ready to serve.

Comments: Will stay fresh for a week if refrigerated.

LEMON-OIL-HERB VINAIGRETTE

Serves: 3-4   Time: 00:10

5 TBL OLIVE OIL
2 TBL LEMON JUICE
1/4 - 1/2 TSP SEA SALT
2 TSP DRIED HERBS (YOUR CHOICE OF MARJORAM, THYME,
BASIL, OREGANO, TARRAGON) OR
1 TBL FRESH CHOPPED HERBS (SUCH AS PARSLEY, CHIVE,
BASIL, TARRAGON, CHERVIL, ETC.)

1. Combine all ingredients and shake very well or whip with wisk or
   blend in blender.

2. Pour over salad greens and toss well.

Comments: _Lovely salad dressing for those who can't have ferments._

MUSTARD DRESSING

Serves: 4   Time: 00:10

2 TBL DIJON MUSTARD
1/2 CP OLIVE OIL
1/4 CP RICE VINEGAR OR
1/4 CP LEMON JUICE
1/4 TSP SEA SALT
1/8 TSP WHITE PEPPER

1. Place all ingredients in a screw top jar and shake hard until well
   blended.

2. Chill to blend flavors.

3. When ready to serve, pour over clean dark greens and toss well.

WALNUT OIL VINAIGRETTE

Serves: 3-4   Time: 00:10

2 TBL WALNUT OIL
2 TBL LEMON JUICE
2 TBL TAMARI SAUCE
2 TBL MINCED PARSLEY (OPTIONAL)

1. Combine all dressing ingredients and shake well.

2. Pour over greens or grain salads and either toss or combine with other ingredients.

8. JUST DESSERTS

Is there anyone who doesn't like the sweet finish to a meal? The desserts here are naturally sweet without using processed sugars. No sugar rush here and no guilt. Enjoy in moderation as with all good things.

COOKIES

ALMOND BUTTER
BARLEY COOKIES
CARROT-RAISIN
FILLED OAT BARS
NUTTY WALNUT DROPS
OATMEAL-RAISIN

CAKES

DESSERT SHORTCAKES
GINGERBREAD CAKE
PEACH DREAM COUSCOUS

PASTRY

CRUNCHY CRUST
FLAKY PIE CRUST
GRANOLA CRUST
STIR & ROLL PIE CRUST
WHEATFREE CRUST

PIES

APPLE CRUNCH
BLUEBERRY
MAPLE CHEESECAKE
PARTY PECAN
PUMPKIN

PUDDINGS

ALMOND CUSTARD
APPLE CRISP
BREAD PUDDING
FRUIT JELL DESSERT
HEAVENLY POACHED PEARS
MOCHA PUDDING
SPECIAL RICE PUDDING
STEAMED PUDDING
STRAWBERRY DREAM
SUMMER FRUIT CRISP
TAPIOCA QUINOA

ALMOND BUTTER COOKIES

Serves: 20   Time: 00:45

1/2 CP ALMOND BUTTER
1/4 CP RICE SYRUP
1 CP SPRING WATER
1/2 TSP SEA SALT
1/4 TSP VANILLA
3 CP WW PASTRY FLOUR
1/2 CP FINELY CHOPPED ALMONDS (OPTIONAL)

1. Combine almond butter and rice syrup and blend well. If butter and syrup are too thick and hard, they can be briefly heated to thin.

2. Add water gradually until well blended.

3. Add this mixture gradually to the flour and salt mixture until you have a firm dough.

4. Add vanilla and chopped almonds if using.

5. Form dough into small balls and place on oiled cookie sheets. Press with tines of fork to flatten slightly.

6. Bake at 350F for 20 minutes or until golden brown. Remove to cooling rack.

7. After cooling, may be stored in cookie tin. Should make about 40 2-inch cookies.

Comments: _Try variations of nut butters and sweeteners._

BARLEY COOKIES

Serves: 6-8   Time: 00:30

1 1/2 CP BARLEY FLAKES
1 CP BARLEY FLOUR
DASH SEA SALT
1/2 TSP CINNAMON
1/2 CP CHOPPED WALNUTS
1/2 CP CHOPPED DRIED APPLES
1/4 CP CORN OR SAFFLOWER OIL
1/2 CP BARLEY MALT
1/2 CP APPLE JUICE

1. Combine all dry ingredients and stir well to blend.

2. Combine all wet ingredients and add to dry ingredients. Stir until well blended. If dough is too soft to hold its shape, add more flour.

3. Prepare cookie sheets and preheat oven to 350F.

4. Drop dough by heaping teaspoon onto baking sheet and bake for 15-20 minutes or until lightly browned and firm.

5. Transfer to wire rack and cool before storing. These will satisfy any sweet tooth.

Comments: _Wheat-free, how sweet it is._

CARROT-RAISIN COOKIES

Serves: 12   Time: 00:45

3 TBL SAFFLOWER OIL
1/4 CP RICE SYRUP OR BARLEY MALT SYRUP
3 TBL WATER
1 CP AMARANTH FLOUR
1/3 CP ARROWROOT
1/2 TSP BAKING SODA
1/4 TSP SEA SALT
1/2 TSP LEMON JUICE
1 TSP VANILLA
3/4 CP GRATED RAW CARROT
1/2 CP RAISINS
1/2 TSP CINNAMON

1. Combine oil, rice or barley malt syrup and water in small saucepan. Heat gently over low heat.

2. Remove from heat and let cool while you prepare rest of recipe.

3. Preheat oven to 325F.

4. Grate carrots.

5. Combine flour, arrowroot, baking powder, salt, and cinnamon in mixing bowl. Add lemon juice and vanilla to the cooled oil and syrup mixture.

6. Pour over dry ingredients and stir until well blended.

7. Fold in grated carrots and raisins.

8. Drop by rounded teaspoon onto oiled cookie sheets and bake for 12-15 minutes until light golden color.

9. Cool on wire rack. Makes about 2 dozen cookies.

Comments: Wheat free, corn free, a treat for anyone.

FILLED OAT BARS

Serves: 12   Time: 00:45

OAT MIXTURE:
2 CP ROLLED OATS
1 1/2 CP OAT FLOUR
1/2 CP OAT BRAN
1/2 CP CHOPPED WALNUTS
1 TSP CINNAMON
1/4 TO 1/3 CP CORN OIL
1/2 CP RICE SYRUP
1/2 CP APPLE JUICE
1/2 TSP SEA SALT

FILLING: (CHOOSE ONE)
3/4 - 1 CP APPLESAUCE/RAISIN
3/4 - 1 CP SUGAR-FREE JAM
3/4 - 1 CP APPLE BUTTER
3/4 - 1 CP BLUEBERRY SAUCE
3/4 - 1 CP COOKED APRICOTS

1. Preheat oven to 350F.

2. Oil a 9x13 inch baking pan.

3. Combine all oat mixture ingredients and mix very well. You may need to use your hands to be sure mix is well blended.

4. Press half of oat mixture into the prepared pan.

5. Spread filling you have chosen over this layer.

6. Sprinkle rest of oat mixture over the filling and press lightly with your hand.

7. Bake for 30-40 minutes or until golden brown. Cool and then cut into squares.

Comments: Wheat free and delicious as a treat or dessert. Can vary fillings.

NUTTY WALNUT DROPS

Serves: 10   Time: 00:30

1/3 CP CORN OIL
1/3 CP RICE SYRUP
1/2 TSP MAPLE SYRUP
1/4 TSP GRATED LEMON RIND
1 CP WW FLOUR
2 TBL WHEAT GERM
2 CP CHOPPED ROASTED WALNUTS
1/2 TSP LEMON JUICE
1/2 TSP BAKING SODA
1 TBL NUT MILK OR SOY MILK

1. Place oil and maple syrup in a small saucepan and heat over very low heat until warm.

2. Remove from heat and stir in the vanilla and lemon rind.

3. Combine the flour, wheat germ and walnuts in a mixing bowl.

4. Place the lemon juice and nut milk or soy milk in a measuring cup and dissolve the baking soda in the liquid.

5. Add the oil, syrup mixture, and milk mixture to the dry ingredients and stir until all combined. Batter should be drop consistency.

6. Drop the batter by heaping teaspoons on oiled baking sheets.

7. Bake at 325F for 12-15 minutes or until light golden color.

8. Cool and store in a tightly covered container.

Comments: A real treat for everyone.

OATMEAL RAISIN COOKIES

Serves: 12   Time: 00:30

2 CP ROLLED OATS
1/2 CP SUNFLOWER SEEDS
1 CP WW PASTRY FLOUR
2 TSP BAKING POWDER
1 TSP CINNAMON
1 CP RAISINS
1/2 CP CORN OIL
3/4 CP RICE OR BARLEY MALT SYRUP
1/4 CP SPRING WATER
1/2 CP FLAXSEED EGG REPLACER *
1/2 TSP VANILLA

1. Preheat oven to 350F.

2. Lightly toast the oats and sunflower seeds until they smell fragrant but not browned.

3. Add whole wheat pastry flour, baking powder, cinnamon and raisins to this mixture in a large mixing bowl.

4. Blend together the oil, rice or barley malt syrup, water, flaxseed mixture and vanilla, and add to dry ingredients.

5. Mix well until a smooth dough is formed.

6. Drop by tablespoon onto a oiled cookie sheet and bake at 350F for 15 minutes or until golden brown. Makes 2 dozen large cookies.

* Flaxseed mixture (egg replacer for baking) See recipe in cooking ingredients chapter.

Comments: _Delicious and good for you._

DESSERT SHORTCAKE

Serves: 6   Time: 00:30

1 CP WW PASTRY FLOUR
1 CP UNBLEACHED WHITE FLOUR
1/2 TSP SEA SALT
1/3 CP CORN OIL
1/2 CP TOFU
1/2 CP SPRING WATER
1/4 CP RICE SYRUP
1 TBL OIL FOR BRUSHING BETWEEN LAYERS

1. Preheat oven to 400F.

2. Combine flours, baking powder and salt in a mixing bowl. Cut in the oil until mixture is crumbly.

3. Blend in a blender the tofu, water and rice syrup. Pour into flour mixture and mix well until you have a smooth dough.

4. Roll out 1/4 inch thick and cut with a 3 inch biscuit cutter into 12 portions. Place half of the circles on a cookie sheet. Brush tops with oil and place another circle on top of each oiled one.

5. Bake at 400F for 15 minutes until light brown.

6. When shortcakes are cool, split and spoon any fruit and sweet dessert topping between and over the shortcake. Serve immediately.

GINGERBREAD CAKE

Serves: 9   Time: 01:00

1 CP WW PASTRY FLOUR
1 CP OAT FLOUR
1/2 TSP SEA SALT
1 TSP BAKING SODA
1 TSP GINGER POWDER
1/2 TSP CINNAMON
1/4 TSP NUTMEG
1/3 CP OIL OF CHOICE
2/3 CP BARLEY MALT SYRUP
1 1/2 CP SOY OR NUT MILK
1/2 TSP PURE VANILLA EXTRACT

1. Preheat oven to 350F and lightly oil a 8x8 or 9x9 cake pan.

2. Combine flours, baking soda, ginger, cinnamon and nutmeg in a mixing bowl and set aside.

3. Combine oil and barley malt syrup in a small pan and heat gently to liquefy.

4. Combine milk and vanilla in a large mixing bowl.

5. Add liquefied barley malt and oil mixture and wisk together well.

6. Add dry ingredients and wisk until well blended. If batter seems too thin you can add up to 1/4 cup more flour.

7. Pour into oiled pan and bake for about 40 minutes until browned and set.

8. Serve hot or cool.

Comments: _Serve with lemon dessert sauce or sweet dessert topping._

PEACH DREAM COUSCOUS CAKE

Serves: 2-4   Time: 00:20

1 CP COUSCOUS
PINCH SEA SALT
1 1/2 CP PEACH NECTAR
1 CP ALMOND MILK WITH THE ALMOND PIECES LEFT IN
1/2 TSP GRATED LEMON RIND (OPTIONAL)
1 CP PEELED AND DICED FRESH PEACHES

1. Place 1/2 cup almonds and 1 cup spring water into blender and blend at high speed until almonds are chopped.

2. Pour into a glass measuring cup and set aside so foam will settle out.

3. Bring peach nectar and almond milk to boiling point in a 2 quart saucepan.

4. Add couscous and pinch of sea salt. Reduce heat and cook for several minutes until grain is almost thick.

5. Add peaches and lemon rind, if using, and cook for minute longer.

6. Have ready a glass loaf pan rinsed with cold water.

7. Pour mixture into loaf pan, smooth out the top, and set aside to cool.

8. Cut into thick slices to serve. Recipe can be doubled to make a 8x8 size cake, which will make 9 servings.

Comments: *Special summer dessert that the whole family can enjoy.*

CRUNCHY CRUST

Serves: 6-8   Time: 00:30

1/2 CP BROWN RICE FLOUR
1 TBL ARROWROOT POWDER
1/2 CP GROUND WALNUTS OR ALMONDS
1/4 CP GROUND SUNFLOWER SEED
1/2 TSP CINNAMON (OPTIONAL)
1 TBL RICE SYRUP
2 TBL OIL OF YOUR CHOICE
2 TBL SPRING WATER

1. Combine dry ingredients in a mixing bowl.

2. Combine liquid ingredients in a small saucepan and heat gently until all are well blended.

3. Pour liquid over dry ingredients and mix with a fork or your hands until a nice even texture.

4. Press into a oiled 9 inch pie plate.

5. Bake at 350F for 15-18 minutes.

6. Cool before filling.

Comments: Use as you would a graham cracker crust, wheat free. This mixture also makes a good topping for a fruit crisp. Just sprinkle over the prepared fruit and bake for 25-30 minutes at 350F.

FLAKY PIE CRUST

Serves: 4-6   Time: 00:15

1 1/2 CP WW PASTRY FLOUR
1/2 CP UNBLEACHED FLOUR
1/4 TSP SEA SALT
1/3 CP + 1 TBL CORN OIL OR OIL OF CHOICE
2-4 TBL SOY MILK

1. Combine flours and salt.

2. Blend in the oil using a pastry blender or your hands. Add the soy milk gradually until the dough forms a ball and leaves the sides of the bowl.

3. Roll out dough to fit pie plate. It is very tender and rather difficult to work with. Don't be afraid to use plenty of unbleached flour on rolling surface and rolling pin so it won't stick.

4. Place in pie plate and flute edges or trim as desired.

5. Bake for 8-10 minutes at 350F before filling, then continue baking until filling is done. Any leftover dough can be used to make strips or cutouts for the top of the filling.

Comments: _Flaky crust for quiche or fruit pie._

GRANOLA PIE CRUST

Serves: 6-8   Time: 00:20

2 1/2 CP GRANOLA (ANY FLAVOR IS NICE)
1/3 CP OIL (SAFFLOWER OR CORN)

1. Grind the granola in a blender to crumb consistency.

2. Pour oil over the crumbs and blend well with your hands until oil is mixed in evenly.

3. Press into a 9 inch pie plate, Pyrex works very well. Press firmly to make crust even and well-packed.

4. Bake at 350F until golden brown, about 10 minutes if using a cooked filling. Crust does not have to be prebaked if you are using a filling which has to be baked.

Comments: _Good with apple crunch pie or with cream type filling._

PRESSED PIE CRUST

Serves: 6-8   Time: 00:30

1 1/2 CP WW PASTRY FLOUR
1/2 CP FINELY GROUND WALNUTS
1/4 CP OIL
4 TBL VERY COLD WATER OR MAPLE SYRUP FOR A SWEET
CRUST
1/4 TSP CINNAMON (OPTIONAL)
PINCH SEA SALT (OPTIONAL)

1. Combine flour, ground walnuts, cinnamon and salt, if using, in a large mixing bowl.

2. In a small bowl, combine the oil and water or maple syrup and beat with a wire wisk until well combined.

3. Stir into flour mixture and mix well.

4. Place dough in a well oiled 9 inch pie plate. Wet hands and press crust evenly onto bottom and sides of the pie plate.

5. Bake at 350F for 12-15 minutes or until golden. Fill with your choice of fruit or vegetable filling and bake again if needed for up to 30 minutes. Cool before serving.

Comments: _No rolling out dough. Can be used for fruit or vegetable pie._

STIR AND ROLL PIE CRUST

Serves: 6   Time: 00:20

1 CP WW PASTRY FLOUR
1 CP LESS 2 TBL UNBLEACHED WHITE FLOUR
2 TBL SOY FLOUR
1/2 CP SOY OIL
1/4 CP SOY MILK OR WATER
DASH OF SEA SALT

1. Combine flours and salt in mixing bowl.

2. Combine liquids in measuring cup.

3. Pour liquids into flours and mix with a fork until it forms a ball.

4. Press in a firm ball and cut in half. Use each half for a crust. Place the half between waxed paper and roll out with rolling pin on dampened work area to prevent sliding. Peel off top paper.

5. Transfer dough, paper side up, to pie plate. Peel off paper and fit into pie plate.

6. Pour filling into pastry lined pie plate and repeat rolling out procedure for the top crust.

7. Tuck edges under bottom pie shell edge and flute edges to seal.

8. Cut slits in top to let steam escape.

9. Bake according to filling directions. Can use recipe for two single crust pies.

Comments: *Almost foolproof pie crust for beginners.*

WHEAT FREE PIE CRUST

Serves: 6-8   Time: 00:30

1 1/3 CP OAT FLOUR
2/3 CP BROWN RICE FLOUR
DASH SEA SALT
2 TBL OIL OF YOUR CHOICE
2/3 CP SPRING WATER OR A LITTLE MORE IF NEEDED FOR PROPER CONSISTENCY

1. Oat flour can be made by blending rolled oats in the blender until flour consistency is obtained.

2. Preheat oven to 350F.

3. Combine oat flour, rice flour and sea salt in a large skillet and roast on top of stove over medium heat until they smell toasty. Do not brown.

4. Mix in oil with a fork.

5. Add just enough water so dough will hold together without becoming sticky.

6. Spread crust mixture into a 9 inch pie plate and press into a thin crust on the bottom and push the extra up the sides to form a rim.

7. Bake for 10-15 minutes until lightly golden.

8. Can be filled and baked for 20-30 minutes until lightly golden. Also can be baked as a pie shell and used for a cooked filling.

Comments: *Pie crust for those who can't use wheat, but delicious for all.*

APPLE CRUNCH PIE

Serves: 6-8   Time: 00:60

FILLING:
3 LB APPLES
1/2 CP RAISINS
1 CP APPLE JUICE
1/4 CP RICE SYRUP
1/2 TSP VANILLA
1/2 TSP CINNAMON
DASH SEA SALT
2 TBL KUZU DISSOLVED IN
1/3 CP COLD WATER
TOPPING:
1 1/2 CP ROLLED OATS
1/2 CP WW PASTRY FLOUR
1/2 CP CHOPPED WALNUTS
1/2 CP RICE SYRUP
1/3 CP OIL & PINCH SEA SALT

1. Prepare a crust using the whole wheat pastry or granola crust recipe.

2. Prepare crumb topping. Combine in a saucepan the oil and rice syrup until all liquid. Pour over the combined oats, flour and chopped nuts. Mix well until it forms a crumbly mixture.

3. Set aside and start the sauce filling.

4. Combine the raisins, apple juice, rice syrup, vanilla, cinnamon and sea salt in a saucepan. Simmer for 5 minutes. Add the diluted kuzu and cook until thick and clear. Set aside.

5. Peel and slice apples into the crust, pour sauce over and then cover with the crunch topping.

6. Bake at 350F for 35 to 40 minutes. Cool slightly before serving.

Comments: Special dessert, very sweet and satisfying.

BLUEBERRY PIE FILLING

Serves: 6   Time: 00:60

1 RECIPE 2 CRUST PASTRY
4 CP BLUEBERRIES
1/2 CP RICE SYRUP
1 TBL LEMON JUICE
4 TBL ARROWROOT STARCH

1. Line a 9 inch pie plate with crust.

2. Combine washed berries with rice syrup, lemon juice and arrowroot starch.

3. Cover with top crust. Cut several small slits in crust for steam to escape.

4. Bake at 450 for 10 minutes, then reduce heat to 350 for 30 minutes or until lightly browned and filling is bubbling.

Comments: _Summer dessert, no sugar, great taste._

MAPLE CHEESECAKE PIE

Serves: 6-8   Time: 00:60

1 1/2 LB TOFU
1/4 CP WALNUT OIL
1 1/3 CP MAPLE SYRUP
PINCH OF SEA SALT
UNBAKED PIE CRUST

1. Preheat oven to 350F.

2. Blend in a blender until smooth and creamy the tofu, oil, maple syrup and salt.

3. Pour into the unbaked pie shell and bake for about 1 hour or until set and lightly browned.

4. Serve cold with sweet dessert topping if desired. Make the pieces small as it is rich.

Comments: _Makes a 8 inch pie._ _Very rich and filling._

PARTY PECAN PIE

Serves: 8   Time: 00:45

CRUST:
1 1/2 CP OAT FLOUR
1/2 CP WW PASTRY FLOUR
1/4 CP CORN OIL
1/4 CP MAPLE SYRUP
PINCH SEA SALT

FILLING:
2 CP ROASTED PECANS
1 2/3 CP SPRING WATER
5 TBL KUZU
1/4 CP BARLEY MALT SYRUP
1/4 CP RICE SYRUP
1 TSP GRATED LEMON RIND
1 TSP VANILLA EXTRACT
1 TBL TAHINI (OPTIONAL)

Prepare crust:
1. Combine flours and sea salt in large mixing bowl.

2. Add oil and maple syrup and blend with fork or clean hands until soft dough is formed. Press evenly into a 9 inch pie plate and bake at 325F for 20 minutes.

Prepare filling:
4. Roast pecans (either in oven or skillet).

5. Combine water, kuzu, barley malt and rice syrups, lemon rind and tahini if using. Bring to boil and simmer until thickened. Remove from heat, add vanilla and pecans and stir to combine.

6. Pour into prepared crust and let cool to room temperature. Serve small pieces as it is very rich. Special dessert topping can be used if desired.

Comments: Special party dessert. Easy to make and very easy to enjoy, rich and satisfying.

PUMPKIN PIE FILLING

Serves: 8   Time: 00:60

1 9 INCH PIE CRUST
2 CUPS PUREED PUMPKIN
1 CP (8 OZ) SOFT TOFU
2 TBL KUZU
1/2 CP APPLE JUICE
1/4 CP MAPLE SYRUP
1 TSP CINNAMON
1/4 TSP NUTMEG
1/4 TSP CLOVES
PINCH OF SEA SALT

1. Combine all ingredients in blender and blend until smooth and creamy.

2. Pour into prepared pie shell and bake at 350F for 45 minutes or until firm.

3. Cool before serving.

Comments: Fall & winter dessert, very delicious as well as being good for you.

ALMOND CUSTARD

Serves: 3-4   Time: 00:15

2 1/2 CP SOY MILK
3 TBL AGAR-AGAR FLAKES
2 TBL KUZU
1/4 CP RICE SYRUP
1/2 TSP PURE ALMOND EXTRACT
1 TSP PURE VANILLA EXTRACT

1. In saucepan combine 2 cups of soy milk and the agar-agar. Bring to boiling point and then simmer over low heat until the agar-agar is dissolved (about 5 minutes).

2. Combine kuzu with remaining 1/2 cup of soy milk.

3. Add rice syrup and combine with the soy-agar mixture.

4. Increase heat to high and stir constantly until mixture comes to a boil and thickens slightly.

5. Add flavorings and pour into individual serving dishes.

6. Chill until ready to serve.

7. Just before serving, top with fresh fruit if desired.

Comments: Nice with a fresh fruit topping, such as berries or peaches.

APPLE CRISP

Serves: 6-8   Time: 00:45

6-8 COOKING APPLES
1 CP SWEET CIDER OR APPLE JUICE
1/4 TSP CINNAMON
1 CP UNBLEACHED WHITE FLOUR
1 CP WW PASTRY FLOUR
1 CP ROLLED OATS
PINCH SEA SALT
1/2 - 1 CP CHOPPED WALNUTS
1/2 CP CORN OIL
1/3 CP PURE MAPLE SYRUP
1/4 TSP VANILLA (OPTIONAL)

1. Peel, core, and slice apples into a 9x12 baking dish.

2. Mix the cinnamon with the sweet cider or apple juice and pour over the apples.

3. Set aside while you prepare the topping.

4. Combine the flours, oats, sea salt and nuts in a large mixing bowl.

5. Add the oil, maple syrup and vanilla if using. Mix all together until crumbly.

6. Sprinkle the topping over the apples and press lightly with hands to firm.

7. Bake at 350F for about 40 minutes or until the top begins to brown and the apples are tender.

Comments: *For special occasion, serve with tofu whipped cream.*

BREAD PUDDING

Serves: 4-6   Time: 00:60

3 CP STALE BREAD, CUBED
1/2 CP RAISINS OR OTHER DRIED FRUIT
1 1/2 CP HOT GRAIN COFFEE
1/2 TSP CINNAMON
1 TBL GRATED LEMON RIND
DASH SEA SALT
1/2 CP CHOPPED WALNUTS
1 TBL OIL OF CHOICE
1 APPLE CHOPPED (OPTIONAL)
WW FLOUR IF NEEDED

1. Combine all ingredients except for the whole wheat flour, in a mixing bowl and let set for 1 to 2 hours.

2. When ready to bake, check for seasoning and add whole wheat flour if mixture is too liquid.

3. Preheat oven to 300F.

4. Spoon into a covered casserole and bake for 30 minutes.

5. Remove cover and bake up to 30 minutes longer or until top is browned and mixture is firm and pulling away from sides of pan.

6. Serve as is or with a sauce of your choice. Lemon dessert sauce is a delicious compliment to this pudding.

Comments: _Healthful dessert, tastes rich and uses up stale bread._

FRUIT JELL DESSERT

Serves: 6-8   Time: 00:15

3-4 TBL AGAR-AGAR
4 CP APPLE JUICE
2 CP FRESH FRUIT, CHOPPED
1 TSP LEMON JUICE
THE LARGER AMOUNT OF AGAR-AGAR WILL MAKE A STIFFER GEL

1. Soften agar-agar in the apple juice for about five minutes.

2. Bring mixture to a boil and simmer for 5 minutes.

3. Remove from heat, let cool slightly, then add chopped fruit and lemon juice.

4. Pour into mold and allow to set. Will set at room temperature in about 1 1/2 hours, or may be refrigerated.

Comments: Very similar to the jello you know.

HEAVENLY POACHED PEARS

Serves: 4   Time: 00:30

4 BARTLETT OR BOSC PEARS
SPRING WATER
2 TSP FRESH LEMON JUICE
1/2 CP RAISINS
1 TBL KUZU
1/2 TSP VANILLA

1. Wash pears and peel if not organic. Remove cores and place in single layer in large saucepan. Cover with spring water and add lemon juice (lemon juice will keep the pears a nice light color). Cover and bring barely to boiling point.

2. Simmer very gently until tender.

3. Remove from cooking liquid and place in large serving dish.

4. Measure out 1 cup cooking liquid and place in small saucepan. Add raisins and simmer for 10 minutes.

5. Dissolve kuzu in 1/4 cup remaining cooking liquid or in cold water and add to raisin sauce mixture. Cook over medium heat until thick and clear. Add vanilla and pour sauce over the pears.

6. Cool to room temperature before serving.

Comments: *A nice company dessert, easy to prepare and delicious.*

265

MOCHA PUDDING

Serves: 2-3   Time: 00:15

2-3 TBL GRAIN COFFEE POWDER
1 1/2 CP SOY MILK
2 TBL MAPLE SYRUP OR RICE SYRUP
1/2 TBL TAHINI
1/4 TSP VANILLA
2 TBL KUZU DISSOLVED IN
2 TBL WATER
DASH SEA SALT

1. Combine grain coffee, soy milk, sea salt, maple syrup or rice syrup and tahini in a small saucepan.

2. Bring to boil and simmer until all ingredients are blended.

3. Dissolve kuzu in water and add to mixture, increase heat and cook until thick and clear.

4. Add vanilla and pour into dessert dishes to serve after it cools and firms up.

5. Can be topped with nuts or sweet dessert topping.

Comments: _Nice dessert after a heavy meal. You decide the toppings._

SPECIAL RICE PUDDING

Serves: 4-6   Time: 00:30

2 CP COOKED LONG GRAIN RICE
1/2 LB TOFU
1/2 CP SPRING WATER
2 TBL TAHINI
1/4 CP RICE SYRUP
1/2 TSP VANILLA EXTRACT
PINCH OF CINNAMON & NUTMEG
1/2 CP RAISINS
1/2 CP ROASTED, CHOPPED PECANS OR WALNUTS
1 TSP GRATED LEMON RIND
CHOPPED APRICOTS CAN BE SUBSTITUTED FOR THE RAISINS

1. Blend tofu, water, tahini, rice syrup, vanilla, spices until very smooth and creamy.

2. Combine with the cooked rice and stir until well blended.

3. Add the raisins, nuts, and lemon rind.

4. Stir well and pour into a oiled baking dish.

5. Cover and bake at 350F for 15-20 minutes.

6. Uncover and cook until top browns and gets crusty.

7. Serve hot or cool to room temperature.

Comments: Nice as a party dessert, but so easy to make you will want it often.

STEAMED PUDDING

Serves: 12   Time: 04:30

4 CP MIXED DRIED FRUITS (RAISINS, CURRANTS, APPLE, APRICOTS, ETC.)
1/2 CP CHOPPED ALMONDS
1 GRATED CARROT
2 CP APPLE JUICE OR CIDER
1 CP GRAIN COFFEE
GRATED PEEL OF ONE LEMON
1/4 TSP BAKING POWDER
1/4 TSP EACH OF CINNAMON, ALLSPICE, NUTMEG, & CLOVES
1/3 CP OIL OF CHOICE
2 CP OF WW FLOUR
1 CP UNBLEACHED WHEAT FLOUR
1 EGG OR EGG SUBSTITUTE
PINCH OF SEA SALT (OPTIONAL)

1. Combine dried fruits, nuts, grated carrot and grated lemon rind in a large mixing bowl. Add apple juice and grain coffee and let stand while preparing pans. You will need either a pudding mold or several tin cans as containers and a deep roasting pan with a rack and cover.

2. Add oil, flour, spices, baking powder and egg or egg substitute to the fruit mixture and blend all together well. Fill pudding molds 3/4 full. Cover tops with aluminum foil and secure with a rubber band.

4. Place in roasting pan on rack and pour boiling water half way up mold. This can also be done on top of stove in a large covered kettle such as a canner.

5. Steam for 3-5 hours, remove from steamer and cool. Can be resteamed briefly before serving with sauce of your choice. Remove from mold, slice and serve on dessert plates. Refrigerate leftovers.

Comments: _Especially nice with Lemon Dessert Sauce._

STRAWBERRY DREAM

Serves: 4   Time: 00:15

1 10 OZ PACKAGE SILKEN TOFU
3 TBL RICE SYRUP
2 CP FRESH STRAWBERRIES SLICED AND ALLOWED TO SIT TO
FORM JUICES
1/2 CP WHOLE STRAWBERRIES

1. Place tofu in a blender or food processor and blend until creamy.

2. Add warmed rice syrup and 1 cup of prepared strawberries, blend
   again and add second cup of strawberries. Blend again at low
   speed. Allow some berries to remain in small chunks.

3. Pour into serving dishes and chill.

4. Garnish with whole strawberry when ready to serve.

Comments: Delicious and healthful dessert. Great snack for the kids.

SUMMER FRUIT CRISP

Serves: 4   Time: 00:45

2 TBL LEMON JUICE
3 CP FRESH FRUIT, CUT INTO BIT SIZE PIECES
(PEACHES, NECTARINES, APRICOTS, BLUEBERRIES, CHERRIES,
STRAWBERRIES, RASPBERRIES)
1/4 CP OIL
1/4 CP RICE SYRUP
1 CP ROLLED OATS
3/4 CP OAT FLOUR
1/2 TSP SEA SALT
1 TSP CINNAMON (OPTIONAL)
1/2 CP CHOPPED WALNUTS OR ALMONDS

1. Preheat oven to 375F.

2. Place prepared fruit in a small baking dish and sprinkle with lemon juice. Set aside.

3. In a small saucepan heat the oil and rice syrup until it becomes thin and warm.

4. Remove from heat and add remaining ingredients.

5. Blend well and then spread evenly over fruit.

6. Bake for 30 to 35 minutes until topping is a golden brown. Serve warm or cool.

Comments: Wheat-free and delicious.

TAPIOCA QUINOA PUDDING

Serves: 4   Time: 00:20

1 CP QUINOA
2 1/2 CP SOY MILK
DASH SEA SALT
2 TBL MAPLE OR RICE SYRUP
2 TBL KUZU DISSOLVED IN
2 TBL WATER
2 TSP PURE VANILLA
1/4 TSP NUTMEG OR CINNAMON (OPTIONAL)

1. Wash quinoa well and drain.

2. Combine the grain, soy milk and sea salt and bring to a boil.

3. Reduce heat, cover and simmer for 20 minutes.

4. Add maple syrup or rice syrup and mix well.

5. Add kuzu mixture and stir constantly until thickened.

6. Add vanilla and spices of choice.

7. Serve hot or cold.

Comments: *Can be served as a hot breakfast or as a dessert for any meal.*

9. BEVERAGES

The usual beverages for a transition diet are spring water, bancha tea, kukicha twig tea, roasted barley tea, grain coffee, dandelion root tea, and various mild herbal teas. Some fruit and vegetable juices are used when prepared from fresh seasonal sources. Try to avoid frozen and prepared drink mixes and especially carbonated soft drinks or sodas. Usually the body does not require the vast amount of excess liquids that people consume today. This diet already contains much liquid when you consider all the water that is used in cooking grains, beans, and soups. Vegetables are already 90% water for the most part. And as Thoreau said "Water is the only drink for a wise man."

BEVERAGES

ALMOND MILK
COOKED GRAIN MILK
SESAME MILK
SODA "POP"
PINK SPARKLE PUNCH

ALMOND MILK

Serves: 4-6   Time: 00:15

1 CP ALMONDS
4 CP SPRING WATER
1 TBL OIL
2 TBL RICE SYRUP
DASH SEA SALT

1. Drop almonds into boiling water to cover. Boil for 30 seconds, remove from heat and let sit for 3 minutes.

2. Drain and remove skins from the almonds.

3. Combine almonds with remaining ingredients in a blender and blend for 2 minutes.

4. Line a colander or strainer with 2 layers of cheese cloth and strain liquid. Squeeze out as much liquid as possible.

5. Store in covered container in the refrigerator. Will keep well for 5 or 6 days.

6. The strained almond meal can be used in baked goods or can be made into almond sprinkles by roasting gently on a cookie sheet until dry and golden. Use to sprinkle over grains or as a topping for desserts.

Comments: Use on cereals, cooking liquid, nice in desserts.

COOKED GRAIN MILK

Serves: 2 quarts   Time: 02:00

1 CP GRAIN, SOAKED 12 HOURS
8 CP SPRING WATER
SMALL AMOUNT OF RICE SYRUP, IF DESIRED
COOK OATS WITH PIECE OF VANILLA BEAN FOR SWEET
FLAVOR

1. Bring soaked grain and water to a boil. Lower heat to a simmer
   and cook for 2 hours.

2. Strain through a cheesecloth.

3. Save residue to use in other dishes, such as burgers, breads, soups,
   etc.

4. Season milk to taste with rice syrup if desired.

Alternative method:
Cover grain and water in a saucepan and cook very slowly on a low
heat overnight. Finish in the same manner.

Comments: Use for drinking or cooking.

SESAME MILK

Serves: 4-6   Time: 00:10

1/3 CP SESAME SEEDS
2 1/2 CP WATER, DIVIDED

1. Wash sesame seeds and drain well.

2. Place in blender with 1/2 cup water and blend on high speed for 1 minute. Add remaining water and blend again.

3. Can be used immediately for cooking purposes or refrigerated for future use. Will keep for up to 5 days.

Comments: Seed milk for use in cooking yields 2 1/2 cups.

SODA POP

Serves: 1   Time: 00:05

1/4 CP FRUIT JUICE (ANY FLAVOR)
1 CP SPARKLING WATER
FRESH FRUIT OR MINT LEAF GARNISH (OPTIONAL)

1. Combine fruit juice and sparkling water in a tall glass.

2. Add ice if desired.

3. Decorate with fresh fruit or mint leaf if desired.

4. Serve with a smile to kids of all ages. A healthful treat that won't decay your teeth or eat the lining of your stomach.

PINK SPARKLE PUNCH

Serves: 10   Time: 00:10

1 QT APPLE-STRAWBERRY OR APPLE-RASBERRY JUICE
2 QT SPARKLING MINERAL WATER
JUICE OF 2 LEMONS
ICE RING WITH FRESH BERRIES AND MINT LEAVES
MINT LEAVES FOR GARNISH

1. Prepare the ice ring the day before you will be serving the punch.

2. In punch bowl or large serving bowl, combine fruit juice, lemon juice and sparking water. Add ice ring.

3. Serve in punch cups and garnish with mint leaves. As the ice ring melts, there will be berries to add to each cup of punch.

Comments: _Beautiful served in a large punch bowl and punch cups._

10. SUPER SNACKS FOR KIDS OF ALL AGES

Healthy snacks are easy to prepare and certainly much better for you than the expensive, fat and sodium laden junk foods that can be purchased almost anywhere food is found in America. Vow right now that no junk food will go into your grocery cart or into your home. It is easy to have a supply of healthy snacks on hand for the family. Rice cakes with a spread, roasted nuts, popcorn, home made cookies, fresh fruits and raw vegetable sticks are all quick and easy healthful snacks. Go easy on even these and concentrate on two or three well balanced meals for best health. If you find you crave or rely heavily on snacks, re-examine the balance of your meals. Are they too heavy on one item or lacking in something else? When you are in need of re-adjustment the body signals this by cravings. Here are some very special treats for healthful splurges.

SNACKS

PEACH FROSTY
POPCORN BALLS
TOFU TURTLES
TRAIL MIX
VERY BERRY SHAKE

PEACH FROSTY

Serves: 2   Time: 00:10

1 CP FRESH PEACHES, SLICED
FRESH LEMON JUICE
1 CP SILKEN SOFT TOFU
2 TBL RICE SYRUP

1. Slice washed but unpeeled peaches and toss with lemon juice to keep from turning dark. Spread in single layer on plate, cover and place in freezer.

2. When ready to make the frosty combine, silken soft tofu with rice syrup in blender. Mix at low speed until blended, add frozen peaches and blend until smooth and thickened.

3. Pour into glasses, garnish with fresh peach slice and a mint sprig if desired.

Comments: *Another healthful snack. Could also be used as a dessert.*

POPCORN BALLS

Serves: 10   Time: 00:30

1 CP ORGANIC UNPOPPED CORN (28 CP POPPED)
1 CP BARLEY MALT
2 TBL MOLASSES (OPTIONAL)
3 TBL REAL BUTTER
DASH SEA SALT

1. Pop the corn and discard any unpopped kernels.

2. Place in a very large mixing bowl.

3. Combine the barley malt, molasses and butter in a small saucepan and bring to a rolling boil. Cook for approximately 3 minutes or until mixture reaches 220F on a candy thermometer.

3. Remove from heat and pour over popcorn while stirring constantly with a wooden spoon.

4. As soon as mixture is cool enough to handle, grease your hands with a little butter and press mixture into 4 inch size balls. Handle quickly before the mixture hardens up and becomes too brittle to shape.

5. Wrap any that are not eaten right away in wax paper to keep from drying out or place in a metal container.

Comments: _Special treat for kids of all ages. Good family project._

TOFU TURTLES

Serves: 12   Time: 00:15

1 16 OZ PACKAGE FIRM TOFU
1/4 CP TAHINI
1/2 TSP SHOYU/TAMARI SAUCE
2 TBL RICE SYRUP OR BARLEY MALT SYRUP
WHOLE WALNUTS OR PECANS

1. Process all the ingredients except for the whole nuts in a food processor or blender until very smooth and thick.

2. Spoon out a tablespoon full at a time onto a large cookie sheet or platter.

3. Press a whole walnut or pecan into the top so it looks like the top of a turtle.

4. Place in freezer and freeze until firm.

5. Transfer to a covered container and leave in freezer until you serve them. They melt very quickly.

Comments: Healthful snack for anyone. Good after school snack for kids. Very nutritious. Kids of all ages like them and there is no cooking. Variations could include chopped nuts or raisins in the batter, but they are good just plain.

TRAIL MIX

Serves: 4   Time: 00:15

1 CP RAISINS
1 CP ROASTED SUNFLOWER SEEDS
1 CP SLIVERED ALMONDS
1 CP DRIED APRICOT OR DRIED APPLES, DICED
THERE CAN BE MANY VARIATIONS TO TRAIL MIX. ALMOST
ANY DRIED FRUIT, SEED OR NUT CAN BE COMBINED FOR A
ENERGY SNACK. THE CHOICE IS YOURS.

1. Roast sunflower seeds and cool.

2. Combine all ingredients and mix well.

3. Put into a glass jar with a tight fitting lid to keep fresh.

4. If using for traveling away from home, simply pour a portion into
   a container and pack it along.

Comments: Healthful snack and great travel food for sports.

VERY BERRY SHAKE

Serves: 2   Time: 00:10

1 CP FRESH BERRIES (STRAWBERRY, RASPBERRY OR BLUEBERRY
2 CP SOY OR NUT MILK (ALMOND MILK IS VERY NICE WITH STRAWBERRY)
2 TSP TAHINI (OPTIONAL)
1/4 CP RICE SYRUP OR MAPLE SYRUP
1/4 TSP VANILLA OR ALMOND EXTRACT (OPTIONAL)

1. Wash berries and blend all ingredients together until very thick and creamy. Be sure milk is very cold before blending.

2. Serve immediately.

Comments: Nice child pleaser, but adults love it too.

11. WHAT'S FOR BREAKFAST?

Rise and shine and get ready for the grueling (pardon the pun) experience. One of the most asked questions is "What can I eat for breakfast?" Without bacon and eggs, sugared prepared boxed cereals, toasted bleached white bread or English muffins, dairy products and lots of fruit juices many think that there is nothing left for breakfast. There are many breakfast dishes that are delicious and very satisfying as well as being good for you. Hot miso soup is the traditional start for a macrobiotic breakfast and is a great way to start the day. Planned-over grains can be turned into delicious cereals and there are many whole grains that can be cooked quickly for a dish that will really "stick to your ribs."

Vegetables also deserve a place in your breakfast plans, either fresh or planned-over from last night's dinner. For people who must have their cold cereal, there are some prepared cereals at the health food stores which are not loaded with sugar and preservatives. Nut milk or soy milk is a good alternative to dairy milk and cream. Here are some recipes to help you and your family through the transition and beyond.

BUCKWHEAT & BARLEY PANCAKES
WITH BLUEBERRY SAUCE
FIT FOR A QUEEN QUINOA
GOLDILOCKS' PORRIDGE
GOURMET OATMEAL
GREAT GRANOLA
SCRAMBLED TOFU
SCRAMBLED TOFU & MILLET
TEFF TREAT
TOFU FRENCH TOAST

Any one of these breakfasts will keep you going full speed all morning. Please don't spoil it all by smothering them in maple syrup or finishing off with a cup of acidic coffee. These will only lead to mid-morning hypoglycemic attacks. Low blood sugar attacks can be pretty nasty and range from mild sweating, nausea, hunger, shaking, weakness or headaches, to full-blown severe symptoms with violent mood swings. So try to avoid setting yourself up for this by keeping breakfast sweets to a bare minimum.

BUCKWHEAT & BARLEY PANCAKES

Serves: 2-4   Time: 00:20

1/2 CP BUCKWHEAT FLOUR
1/2 CP BARLEY FLOUR
1 1/2 TSP BAKING POWDER
1/4 TSP SEA SALT
1 1/2 TBL RICE SYRUP
1 EGG OR EGG SUBSTITUTE
3/4 CP SOY OR NUT MILK
1 1/2 TBL OIL

1. Combine all dry ingredients in a mixing bowl.

2. Combine all wet ingredients, and add to dry ingredients.

3. Mix until all ingredients are blended. Add additional liquid if mixture is too dry.

4. Cook on a medium hot griddle. These pancakes take a little longer to cook than wheat flour pancakes.

5. Serve with apple butter and/or maple syrup.

Comments: _Recipe can be doubled, wheat-free._

BLUEBERRY SAUCE

Serves: 2   Time: 00:10

1 CP FRESH BLUEBERRIES
1/2 CP SPRING WATER
2 TBL MAPLE SYRUP
1 TBL KUZU
DASH SEA SALT
DASH CINNAMON (OPTIONAL)

1. Dissolve kuzu in 2 tbl of water.

2. Add to rest of ingredients and bring to boiling point.

3. Simmer gently until thick and translucent.

4. Serve warm over pancakes or waffles.

Comments: *Makes a good filling for dessert crepes or a fruit sauce for pudding.*

FIT FOR A QUEEN QUINOA

Serves: 1-2   Time: 00:15

FOR EACH SERVING YOU WILL NEED:
1 CP COOKED QUINOA
1/2 CP APPLE JUICE
1-2 TBL CHOPPED WALNUTS
DASH OF CINNAMON

1. Combine all ingredients in a small saucepan and bring to a boil,
   reduce heat and simmer gently until the apple juice is absorbed.

2. Serve in cereal bowl and enjoy.

Comments: For those who like a sweet gourmet breakfast occasionally.

GOLDILOCK PORRIDGE

Serves: 1-2   Time: 00:20

FOR EACH SERVING YOU WILL NEED:
1 CP OF COOKED MILLET
1 TBL CHOPPED DRIED APRICOTS
1 TBL ROASTED SUNFLOWER OR SESAME SEEDS
1/2 CP APPLE-APRICOT JUICE
IF YOU DON'T HAVE COOKED MILLET ON HAND. THIS CAN
BE PREPARED QUICKLY BY USING CRACKED MILLET CEREAL
AND WATER AND JUICE COMBINATION.

1. Combine all ingredients and simmer until hot and juice has been
   absorbed.

2. Serve.

Comments: Especially easy if you have planned-over millet on hand.

GOURMET OATMEAL

Serves: 3   Time: 00:15

2 CP SPRING WATER
1 CP APPLE JUICE
1 APPLE, DICED
1/4 CP RAISINS
1/4 CP CHOPPED WALNUTS
1 CP OLD FASHION ROLLED OATS
DASH OF CINNAMON

1. Combine water and apple juice in a large saucepan.

2. Add diced apple and raisins and bring to a boil.

3. Add oatmeal, walnuts and cinnamon.

4. Reduce heat and simmer for 5-10 minutes.

5. Remove from heat, cover and let stand for 4-5 minutes to blend flavors and allow oatmeal to finish cooking.

6. Serve with your choice of apple juice, soy milk, or nut milk.

Comments: _Totally different taste than expected from oatmeal._

GREAT GRANOLA

Serves: 10   Time: 01:45

3 CP ROLLED OATS
1/2 CP WHEAT GERM
1 CP SUNFLOWER SEEDS
1/4 CP SESAME SEEDS
1 CP SLIVERED ALMONDS
1/2 CP COCONUT SHREDS (OPTIONAL)
1/4 CP OIL
1/2 CP APPLE JUICE
1 CP RAISINS

1. Preheat oven to 250F.

2. In a large mixing bowl combine rolled oats, wheat germ, seeds and nuts. Add oil and stir until well mixed. Add coconut if using. Add apple juice a little at a time mixing until crumbly.

3. Pour into a large, shallow baking pan which has been brushed with oil.

4. Bake for 1 1/2 hours. Stir every 15 minutes.

5. When the mixture is dry and light brown remove from oven and cool.

6. Add raisins when cool and store in sealed jars to keep fresh.

Comments: *Good served with soy milk or nut milk.*

SCRAMBLED TOFU

Serves: 1   Time: 00:15

4 OZ OF FRESH TOFU
1 TSP OR MORE OF CHOPPED CHIVES OR SCALLIONS
DASH OF TURMERIC
DASH OF SHOYU/TAMARI SAUCE
1 TSP OIL OF CHOICE
DASH OF SEA SALT OR HERBAL SEASONING (OPTIONAL)

1. Drain tofu and crumble into a small mixing bowl.

2. Heat oil in a small skillet.

3. Combine remaining ingredients with the crumbled tofu and saute in skillet until hot and the consistency of scrambled eggs.

3. Serve with toasted sourdough bread or homemade muffins for a great start to the day.

Comments: _Recipe for one serving, can multiply for more._

SCRAMBLED TOFU & MILLET

Serves: 2   Time: 00:15

4 OZ OF FIRM TOFU
1 CP COOKED MILLET
2 CHOPPED SCALLIONS OR
2 TBL CHOPPED CHIVES
1 TSP OIL
1 TSP SHOYU/TAMARI SAUCE
1/8 TSP TURMERIC

1. Saute the scallions very briefly in the oil.

2. Add crumbled tofu, cooked millet, shoyu sauce, and turmeric and mix well. Continue to saute about 10 minutes until the mixture resembles scrambled eggs.

3. Check for seasoning and serve hot.

4. If using chives instead of scallions, simply combine all ingredients and saute. The turmeric is important because it colors the mixture.

5. Sourdough toast or basic bran muffins go very well with this dish.

Comments: Recipe can be doubled or tripled if desired.

TEFF TREAT

Serves: 1   Time: 00:15

RECIPE CAN BE DOUBLED OR TRIPLED OR QUADRUPLED TO
FEED AS MANY AS YOU NEED.
1 CP SPRING WATER
1/2 CP TEFF (LIGHT OR DARK)
1/4 CP CHOPPED DRIED APPLE
DASH SEA SALT

1. Bring water and salt to a boil, add chopped dried apples and teff.

2. Reduce heat and cook until thickened, about 10 to 15 minutes.

3. Pour into cereal dish and lightly drizzle a little pure maple syrup over the top. DELICIOUS!

Comments: New taste treat for breakfast.

TOFU FRENCH TOAST

Serves: 4   Time: 00:20

1 1/2 CP CRUMBLED TOFU
1 1/2 TSP CINNAMON
2 TBL RICE SYRUP
1/2 CP SOYMILK
1/2 TSP SEA SALT
1 TBL OIL
IF TOO THICK ADD SOYMILK
8 SLICES OF BREAD

1. Blend in a blender until smooth and creamy the first 6 ingredients.

2. Dip slices of whole grain bread in batter and then fry in a hot oiled skillet until browned on both sides.

3. Serve hot with maple syrup or applesauce or apple butter topping.

Comments: Great for breakfast with real maple syrup, applesauce, or apple butter topping.

12. THE HEALTHFUL LUNCH

If you are home during the day, lunch is pretty easy, as it can be last night's dinner's planned-overs. But when you are away from home it does require some advance planning to avoid the fatal fast food trap. Almost anything you prepare at home can be transported to work with the help of a wide mouth stainless steel thermos bottle. The stainless steel type is more expensive but much more durable and healthy for you than the plastic variety. I find they also do a much better job of keeping foods at hot or cold temperatures for a longer time. Stainless steel dishes with locking covers are also available at oriental stores. They are wonderful for carrying portions of grains, vegetables or even desserts. They don't leak because of a rubber gasket and they don't break. What more could you ask for?

Soup and salad or soup and sandwich is the old traditional lunch and it can easily be modified for your transition diet lunch either at home or away. Try some of these ideas.

SOUP OR STEW

CREAMY SPLIT PEA SOUP
SUMMER MINESTRONE
VEGETABLE-BARLEY
MIDAS ROOT SOUP
GINGERED LEEK & LENTIL
MY GARDEN STEW

SALAD OR SANDWICH

TOFU-VEGGIE IN PITA BREAD
TABOULI SALAD
BBQ BURGER ON SOURDOUGH
KNISHES W/VEGGIE-RICE FILLING
NORI ROLLS
RICE CAKES W/SWEET VEGETABLE BUTTER

I'm sure you can come up with many ideas of your own. Almost any leftover grain can be made into a salad by adding green onion, red radishes, celery, minced parsley, and seasonings of your choice. A quick garnish of chopped chives or watercress turns it into a gourmet dish. Any leftover cooked vegetables can also be added. Barley and corn make a great summer salad made in this manner.

If you are doing the two or three step plan ahead meals, you will always have something in the refrigerator with which to create your own special dishes. You can also add a home made cookie or special dessert to your lunches if desired.

Here are some especially good travelers.

KNISHES W/VEGETABLE RICE FILLING
SPECIAL PUFF PASTRY
NORI ROLLS

KNISHES W/VEGGIE-RICE FILLING

Serves: 12   Time: 00:30

2 MED SIZE CARROTS
1 MED SIZE ONION
2 STALKS CELERY
2 INCH PIECE DAIKON OR
4 RED RADISHES
1 PURPLE TOP TURNIP OR A KOHLRABI BULB
1/4 HEAD OF SMALL CABBAGE, CHIVES, PARSLEY,
WATERCRESS, AS AVAILABLE AND DESIRED
1 TO 2 CP BROWN RICE
1/2 CP SUNFLOWER SEEDS
SHOYU/TAMARI SAUCE TO TASTE
UMEBOSHI VINEGAR TO TASTE

1. Finely chop the first five ingredients saute in water or oil for 3 - 4
   minutes in a large skillet. Slice the cabbage finely and add to the
   ingredients, cover and steam for a few minutes until all the
   vegetables are softened but slightly crisp. You will have about 3
   cups of vegetables.

2. Add rice and seeds to mixture. Season with chives, parsley,
   watercress if desired.

3. Add shoyu/tamari sauce and umeboshi vinegar to taste (umeboshi
   vinegar delays spoilage when carrying for lunches or travel).

4. Roll out the pastry dough 1/2 at a time. Divide each half into 6
   equal size pieces and fill with the vegetable-rice filling. Fold
   dough around filling and seal well. With your hands shape into a
   nice round bun and place sealed side down on a baking sheet.

5. When all are ready, bake at 350F for 30-45 minutes or until nicely
   browned. Eat hot or cool and store.

*Comments: Great traveling food. Great filling for Special Puff Pastry, good
for lunch bags and picnics.*

SPECIAL PUFF PASTRY

Serves: 6-8   Time: 00:15

1 CP SPRING WATER
PINCH SEA SALT
1/3 CP 1 TBL OIL (SESAME, CORN OR SAFFLOWER)
1 1/2 CP WW FLOUR
1 CP UNBLEACHED WHITE FLOUR
1 CP FINE CORNMEAL

1. Combine flours in a large mixing bowl.

2. Bring water to a boil in small saucepan. Add salt and wisk the oil into the water. Pour this mixture into the flour mixture and blend in quickly to form a smooth dough.

3. Knead for 1 minute.

4. Return to mixing bowl, cover tightly and let cool to room temperature before rolling out.

5. Divide dough in half for pie crusts.

6. Roll thinly for strudel or knishes.

IT IS VERY IMPORTANT TO USE BOILING WATER AND TO BE SURE OIL IS THOROUGHLY WISKED INTO THE MIXTURE TO OBTAIN A TENDER CRUST. COLD WATER WILL NOT WORK.

Comments: _Nice light pastry for pies, strudel, and knishes._

NORI ROLLS

Serves: 1   Time: 00:30

1 TO 1 1/2 CP COOKED SHORT GRAIN BROWN RICE
1 SHEET NORI
1 SMALL CARROT, CUT IN THIN STRIPS
1-2 GREEN SCALLIONS
1/4 - 1/2 TSP UMEBOSHI PASTE
SEA SALT
SPRING WATER
FLAVOR CAN BE VARIED BY ADDING DIFFERENT VEGETABLES
OR SEEDS TO THE FILLING.

1. Recipe can easily be multiplied.

2. Add pinch of salt to small amount of water in pot. Bring to a boil. Add carrot and simmer until soft. Remove and drain, save cooking liquid.

3. Blanch scallions briefly. Remove and drain. Save liquid for soups. You can also vary the vegetable filling for the nori rolls.

4. Open sheet of nori, place on sushi mat (bamboo mat) or use several sheets of paper towels or wax paper.

5. Moisten right hand with water. Evenly press 1/4 inch layer of rice on nori sheet. Leave 1/2 - 3/4 inch at top edge and 1/4 inch at bottom edge uncovered.

6. One inch up from bottom edge make a narrow track in the rice. Spread lightly with umeboshi paste. Place a few carrot and scallion strips over the paste, they may be blanched or raw.

7. Roll up, pressing firmly. Moisten flap end of sheet to seal.

8. Cut into 1/2 inch slices to serve.

Comments: _Pretty to serve and a very good traveling food._

13. EATING OUT: A SURVIVAL LESSON

Let's face it. There are times when you have to eat out and there are some things you have to know in order to survive the event. If you are traveling you can check the local phone directory and try to locate a macrobiotic or a vegetarian restaurant. The second choice would be to find an ethnic restaurant such as Italian, Greek, or Oriental (Chinese, Thai, Japanese, etc) where you would be able to find meatless entrees and more vegetable dishes. The third choice is to find a regular American restaurant and opt for the broiled fish, rice pilaf and garden salad. Don't be afraid to speak up and ask for exactly what you want. Fish broiled plain (that means no butter and extra seasonings), no dressing on your salad (ask for lemon and skip the oil). If they do serve fresh vegetables, feel free to ask for a double portion. Remember the restaurants are in business to please you and will try to give you what you want and need. Some restaurants offer a salad and soup bar which can be a lifesaver if you choose carefully.

Breakfast is easy. Just order the oatmeal. If you always carry a few individually wrapped kukicha tea bags or roasted barley tea bags, you can order a pot of hot water and have a hot drink.

If you are traveling far away from home, you really need a kitchen suitcase to stick to your diet. A kitchen suitcase will hold an electric hot plate, saucepan with cover, eating utensils and some food supplies with which you can create some meals, especially breakfast and lunch. The choices are many since grains, beans, and sea vegetable are all easy to carry in their dry state and need no refrigeration. Fresh vegetables and fruits can be purchased along the way. Read the strict phase macrobiotic healing diet in The Cure Is In The Kitchen: The Strict Macrobiotic Healing Phase Diet, by S.A. Rogers, M.D. (Prestige Publishing, Syracuse, N.Y.) for all the details and lists of what to bring with you if you need to stay on this plan in order to remain well. If you are a camper, boater, biker, or hiker, you can also stay on your healthful diet. With a gas camp stove (there are many types from small to large), your staples, and a preplanned menu, anything from a day trip to a long touring trip is possible and fun for all. The most difficult eating out situation is when you are invited to someone's home where the SAD (standard American diet) is the way of eating. If it is someone you know well, you can offer to bring a dish for the meal. That way you'll know there is at least one thing you can safely eat.

Otherwise just take a very tiny portion or pass by the dishes that are not good for you and take larger portions of the safer foods and don't make a fuss over it. Just relax and enjoy the good time. Some people eat at home before going to an event to take the edge off their appetites, and make it easier to stay in control of their intake of less desirable food. Of course, the other choice could be your decision to just eat whatever is served and call it your splurge, which is fine as long as it is your decision. We all need to have a special splurge occasionally, but it should never be followed by guilt and it won't be if it is your decision.

Be sure to check back to the previous chapter, The Healthful Lunch, for some recipes for good traveling foods.

CHAPTER VIII

MY STORY: HOW I BECAME MACROBIOTIC

When I started working for Dr. Rogers, over fourteen years ago, I thought I was a pretty healthy person, although I knew I had a few problems. I was always fighting 10 or 15 pounds of weight that I didn't need. I had been on and off high blood pressure medications. I seemed to have a regular routine of urinary infections, my nose always ran, and my head always ached. Every summer I would break out in rashes when I tried to work outside in the garden. But, basically, I thought of myself as a very healthy person.

As I learned more about allergies, I realized that many of my problems might be allergy related. I was tested and started on injections for pollens, dust and molds, and these helped greatly. My nose stopped running, and my headaches were not quite as bad, but they were still there. As time went by, new things started to happen. I found that when I was exposed to cigarette smoke I would have laryngitis, and I noticed that chemical things were starting to bother me more, like going in stores or smelling perfume or aftershave on someone. Now I was developing chemical allergies, as well.

And then one day our office administrator said to me, "Why don't you try testing a few of those foods." I thought, "I'm not allergic to food, I can eat anything." But I went ahead and tested some foods, and found out, to my amazement, that many of the foods I tested, such as milk, egg, chocolate, coffee, and mushroom, were the ones that gave me the headaches. And sure enough I could turn them right off with the neutralizing doses. This was just wonderful, so I started some food injections, and along with that a very strict rotation diet. I did lose some weight and I felt good, but I knew if I didn't stick to my diet, the symptoms would all come right back, even with the food allergy injections.

Several amazing things did happen; my blood pressure problems went away, and I no longer required any medication. Also, I no longer seemed to have the recurrent urinary infections.

Next, a couple of girls at the office started on macrobiotics and I saw how much it was helping them, and I thought that I would like to try it. So on one of my husband's annual two week hunting trips, I stocked up on rice and millet, and even bought some miso, not knowing what to do with it, and started reading a little bit. I call this my false start because I found that it was just too foreign to me, and I still in my mind was thinking that I had to rotate my foods. So it soon became something that I just didn't think I could work into my life.

Then in April of 1988, I came down with shingles (Herpes zoster). It was a very painful disease and it certainly was an opportunity to realize that something was definitely wrong with my immune system. It gave me the incentive I needed to try macrobiotics again; basically, because I had seen how well the doctor had done on her macrobiotic regime. I knew it would entail a huge lifestyle change, but I thought I had better try. The second time I got considerably more serious, and had a consultation regarding my foods. The list of foods you must avoid, at least temporarily as all macrobiotic people know, includes a lot of don'ts and then a lot of foreign sounding foods. With a beginner's cookbook and You Are What You Ate, off I went to find some of these foods and to begin to learn how to cook them. Fortunately my interest from before had helped a little because I had become a recipe collector. I had read quite a bit and figured out where to start. I am also very fortunate to have an understanding husband who has been extremely supportive in this venture.

Luckily I enjoy cooking, but for the first macrobiotic meal I tried to prepare, I could have used three more stoves and sixteen more feet of counter space. For the first two weeks it seemed as though I spent hours in the kitchen, whereas before I had been able to put a meal on the table in a fraction of that time. Of course this was very frustrating for me at this time of the year, because I wanted to be outside working in my garden and doing fun things; instead I was in the kitchen cooking and cooking and cutting and cutting and cooking.

Step by step I got better at it, and mastered progressively more hurdles. Of course, you must remember that at this time I was always cooking two meals, because my husband was not eating macrobiotically. Trust me when I say that it is quite a feat to prepare a pot roast dinner along with a macrobiotic dinner. But once I was really on the macrobiotic diet, I had so much more energy, more than I had in a long time. I felt my headaches clearing totally, and the pounds melted away. I lost more pounds that I ever remembered losing, to the point where people were starting to say, "What are you doing, you're so skinny?" I didn't feel skinny, I just felt good.

A lot of funny things happened along the way. We tried to

take a trip to Cape Cod early in June. We packed for a camping trip and I found out just how difficult it is to cook macrobiotically on a two burner Coleman stove. But I did do it and succeeded, even when I had a macrobiotic discharge on the vacation and my husband was ready to bring me home because he was so worried about me.

A discharge, macrobiotically speaking, is the way your body periodically gets rid of all the old, unnecessary "toxins" that have accumulated and are keeping you from being truly healthy. Although it is not a pleasant process, there is something about it that makes you feel that this is supposed to be happening and you know you are improving because of it. It is very hard to explain to other people, though, because though you feel miserable, you are thankful for it, and you know you will eventually be healthier.

I have now been macrobiotic for three and a half years. I do have my moments of cheating, but they are few. And all the time it becomes easier to stay on the diet. As a matter of fact, I am at the point now, where if I don't have my daily fix of greens, grains, weeds, and seeds, I feel that something is missing.

After three and a half years on this diet, I cannot imagine ever eating the way I used to again. I may not be totally macrobiotic forever, but I know I will be mighty close to it. It has been a really wonderful experience to find my body becoming rejuvenated just from what I eat. When you see the bags disappearing from under your eyes, the old age spots on your hands starting to fade, and you feel an energy that you haven't had since you were a teenager, you know you have to be doing something right.

I give my thanks every day of my life to have been fortunate enough to have come to work for Dr. Rogers, and to learn all the wonderful things I have learned in these years. Hopefully I will be able to pass this on to other people so that they can also find the way that I think God meant for many of us to eat and to improve our lives, and hopefully the lives of all the world.

CHAPTER IX

HOME REMEDIES FOR COMMON COMPLAINTS

Each number is a separate remedy. Recipes follow when not given. As with any remedy, if it is not immediately effective, see your doctor.

Constipation

1. Be sure that you are chewing your foods very well. Preferably 50 times per mouthful.
2. Hot apple juice, one cup daily, first thing in the morning.
3. Agar-agar with rice syrup or barley malt, 1 1/2 tsp agar-agar flakes, 1 tbsp rice syrup or barley malt, 1 cup of water, a pinch of sea salt. Bring all together to a boil, simmer for 5-10 minutes, cool and eat it after it gels.
4. One to three tsp flax seed sprinkled on cereal grains at each meal.
5. Cook grain with more water and increase grains. Also increase raw foods.
6. Take buffered C (see The E.I. Syndrome for directions.)

Diarrhea

1. Kuzu/Soy/Plum/Ginger drink one hour before breakfast for two to three days. Also known as ume/sho/kuzu with ginger.

Achy Joints

1. Rub on ginger oil.
2. Hot ginger compress.

Inflamed Joints

1. Tofu compress.
2. Buckwheat compress.

Headache

1. Kuzu/bancha tea.
2. Tamari/bancha tea.
3. Ginger oil (rub into painful area).

4. 1 tsp of sesame salt (gomashio), chew very well.
5. Rice syrup tea.

Weakness
1. Umeboshi/kuzu drink or umeboshi/sho/kuzu drink.

Asthma - Coughing
1. Rice syrup/kuzu tea.
2. Lotus tea.

Kidney Pain
1. Aduki bean juice, 1/2 cup, 1/2 hour before meals for two days.

Depression
1. Roasted, salted peanuts. (Limit 1/2 cup per day, maximum 3 days in a row.)

Fatigue
1. Kuzu drink. 2. Plum/soy/ginger/bancha drink (ume/sho/bancha with ginger or just shoyu/bancha drink.

Indigestion
1. Umeboshi plum. Be very careful not to bite or swallow the hard stone pit.
2. Plum/sho/ginger/bancha drink.
3. Ume/Sho/Bancha tea

Insomnia
1. Raw scallions mixed with raw miso and eaten before bedtime.

Nervousness
1. Kombu tea.
2. Tamari/Bancha tea.

Pain
1. Hot ginger compress, or ginger oil rubbed into affected area.

RECIPES FOR HOME REMEDIES

Ginger Oil

Juice from a large grated ginger piece. Equal amounts of sesame oil.

Directions:

Mix the ingredients. Massage into skin in the area of pain.

Ginger Compress

3 quarts of water
8 oz. or 1/2 cup grated ginger

Preparations:

Grate ginger and place in cheese cloth. Squeeze the juice into the hot water.

Note:

Heat to boiling point but
DO NOT BOIL.

Directions:

Carefully wring out a small cotton towel in the hot solution (twisting it around a wooden spoon handle so as not to touch or burn yourself.) Place on the affected area after checking carefully that it is not hot enough to burn the skin; never use uncomfortably hot towels. Cover with a dry cotton towel. Replace every 3 minutes or so, until the area is bright red.

Note:

It is best to have someone help you with this, as it is very difficult to do by yourself.

Kuzu Drink

1 level tsp of kuzu
3/4 cup of water
1 tsp of shoyu sauce

Directions:

Dilute kuzu with a little cold water. Add rest of water. Bring to a boil. Reduce heat, add shoyu sauce. Simmer for a few minutes. Drink while warm.

Plum/Soy/Ginger/Bancha Drink
(ume/sho/bancha with ginger)

>1/2 umeboshi plum
>1/4 tsp freshly grated ginger juice
>1 tsp tamari sauce
>1 cup bancha tea - very hot

Directions:

>Combine all ingredients, simmer a minute or so. Drink it hot.

Shoyu/Bancha Tea

>1 cup bancha tea
>1-2 tsp shoyu sauce

Directions:

>Heat tea. Add shoyu sauce, simmer for a minute. Drink while hot.

Ume/Sho/Bancha Tea

>1 cup bancha tea
>1/2-1 umeboshi plum
>1 tsp shoyu soy sauce

Directions:

>Pour hot tea over umeboshi plum and shoyu in cup. Stir. Drink hot.

Rice Syrup/Kuzu Tea

>1 tsp kuzu
>1 cup spring water
>1 tbsp rice syrup

Directions:

>Dissolve kuzu in small amount of water. Add rest of water and rice syrup. Cook over medium heat to boiling point. Reduce heat. Simmer for 10 minutes - stir to prevent lumps. Drink hot.

Lotus Tea (Fresh)

Note:

>Powdered form of this tea is available at macro-biotic food sources.

Directions:

>Grate 1/2 cup of fresh lotus root. Wring in cheesecloth squeezing juice into a pot. Add water

to make a full cup. Cook 5 minutes. Add pinch of sea salt or tamari to taste. Drink hot.

Kombu Tea

3 inch strip kombu seaweed
1 quart spring water

Directions:

Add kombu to water. Bring to boil & cook for 30 minutes to reduce liquid by 50 percent. Remove kombu piece. Drink while warm. Up to 1 cup 1-3 times a day.

Hint:

Planned-overs can be reheated.

Buckwheat Compress

(Draws retained water and excess fluid from swollen areas of the body).

Directions:

Mix buckwheat flour with enough hot water to form a stiff, hard dough.

Usage:

Apply in a 1/2 inch layer to the affected area.

Hints:

As it draws out fluid, the dough will become soft and watery. You can replace with a fresh plaster every 3-4 hours as needed.

Tofu Compress

(Reduces fever, stops inflammation, prevents swellings, or decreases swellings, treat burns)

Directions:

Squeeze water from tofu. Mash well. Add 5% grated ginger. Add 10-15% white flour (enough to make a sticky paste)

Usage:

Spread on cotton gauze or towel in 1/2 inch layer. Apply directly to skin and cover with a layer of cotton towel. Replace when it dries out (usually 1-2 hours)

Note:

Very safe and effective.

These suggestions are only temporary measures for mild ailments. If the problem persists, you need to seek medical advice.

CHAPTER X

THE GARDEN OF EDEN

****

Everything stress is, gardening is not. Stress is hurried and harried, gardening has the pace of nature's season-long rhythms. Stress is feeling powerless and victimized; gardening is control over both your food supply and your immediate environment. Stress is alienation, isolation; gardening is taking part in the great cycles of the earth, the cycles of growth and nourishment, death and rebirth. Gardening is a daily and joyous ritual of participation in the unity of life. As you garden, you are healed - body and mind, heart and soul.

William Gotleib in Organic Gardening.
****

****
THE GARDENING CALENDAR
****

JANUARY
****
"Now under a blanket of snow earth rests in winter's beauty."

W. Manderfield, Driftings
****

The holidays are over and the seed catalogs have started arriving and it is time to plan your garden, and order your seeds.

You should look for untreated seeds, as much as possible. Vermont Seed Co. has untreated seeds, (no fungicides) and many of the older, sturdier varieties (so they do not need pesticides). Hybrids, which are progressively more the norm for most seed companies, are generally newer varieties and often bred for qualities other than disease resistance. They have not withstood the test of time: which results in survival of the fittest. Other seed sources will be listed in the resource section.

Before ordering your seeds you need to answer several questions:

1. How many people am I growing food for?
2. Do I want to furnish all of our fresh vegetables or only a partial amount? (Much of this depends on how much room you have.)
3. Do I want to grow enough to preserve some for winter use?
4. How much space can I devote to a garden?
5. How much time can I devote to a garden?
6. What kinds of vegetables will my family eat? (There is no use in growing them to throw them away.)
7. Do I want to grow enough to sell or give to others?

A seed catalog is a wonderful source of information. It will tell you your planting time, length of growing time, expected yield, and many other details.

Please do not make the mistake of planting a whole package of seeds at one time, or you will have the whole crop ready at one time, with more produce than you can possibly weed, use or even give away. Later on, we will discuss succession planting for a continuous harvest. And don't forget some flower and herb seeds to add variety and color to your gardening.

To brighten up the winter months inside, you might start forcing some paper narcissus, which will give you an early arrival of spring, at least indoors.

FEBRUARY

****

"If February gives much snow, a fine summer it doth foreshow."

English rhyme

****

We are deep into winter now, and there is nothing to grow. Wrong! Let's start a window sill herb garden and learn how to make fresh sprouts to brighten up meals. It is also great for children to watch nature at work and to learn where real food comes from.

Many common herbs grow very well in a bright window location. Find some clay pots, small ones at this point, potting soil (later on you will plan to have a pile in your backyard to use so you'll know it is "alive" and chemically untreated), and some seeds, and sow your mini garden. Suggestions would be chives, parsley, thyme, savory, and sweet basil. Actually these should have been started last fall, but they will see you through until summer when your outdoor planting starts producing.

Parsley is very slow to germinate, and will do best if soaked in water for about 1 hour before planting. Be sure to keep your newly planted pots warm, moist, and covered with clear plastic until the seeds sprout.

While you are waiting for your herbs to grow, you can learn how to sprout fresh food for the table. Alfalfa seed is the easiest and most common. But as you go along you may want to try many of the other varieties available. There are several types of commercial sprouting kits on the market. But all you really need is a quart size, mason-type jar, a double layer piece of cheese cloth to cover the opening with about 1 1/2 inches extra all around, and a sturdy rubber band.

Fill the jar about half full with luke warm water, add a heaping tablespoon of seeds and soak for 8-12 hours. Drain off the water, rinse well, drain off again, and then place the jar on its side in a dimly lit area. Rinse at least two times daily. The more often they are rinsed, the better the sprouts will taste. When the growing sprout reaches about 1/4-1/2 inches, you should continue the rinsing process, but now place in a bright window so they will manufacture magnesium-rich chlorophyll and turn green.

When they are about 1 inch in length, and pale to dark green, they are ready to eat. Rinse off the loose seeds that did not sprout. Pat dry and store the sprouts in the refrigerator and enjoy them daily They keep very well.

If they won't sprout, the commonest cause is city water chemicals. Switch to spring water. If you want to do an experiment start two identical jars of sprouts but use bottled drinking water for one, and city tap water for the other, and note the different rates of growth. Good for the children's science project.

MARCH

"March comes in like a lion and goes out like a lamb."
English proverb

Countdown is starting for the summer gardening and if you are going to start your own seedlings for tomatos, broccoli, cauliflower, peppers, etc. now is the time. You have ordered and received your seeds. Right? If not, do it NOW!

Starting your own seedlings can be economical and give you fresh plants all during the gardening season to keep a continuous harvest growing when commercial seedlings are no longer available.

Seedlings are what make intensive planting and succession planting work in a small garden, which means over the growing season you can get two or even three crops from the same piece of ground. Starting your own seedlings will also enable you to use many varieties which are not available commercially.

There are many plants that can be started from seedlings. Here is a list:

beans, lima	leeks
broccoli	lettuce
Brussel sprouts	melons
cabbage	onions
cauliflower	parsley
celery	peppers
Chinese cabbage	spinach
cucumbers	squash
eggplant	sweet
potatoes	tomatoes
kale	kohlrabi

Commercial peat pots are the best medium for the beginner and the easiest to transplant into the garden without damaging the root system of the seedling. With proper planning, you can have fresh seedlings ready to pop into the ground whenever a new space opens up. Unless you are lucky enough to have a greenhouse, the best method I have found is to set up a fluorescent adjustable light fixture with special full spectrum grow lights to provide good lighting for 14-16 hours daily. Many gardeners set up a table and light fixture in their basements which have a fairly steady room temperature of between 60-70 degrees, but you can set up in any room in your home.

Start the seedlings with lights about 3 inches from the sprouts. As they get their first true leaves, raise the light to 4 inches and then when seedlings are a few inches tall raise to 6 inches. A self timer on the lights is a great help.

Seedlings need to be kept moist but not wet. Drying out totally is usually death to a tiny seedling.

Timing is now the important part of the program. You need to start most plants 6-8 weeks before they go into the garden and you need 5 or 7 days to "harden them off" before you actually plant them. "Hardening off" means setting the plants outside on warm sunny days, and bringing them back inside cold nights to help them adapt to the outdoor environment.

This is a busy month because it is also time to prepare your garden layout plan. Two books which I would suggest for the new backyard gardener are:

1. Square Foot Gardening, by Mel Bartholomew.
2. 60 Minute Garden, by Jeff Ball. These are both available through Rodale Press, Emmaus, Pa. (You might also want to subscribe to Organic Gardening magazine from the same source).

The raised bed system works best for me, as it is a high yield, low work garden system, which can be easily modified to extend the gardening season from very, very early spring, to very late fall in our local area. The beds can be as long as you want, but should not be more than 3 1/2 to 4 feet wide so that you can reach to the center easily for planting, weeding and harvesting. If you don't have room to grow all your own vegetables, there is still much you can do with even 4 square feet of space or a few container gardens on your porch, patio, or even your balcony for high rise living. A four square foot area can provide greens for two people all summer long. And everyone should have at least chives and parsley ever ready at their kitchen door.

Here is a fun project for the month: Try sprouting some brown rice organic vs. commercial white rice. If it sprouts you will know it is truly organic and you are eating live food. Show your family what "live food" really means.

313

****

"Sweet April showers do bring forth May flowers."
Tussar, <u>Five Hundred Points of Good Husbandry</u>
****

Things are greening up. Start looking for dandelions in your own back yard or anywhere that you know that they do not spray weed killer. Try to dig them root and all, as the root is a very strengthening food, as well as delicious. The cooking section will tell you how to cook them. It is also time for the March marigold or "cowslips." They grow in marshy areas and taste best before they blossom.

How about a hike in the woods? The wild onions "ramp" will be starting late this month and into May and June. Wild onions grow in open spaces of the woods, usually in moist areas. The leaves look like green scallions which you buy in the grocery store. They look like a green onion, but are much stronger in flavor. When you pull one from the ground there is no mistaking the odor. If they look like onions but don't smell like them - DON'T EAT - Eat only the ones that have the onion aroma. Go easy with them in cooking - the flavor is more like garlic.

If you find that you enjoy foraging for wild food you will need to obtain a book to learn what is SAFE to bring home for dinner. Suggestions are: <u>Exploring</u> <u>Nature's</u> <u>Uncultivated</u> <u>Garden</u>, by Deborah L. Hoag, privately published but available in most macrobiotic book stores, or <u>Field</u> <u>Guide</u> <u>to</u> <u>Edible</u> <u>Wild</u> <u>Plants</u>, by Bradford Angier published Stackpole Books, Harrisburg. There are many others but these are my favorites.

As soon as the soil is workable (does not clump) you should start bed number 1 with seeds of green peas, kale, collards, mustard greens, radish, lettuce, beet, carrots. If the plants are available, start broccoli, cabbage, cauliflower, onions and parsley. These are hardy vegetables that can usually take any cold weather. For even faster growth, plastic row covers can be used for a green house effect. Be sure to limit the quantities the first year so you get a feel for your garden and do not overwhelm yourself with the demands of weeding. Keep it small and enjoyable.

It is also time to ready your garden supplies. If you are doing a large traditional garden, arrange for the plowing or rototilling so it will be ready for early plantings. You will need garden gloves, kneeling pad, straw hat, and old work clothes, just for yourself. Plus trowel, hoe, rake, spade shovel, and wheelbarrow or garden cart. Don't forget the little things like stakes and string to mark your plantings. Also a little notebook is handy so you know where you planted what. This also serves as instant directions for next season and helps you keep track of changes you wish to make.

MAY
****

"Come the spring with all its splendor, all its birds and all its blossoms, and its flowers, and leaves and grasses."
Longfellow, <u>Hiawatha</u>
****

It is time to get serious about planting your garden. If you didn't do an April planting for hardy vegetables, get started now by May 15th at the latest. If you did an April garden, plant those same seeds again for a continuous harvest of these early vegetables for as long as possible.

By the end of May when the soil is warm, you can plant the more tender vegetables such as string beans, peppers, tomatos, squashes, melons, pumpkins and corn. Also try to get some herbs and flowers started. Everyone should have, at a minimum, parsley and chives. And a package of zinnias can bring delight to not only the garden but the table.

Chives is a perennial which means you plant it once and it will survive the winters and start growing again in the spring. As the plant gets larger, you can divide it up and make new plants. Parsley is a biennial, which means it will grow and be usable the first year, but if left in place it will restart in the spring and be good to use for a couple of months until your new planting is ready for use. Both parsley and chives are easy to start indoors and then move outdoors when the weather is warm enough. Or, you can buy started plants at a garden nursery store.

The other herbs which you will enjoy using to flavor your foods are many, but the easiest to grow are chervil, summer savory, sweet basil, and dill, which are all annuals. Others are sage, thyme, and tarragon, which are perennials. Rosemary is a tender perennial, which means it must be taken indoors for the winter, and then

315

replanted outside again when all danger of frost is past. There are a couple of other plants which you may want to try. The first is comfrey, which is a perennial herb. It is a very large plant and the leaves make good greens which contain vitamin B12, which is often lacking in a vegetarian diet, as it is usually not available from a plant source. It also has a pretty blue flower. The leaves as well as the roots, can be used for healing purposes. The leaves also make excellent compost.

Jerusalem artichoke is another perennial, which will grow rampant if you are not careful. The tubers are planted in the early spring and grow into very tall sunflower type plants. In late summer they will have a yellow flower. After the first heavy frost they can be dug and used as a vegetable in almost any way you would use a white potato. And what you don't use immediately can be left in the ground all winter and dug during the winter and the early spring. The root system is very large, and it is impossible to get every small tuber, so they will grow back again year after year. Plan carefully where you put them, they grow about 9 feet tall.

There are certain flowers that belong in your vegetable garden also. Marigolds repel beetles and nematodes, and should be used generously throughout the garden as they benefit all plants. Nasturtiums repel bugs, aphids, and bean beetles, and usually improve growth and flavor as a bonus. Both the leaves and the flowers can be used in salads as they are edible and have a nice spicey flavor.

Also many of the herbs which you are starting are good allies in your garden for certain things. Summer savory is an excellent one for growing along with green beans, as it deters the bean beetles, and improves growth and flavor. Also summer savory cooked with the beans is delicious.

Below is a list of the companions, allies and enemies of your garden. If you try to grow things that are mutually beneficial you will have a much more productive garden and provide natural protection for your plants.

316

COMPANION PLANTING CHART

Vegetable	Companion	Allies
bush beans	beets	summer savory
pole beans		summer savory
cabbage family (broccoli, Brussel sprouts, cabbage, cauli flower, kohlrabi, Chinese cabbage, etc.)	beet celery chard lettuce onion spinach	marigold nasturtium rosemary garlic sage dill mint thyme
beets	bush beans lettuce onion	garlic
carrots	beans lettuce onion peas pepper radish tomato	chives rosemary sage
celery	beans cabbage family tomato	chives garlic nasturtium
chard	bean cabbage family onion	
corn	beans cucumber	marigold

	melon	
	parsley	
	pea	
	potato	
	pumpkin	
	squash	
cucumber	bean	marigold
	cabbage	nasturtium
	family	
	corn	oregano
	pea	tansey
	radish	
	tomato	
eggplant	beet	marigold
	pepper	
lettuce	beet	chives
	cabbage	garlic
	family	
	carrot	onion
	radish	
melon	corn	marigold
	pumpkin	nasturtium
	radish	oregano
	squash	
onion	beet	summer savory
	cabbage	
	family	
	carrot	
	chard	
	pepper	
	tomato	
parsley	asparagus	
	corn	
	tomato	

potato	beans	horseradish
	cabbage family	marigold
	corn	
	eggplant	
	pea	
pumpkin	corn	marigold
	melon	nasturtium
	squash	oregano
radish	bean	chervil
	carrot	nasturtium
	cucumber	
	lettuce	
	melon	
	pea	
spinach	cabbage family	
squash	corn	borage
	melon	marigold
	pumpkin	nasturtium
		oregano
tomato	carrot	basil
	celery	bee balm
	cucumber	chives
	onion	mint
	parsley	borage
	pepper	marigold
turnip		peas

Somes notes on the allies:
Catnip, hyssop, rosemary, and sage repel cabbage moths.
Thyme deters cabbage worms.
Marigold deters beetles and nematodes.
Borage deters tomato worms.

319

Garlic and chives improve growth and flavor.
Oregano deters pests in general.
Basil repels fleas and mosquitoes.
Nasturtium deters bugs, beetles, and aphids.

Somes notes on the enemies:
Pole beans and beets stunt each others growth.
Kolhrabi and tomato stunt each others growth.
Dill retards carrot growth.
Tomato and corn attract the same worm.
Onions stunt bean and pea growth.

Information on companion planting furnished by ORGANIC GARDENING, Rodale Press, Emmaus, PA

As you see, there is a lot more to having a good garden than putting some seeds in the ground. But you will find by looking this over, that most of the families that taste good together, and are cooked together, also grow well together. Things that are not usually cooked together, or served together, are things that are not compatible.

This is just a general guideline to get you started. You will find as you grow things and experiment, what works best for you.

Make sure you are keeping a garden notebook as you go along so you will know what you have planted in different places, seed sources, germination times, etc.

JUNE

" And what is so rare as a day in June? Then if ever,
come perfect days".

Lowell, Visions of Sir Launfal

Your April planted vegetables should be ready to eat now.
As you use them, you will have open spaces in the garden which can
be replanted according to your needs. Seeds can be used, but you can
also keep seedlings going all summer, so a started plant can be
popped in where ever you have a space.

This is a very important month for the garden care. Weeding,
watering, and pest control top the list of things to do. Companion
planting, which we talked about last month, is a very important part
of this, as it is a natural insect repellent.

The other things that you can use, that are safe for the
garden, include Safersoap which is a safe, mild insecticide made from
fatty acids. It controls most soft body insect pests, including aphids,
mealy bugs, white flies and spider mites. It is generally easily
available, and is mixed according to the directions on the bottle and
sprayed.

The next organic pest control would be Bacillus thiurigensis,
a type of bacteria sold under the trade name of Dipel. This is used for
leaf eating caterpillars, such as a tomato worms, leaf rollers, and
Gypsy moths. It kills by paralyzing the digestive systems, but it is
harmless to all other insects.

Another pesticide would be diatomaceous earth. It is made
from the petrified cells of ancient sea life. These tiny shells are
sprinkled about either on the plants or the soil surface. The shells
pierce the body of the slugs, scales, and snails, or other soft body
insects and they cannot survive.

The last choice of one which can be purchased would be
rotonone or pyrethrum. It is a plant derived, organic pest control, but
I would only use it in cases of last resort. Even though it is plant
derived, it is not 100% safe. Avoid it if possible.

These are the general ones, but there are many others. One of
the simplest tricks is to use your blender to make a combination of
garlic and water to spray on your plants. Almost all garden pests are
repelled by garlic.

Pest control is a very selective process and it is best to avoid use of any products unless they are absolutely necessary. Reading your garden books will teach you what to watch for and when it is necessary to resort to any one or many organic pest controls. For example some remedies are just common sense like checking apple trees weekly for worm nests and physically removing them.

June is a wonderful month. The garden is starting to produce, the flowers are blossoming, and the weather is usually beautiful. It is also time to be picking strawberries and enjoying their lovely flavor. How about freezing some or making a sugar free jam for future use?

JULY
****
"You appreciate the rain when you have a garden."
W. Manderfeld, Driftings
****

As your produce is being used, and leaving more empty spaces in the garden, it is time to start planting your late fall garden to keep those greens coming. There is still time to replant carrots, beets, kohlrabi, radishes and daikon. You will have results in September, long before we have a frost, and they will keep growing until a severe killing frost.

One of the most important things is to make sure your garden is receiving enough water. Plants do not grow well without receiving enough water to keep the soil from totally drying out. If you do have to resort to watering by hand, make sure that you do not just superficially water, but water enough to soak the ground well, and then do not water again for a few days. Frequent top watering does not allow the roots to grow deeply, and is not good for the plant.

Towards the end of July, you will need to plant the hardy vegetable seeds of kale, collards, bok choy, some of the hardier lettuces, and mustard greens. Kale, especially, is extremely hardy. This year I plan to grow a row of it right by my back door, so that when the snows come I can just reach out the door and pick my kale for dinner. It is also a very attractive plant and will keep growing well into the snow season, and if left in place will start growing again the early spring for fresh greens until your garden starts producing.

You should also have plants of broccoli, cauliflower, and

even cabbage ready, because if you get them in now you will still be harvesting them right up to the frost season and beyond.

One of the most important things to do now is to be sure that you keep on picking your vegetables as they are ripe. If you let them grow to an unusually large size, you are sending a message to the plant that it is making seed and it doesn't have to produce any longer. So be sure and pick things while they are young and tender, and they taste best at this stage, too.

At this time of the year, many people go on vacations. If you are going away, try to find a neighbor who will pick the produce from your garden and use it, as it will be better for the garden over all, than just leaving it to go to seed.

And don't despair on those rainy days. The garden provides a good excuse to get outside even when it isn't sunny, for the weeds are easier to pull from moist soil than hard dry soil.

Remember to keep weeding, watering, and enjoying. From now on through the rest of the summer, is the height of your produce time, and you will have to figure ways that you are going to use it, give it away, or preserve some of it for the future. We will talk about that a little later.

AUGUST
****

"The purpose of agriculture is not the production of food, but the perfection of human beings."
Nasanobu Fukuoka, One Straw Revolution
****

Summer is in full bloom and the sweet corn and the watermelon alone make this a gardener's delight. We are ready to sit back and enjoy the veritable fruits of our labors.

But please don't stop gardening now. There is still much to do. Gardeners are always planning ahead and we need to constantly rejuvenate the soil. The best method of doing this is to learn to make compost. Compost is fully decayed vegetable material, such as garden waste, old mulching materials, leaves, grass clippings and kitchen waste (vegetable and fruit parings, coffee grounds, egg shells -no meats or fats should be used as they will attract rodents and smell bad as they decompose).

There are many methods of making compost, but the easiest

323

is to just set aside a four foot square area and start collecting vegetable waste. When the pile is about four feet high, water it well, cover with a plastic sheet, and let mother nature start the decomposition. Every two to three weeks uncover, and with a garden fork rearrange the piles so that the outside edges get turned towards the middle. Add more water if needed, the pile should be moist but not dripping wet, and cover again.

When you turn the pile you will notice the heat that the center of the pile is producing. This heat is the catalyst which helps the microorganisms break down the cellulose and the plant fibers so the end result is a pile about one to two feet tall of dark, crumbly compost which will enrich and improve your garden soil.

Ideally, each year before you plant your garden, about one inch of compost should be spread over your garden soil to replace the nitrogen and other nutrients which plants need for growth. Compost will also improve the texture and the moisture holding ability of your garden soil. Best of all, it is free and really teaches us what recycling in nature is all about.

The other organic fertilizer you can use, if you have a source, is well rotted animal manure. Dried manure is also available at garden centers, and a little goes a long way.

Compost and manure will add nitrogen to your soil, some potassium and trace minerals. Plants also need phosphorus and more potassium, which can be obtained organically by using rock powders. Rock phosphate added to your garden in the fall will supply next season's garden, and will continue for one to two years as it is slowly assimilated by the soil. A good potassium supplement is granite dust, or green sand. All of these supplements are available at garden centers.

The rock powders break down very slowly so it is almost impossible to use too much. But just to be sure, you could obtain a soil test kit and find out exactly how your garden soil checks out and what supplements it needs to maximally yield health giving vegetables. Plants are like people, they don't do well unless well-nourished.

SEPTEMBER

****

"Nature is the art of God."

Latin

****

One of the most important parts of being a good gardener is to learn ways to preserve some of the harvest for the long cold winter, when we can't rely on our own vegetable garden to provide us with all our fresh food.

Macrobiotically speaking, locally grown fresh produce is best. Next is cold stored, such as squash, pumpkins, onions, carrots, etc. Third would be dried (dehydrated). And last would be frozen or canned.

Healthwise, we know that organic produce in any form is much superior, nutritionally, as well as being safer because there is no use of poisonous pesticides. Therefore, I personally see no harm in using some home frozen and canned produce. Nutritionally speaking, fresh is best, frozen second, dried third, and home canned fourth. It is a decision that we all have to make for ourselves. But I know that frozen broccoli or green beans, which I have grown myself, are far better for me than any I could buy at the local grocery store.

We all know how to use the fresh foods, but we need to learn more about preserving the harvest. Cold storage is the oldest form of preservation. Our grandparents had large homes with cold basements, root cellars, big attics, and lots of storage area. Unfortunately, this is not available to the majority of us anymore, who live in suburbia, apartments, condos, or mobile homes.

If you are lucky enough to have a cool basement and an airy attic, you are in luck. But if not, don't despair, there are ways. Some of the possibilities are an unheated bedroom, unheated garage or pantry, a balcony or fire escape, space underneath a porch, basement stairwell, and your garden itself.

Root vegetables, such as carrots, parsnips, salsify, Jerusalem artichokes, horseradish, turnips, and daikon radish will keep well through frost and snow, if protected by mulch such as dried leaves or straw. The flavor of these vegetables is improved by the cold and they can be dug during the winter and very early spring. Be sure you mark the location in the garden so that you can easily find them in the winter when they are covered by snow.

Root vegetables can also be stored in a cold basement, or an

325

unheated garage by packing them in sand. If you are using a garage, wrap your containers well to protect them from any toxic car fumes, if you have room in your garage for a car! The dormant summer picnic cooler, a clean trash can or other container with sand will protect your produce from freezing. Root vegetables can also be stored in a heated basement by creating a "cool room". Get your hammer out and partition off an eight by ten area, insulate with fiberglass, add some shelves, and you will have room for many bushels of produce. We made such a room in the corner of our garage and it is a great place to store all our food supplies which we want to keep cool. It is so well insulated that on long below zero periods just the heat from a sixty watt light bulb will keep it around forty degrees. The concrete floor is so cold that the room even stays cool during the heat of summer.

In such a cool room, root vegetables should be stored in plastic bags to maintain humidity so that they won't shrivel. Ripening tomatoes, apples, and melons produce ethylene gas which promotes sprouting of potatoes and bitterness in carrots, so these should not be stored together.

Certain vegetables, such as onions, garlic, and beets, require air circulation to prevent spoilage. Onions and garlic can be braided and hung, or they can be stored in net bags. Be sure to cure the onion family outdoors for five to seven days before you store them. Carrots and beets should be left outside in the shade for one day before storing, potatoes for seven to ten days, and squash and pumpkin for two days. Do your curing on a wire rack, or turn the vegetables over daily to dry evenly so that they will resist molding. Squash should be stored without touching each other to prevent molding. If you have a cool attic, squash can be stored there also. The one thing that seems to be the worst for squash is high humidity as it causes molding. If these methods of cold storage preservation are not possible, there is still one more solution. You could purchase an old refrigerator to store your root vegetables. It can go in your garage or any place you have room. The older the better, because a frost free model would cause your produce to dehydrate. If you are in the market to purchase a new refrigerator, I would just save the old one for this purpose. Remember too, that even if you can't grow all your own vegetables, there are wonderful bargains to be found at the local farmers' markets. When produce is at its peak, you will especially want to purchase and preserve some for future use. If you check carefully, you will be able to find organic farmers in your area. And we certainly want to support the organic farmers.

Drying or dehydrating is the oldest form of preservation. Dried roots, fruits, grains, and animal foods have been staple foods of native populations for eons. Certain dried foods are very familiar to us, such as dried fruits and herbs, and these are the simplest to preserve in this manner. The main purpose of drying is to remove the moisture content of the product to prevent spoilage organisms (mold and bacteria) which can multiply during storage. Dried foods have excellent keeping qualities and the process reduces the bulk so that they are easily stored.

A word about mycotoxins is in order. They are chemicals made by molds that can cause genetic damage and even cancer. The best way to avoid them is to be sure moisture is at a minimum, for where there is no mold, there can be no mycotoxins. When in doubt, discard discolored or rancid smelling grains, seeds, nuts and produce.

Foods can be dried outdoors, in your oven, or by using the home made or electric dehydrators which are now available. As in any type of food preservation, you should use the freshest food in prime condition, using the utmost cleanliness. Uniformly sized pieces of thinly cut produce will produce the best results. Good drying should be done as quickly as possible without actually cooking the food. Properly dried produce should be stored in glass jars and kept in a cool place, such as your cool room. Keeping them under 40 degrees Fahrenheit will increase the storage life.

If you decide to really get into drying your own produce, I would suggest you read Putting Foods By, by Ruth Hertzberg, Beatrice Vaughn and Janet Greene. This book also has directions for many other forms of food preservation, such as freezing, canning, and even root cellaring.

In our part of the world, the great northeast, outdoor sun drying is very limited because of our higher humidity. It also requires daily attention, every few hours, so it is not practical for working people. Also you should not attempt outdoor drying in any polluted areas, such as near a super highway. Food will absorb toxins from the air.

Indoor room drying is often used for herbs in either the kitchen or a dry airy attic. Basil, the mints, parsley, sage, thyme, tarragon, or any other herb which you grow and use are easiest to preserve by dehydration. They should be dried at 100 degrees Fahrenheit or lower, or they will lose the aromatic oils which give them their distinctive flavors. Excluding light will also help them to keep their color. Use only the prime produce, preferably only the most tender and flavorful leaves from the top six inches of the stalk. Cut them on a dry sunny morning, just before they actually bloom. Cut with as long a stem as possible, strip off the tougher lower leaves and remove any blossom heads. Gather into small bunches and swish through cold water to remove any dust and dirt. Shake off the water and lay them on absorbent toweling until the surface moisture evaporates.

To bag dry them, collect six to twelve stems and tie loosely together. Then place them, leaves down, in a brown paper bag (large enough so that the herb leaves do not touch the inside of the bag). Tie the top of the bag loosely around the stems and leave enough strings so that the whole pack can be hung high in a warm airy room to dry. When the leaves have dried and feel brittle to the touch, they are stripped from the stems and stored whole or crushed and stored in glass jars for future use.

Herbs can also be tray dried, but this is a much more work intensive project, as they will need to be turned at frequent regular times to insure an evenly, well dried, finished product. Celery leaves are excellent dried in this manner.

Some people merely freeze fresh herbs from the garden in glass jars. A small fingerful crushed before it defrosts adds zest to winter cooking. But be sure to take what you need quickly and return the jar to the freezer.

If you decide to dry other fruits and vegetables, you will need to either make or purchase an electric dehydrator, and learn much more about this preserving technique than can be explained here. Whole books have been written about this one subject alone.

Preserving food by freezing is a relative newcomer to modern life, but our forefathers and people living in arctic countries learned to use this method out of necessity. Granted, it was usually animal food that was preserved in this manner, but now almost any food which can be preserved by any other method, can also be frozen. Freezing does preserve some of the vitamin content of vegetables, fruits, and meats, but it drastically changes the life force energy. Freezing requires the expense of purchasing a freezer, plus all of the storage material needed to safely package the food. It does offer great convenience and wide variety in our menus. The decision to freeze, or not to freeze, has to be an individual choice. If you decide it suits your needs, there are countless books to give you explicit instructions on freezing procedures.

Canning is the final choice of food preservation. Many of us remember our grandma's fruit cellar with rows of sparkling glass jars filled with fruit, jams, pickles and relishes, and the fun it was to be sent there to choose a jar of pickles to go with supper, or a jar of fruit to be made into a pie. In many homes "the canner" came out in early summer and was a permanent fixture in the kitchen until late autumn. Some homes even had a summer kitchen where the preserving was carried on in earnest to provide food for the family during the long cold winter ahead.

With the invention of the home freezer, canning has been greatly reduced. But many people still preserve the homemade jams, jellies, pickles and relishes. If this is a tradition in your family, I suspect you will continue doing it. But now you will be looking for sugar-free jam and jelly recipes, and simple salt brine cured pickles. Walnut Acres catalog has a jelling agent you can use to make sugar-free jams and jellies. Send for their catalog listed in the resource section.

Every method of food preservation does alters the life force of the food. Locally grown fresh food should always be your first choice. Each of us has to make the decision of not only what but also what is most compatible with our life styles to promote health and harmony in our lives.

OCTOBER
****
"The wonders of nature should make men humble."
W. Manderfield, Driftings
****

The golden month has arrived, and the first frosts have ended the harvest of much of the garden, but you should still have kale, Brussel sprouts, and other hearty greens, carrots, daikon radish, and perhaps broccoli and green bunching onions. Your Jerusalem artichokes will be ready to start digging after a good hard freeze. You should also still be stocking up for the winter.

It is apple harvest time, which means sweet cider time. Ask your friends, or the merchants at the farmers' market how to find the least contaminated source of fresh apples and cider.

Now is also the time to prepare the garden for winter. Many gardeners are ready to put the tools away and forget gardening until next spring. But what you do now will determine how great next year's garden will be, and will save you time in the spring when perhaps your garden muscles are not yet in shape.

A clean garden is essential for pest and disease control. Start by clearing out all the dead plants; any that are diseased should be destroyed, but healthy plants can be added to your compost pile. In the fall, the soil is easy to work; so by adding compost and turning it into the soil the garden will be ready for early spring crops, when the ground is cold, wet and difficult to work.

If you are using a raised bed garden system, it is easy to do one bed at a time. This is also a good time to do a soil test again and see exactly what your soil needs. Soil testing kits are very inexpensive and readily available at your local garden center.

The pH test is the most important. This measures the acid/alkaline level of your soil. To grow good vegetables, the pH should be between 6 and 7. Slightly alkaline soil can be adjusted by adding peat moss. Wood ashes can adjust the acid soil quickly, as can lime. It takes about six months for the lime to react and change the pH of the soil, so adding it in the fall is preferable to the spring. After your pH corrections are made, add as much compost, leaf mold, or manure as possible. This would also be the time to add your natural fertilizers, such as bone meal, rock phosphate, green sand or granite dust.

Next, take your spading fork, or some form of a tiller, and work these soil improvements in well. Then break up any clods of earth and remove any sticks or stones, rake, smooth, and level. To keep the soil in this perfect condition, cover it with a three to six inch layer, or more, of mulch. You can use hay, straw, or leaves that you have raked, up from your yard. This will protect the soil from winters harsh weather, and when early spring arrives, you can take the top mulch off and start planting.

The mulch which you rake off is the basis of your new compost pile. Don't try to rake it into the soil, as it will not have decomposed enough, and will defeat all the work you did in the fall to have the garden ready to plant.

You will find that getting the garden in shape in the fall will automatically give you crop rotation, as you will have your cold weather crops still growing in some areas which will not be worked up until spring. Therefore, the area you have just prepared for spring planting will take the hearty vegetables, and where they grew last year will be prepared in the late spring for the heat loving vegetables.

If you are a real die-hard raised bed gardener, you can even plant one of your freshly prepared beds for next spring now. The seeds of kale, carrot, green bunching onions, daikon radish, and any other very early spring planting variety can be used. After planting the bed, you need to cover it with a commercially purchased floating row cover. They go by the trade name of Remay. Somehow, they protect these tiny little seeds, and they do start popping up long before you could possibly be out in the garden working. Adding a plastic cover over this will even give them more protection, but it will have to be removed once they do start.

If you are not brave enough to try planting vegetables in the fall, you could consider planting a cover crop to improve your soil. This should probably be done in only one bed, and this would be rotated each year so that eventually all of your areas would have this treatment. A cover crop would add vital green organic nitrogen producing material to the soil for next year.

Here is how it works: In the area where you are growing your fall crops of lettuce, beets, carrots, cabbage, etc., as you harvest a crop sow a new crop of winter rye grass, or winter hairy vetch. Since this area won't be needed until late spring for next season's warm weather crops, winter rye will sprout and grow in the coldest weather, and any warm days thereafter it will just keep growing. In the spring when the crop is at its most lush condition, it is turned under to add nitrogen rich organic matter to the soil. This is just one more way to constantly improve your garden soil, so you can grow the healthiest vegetables to create the best and healthiest bodies.

NOVEMBER
****

"To be interested in the changing seasons, is a happier state of mind than to be hopelessly in love with spring".

George Santayana
****

Aren't we lucky? Most gardeners have put their tools away for the year, but we are still harvesting kale, Brussel sprouts, daikon radish, carrots, leeks, parsley and Jerusalem artichokes, at the very least, from our garden, and collard, chives, cabbage, and spinach if using a plastic tunnel device which we talked about for early spring planting (the Remay).

Speaking of tools, this is also a great time to check over your garden equipment and clean it up for winter storage. If you use any type of gasoline powered equipment, the fuel must be run out to prevent it from gumming the engine, or add a storing agent such as Pour and Store. And while you are at it, why not check any spark plugs and replace if needed so you will be ready to go next spring?

Don't forget the hand tools; clean them, sharpen with a file, and oil them lightly. Check the handles and repair or replace if needed. Hopefully you will have a spot to store each tool, so that you will always be able to find what you need, when you need it. Remember your tools are one of the most important parts of a good garden. Some prefer a handy basket full of hand tools that can be taken to the garden.

Also, check on your other garden supplies, such as fertilizers, peat moss, potting soil, starting mix, and so on. Seal and store these in a dry area. If some of these supplies look old and you are not sure they are still usable, just add them to the compost pile. Sprinkle over layers of vegetable matter in the pile and let Mother Nature do her work.

Take one final check of the garden to be sure it is all tucked in for the long winter sleep.

You will have much to be thankful for as you sit down to dinner on Thanksgiving Day and enjoy the bountiful fruits of your labor.

DECEMBER
****

"For everything there is a season, and a time for every matter under heaven: a time to be born, and a time to die, a time to plant, and a time to pluck up what is planted."

Ecclesiates 3
****

The garden is now probably blanketed with snow and there is not much you can do out there. You could still dig some Jerusalem artichokes if the snow isn't too deep, providing you have marked them well.

So now is the time to do your notebook. Study your garden notebook and see what you want to do differently next year. More or less of the same vegetables? Do you want to try some new varieties?

Do you want to expand the garden and make it larger, or was it too big and you need to reduce the size? How about starting a strawberry bed in the spring, or planting some berry bushes, or fruit trees? Or how about more perennial foods like asparagus that comes up year after year? Would you like more flowers and herbs? Do you want to learn more about gardening? Maybe this is the time to put in your little note to Santa that you would like some gardening books. Maybe there is a special one you have your eye on. Check the local library.

Many of your garden projects could have left you with the means of furnishing Christmas gifts to others. The herbs can be dried into seasonings, added to decorative bottles of herbal rice wine vinegar, or made into herbal wreaths to scent the home. Many of your vegetables could have been made into macrobiotic pickles which your macrobiotic friends would enjoy receiving. There is also a recipe for cranberry relish in the recipe section which is easy to make and would make a nice gift.

It is also a time that you might want to get interested in some house plants. Greenery in your home is a wonderful addition and keeps you in touch with nature all during the cold months. And don't forget this is an excellent month to grow sprouts to eat now.

There truly is just no end to gardening, only to each season. But gardeners are always looking ahead and learning and planning, and what do you know? Here comes the first new seed catalog. Time to start all over again, but let me leave you with this thought. As the author of one of our favorite gardening books (Perennial Gardening, Elizabeth Van Pelt Wilson) said, her garden has been a source of solace for her through the year and helped her weather the vicissitudes of life.

HANDY SUMMARY OF MONTHLY
GARDEN PROJECTS

JANUARY
Plan gardens.

Order seeds.

Start forcing paper narcissus.

FEBRUARY
Start windowsill herb garden.

Learn how to make fresh sprouts.

MARCH
Start seedlings of tomato, broccoli, cauliflower, peppers.

Prepare garden layout plan.

APRIL
Start looking for wild dandelion greens to harvest.

Take a walk in the woods and look for wild onions "ramps".

Start seeds of green peas, kale, collards, mustard greens, radish, lettuce, beets and carrots as soon as soil is workable.

Purchase garden supplies.

MAY
Replant the early vegetable seed for a continuous harvest.

Toward end of May, plant string beans, squashes, melons, pumpkin, corn, tomatoes, peppers.

Start a herb garden.

Start a flower garden.

Learn about companion planting.

JUNE

Replant as you harvest vegetables planted in April.

Water as needed.

Weed the gardens as needed.

Learn about natural methods of pest control.

Pick strawberries, eat, freeze or make sugar free jam.

JULY

Learn about composting.

Keep watering and weeding and replant as spaces open up in garden.

SEPTEMBER

Learn how to harvest & preserve bounty from your garden.

OCTOBER

Continue to harvest hearty vegetables.

After a hard frost, dig some Jerusalem artichokes.

Stock up at Farmers Market.

Purchase apples and sweet cider.

Prepare garden for winter and mulch.

Do soil test and correct soil as needed.

Plant area for early spring & cover with floating row cover or plant cover crop for nitrogen.

NOVEMBER

Continue to harvest hearty vegetables.

Clean and prepare tools and equipment for winter.

DECEMBER

Review your notebook and plan for next gardening season.

Prepare natural Christmas gifts.

Start raising some house plants.

Start sprouting again.

HAPPY GARDENING!

CHAPTER XI

****

A NOTE FROM THE DOCTOR

****

MEDICAL ASPECTS OF THE TRANSITION PHASE

To macrobiotic people, the transition phase is the intermediary step from the standard American diet (SAD), high in fats, sugar, salt, alcohol and processed foods, to a full-fledged strict healing phase macrobiotic diet which many have used to conquer cancer (see The Cure is in the Kitchen, Prestige Publishing, Syracuse, NY). But the transition phase you have just learned is also slowly becoming the goal of the increasing numbers of knowledgeable health-conscious people around the world who realize drugs cannot cure.

Moreover, these people know they must spend money on food, and they must spend money for health care. But if they chose the former wisely, the latter becomes inconsequential. And as they progress toward their goals, they know when they are on the right track when they start to feel macro mellow.

The January 2, 1990 cover of USA Today newspaper gave a statistical look at how average American families spend their money. 14% of every dollar is spent on health and another 14% of every dollar is spent on food. What most people do not know is that by eating macrobiotically, they can reduce that total 28% to about 10% and that's probably a conservative estimate.

You spend far less money on food and medicine when you eat macrobiotically, because you don't have all of the processed, over-priced items and the expensive meats, as well as the symptoms that stem from plugging organs with fat as you concentrate on fresh vegetables and whole organic grains. As you eat this way, you automatically become healthier and do not have the medical expenses that most people do. In the medical journal entitled Journal Of Chronic Diseases, the article, "Essential Metals and Man" by Schroeder, H. A. and Mason, A.P., (Vol. 21, pg 815-884, 1969) provided some very interesting statistics that 99% of physicians are not aware of.

Before I give you these facts, though, let me give you a little background information. Basically, in the 80's we did some research which showed that over 51% of our patients were magnesium deficient. (Rogers, SA, Magnesium Deficiency Masquerades as Diverse Symptoms. Evaluation of an Oral Challenge Test. International Clinical Nutrition Review, 11:3, July 1991). Since then we have continued the work in over 500 patients.

Other researchers have found similar statistics, as well. We were stimulated to do this research because Science News, June 1988, reported that the United States government had performed a study showing that the average American diet only provides 40% of the magnesium that people need each day. Furthermore, the most prominent researcher (M. Seelig, M.D.) in the world in magnesium, estimated that 80% of the U.S. population has a significant magnesium deficiency. Magnesium is only one of over 4 dozen nutrients that are extremely crucial in the body. It just serves as an example of what is happening many times over within the U.S. medical system today. If that weren't enough to stimulate my interest, the Journal of the American Medical Association (Whang, et al, June 13, 1990) reported that well over 54% of 1033 hospitalized patients were magnesium deficient. What is worse is that 90% of the doctors never even thought of testing for it, and the 10% that did used a test that misses at least 30% of those who are deficient.

Since magnesium is in over 300 enzymes, a deficiency of it can produce just about any symptom you can think of. Indeed, among the patients who were magnesium deficient, we found that the symptoms that improved when we corrected the magnesium deficiency were anything and everything. Some people just felt stronger and more energetic, less tired, no longer needed naps; others had relief from depression; others were markedly less chemically sensitive for the first time in their lives; others lost food allergies that they had had for ages; others were dramatically relieved of chronic back pain, muscle spasms, cardiac arrhythmia, high blood pressure, high cholesterol and the list goes on.

Some of the symptoms that were relieved in people, they had had for over 20 years. A common symptom was that of always feeling cold, regardless of what the ambient temperature was. This is explained by the fact that when one is magnesium deficient, it causes muscle spasms. These spasms can be in the brain blood vessel smooth muscles and cause a migraine, in the muscles of the bronchi in the chest in the form of asthma, in the gut muscles in the form of colitis, in the back in the form of muscle spasms, in other muscles producing eye twitches, or they can be in the uterine muscle causing

338

repeated abortions or infections. They could also be in the heart vascular muscles and cause cardiac arrhythmia, high blood pressure, or poor circulation, again leading to the feeling that one is always cold.

So you can begin to appreciate that the lack of one tiny mineral can produce any symptom you can think of. The scary part is that, what we also showed in this research and many other researches throughout the world have shown, is that there is no single blood or urine test in the whole world that will tell for sure if someone has enough magnesium. It requires a loading test. Anyway, couple this with the fact that the diet is becoming progressively more deficient in magnesium, and you have set the stage for a world where the sick get sicker and nobody knows why. And what do we do in medicine? We just keep drugging them. As shown by a study in the 1990 Journal Of The American Medical Association, 90% of the doctors miss magnesium deficiencies, in that they do not order tests for it when the patients actually have deficiencies. And this study was done on 1033 patients who were in the hospital. So if 90% who are so dire as to be hospitalized are missed, what about those who are out-patients? My friend, researcher Dr. Jeffrey Bland, calls these people the "walking wounded".

Let's now look at some of the statistics drawn from Schroeder's paper. Below you will find the amounts of magnesium in various common foods:

FOOD	AMOUNT OF MAGNESIUM (mcg/gm)
Milk	102
Cheese	268
Broccoli	321
Parsley	566
Brown Rice	1,477
Processed Rice	251
Millet	1,670
Whole Wheat Flour	1,502
Refined Flour	299
Kellogg's Special K	412
Sugar Cane	190
Refined Sugar	2
Raw Carrots	185

Cooked Carrots	62
Cooking Water	119
Chicken	195
Steak	383
Lettuce	85
Seaweed	13,658
Butter and oils	1-6
Cat Chow	1,716
Cattle Feed	2,302

You can readily learn many things from this short list. First, you see that when grains like rice or wheat are processed, as they are in the standard American diet, there is a tremendous loss of magnesium (as well as many other precious minerals). Brown rice goes from 1477 to 251 micrograms of magnesium per grain of rice, and wheat flour goes from 1502 to 299. Likewise, sugar cane goes from 190 to 2 mcg/gm of magnesium in refined sugar. Also you'll see that raw carrots provide 185, while cooked only yields 62. And the cooking water, which we normally throw out in American cooking, retains the 119. In macrobiotic cooking, the cooking water is always saved and used in soup stocks or as a drink.

Butter and oils, which make up anywhere between 1/3 to 1/5 of the American diet, have practically no magnesium in them. But they require lots of magnesium to be metabolized properly. Now, if you take the average breakfast, and say you have an egg, Kellogg's Special K and some milk, you'll see that the total is 113 plus 412 plus 102, or which equals of 627. Now say you just had the simplest macrobiotic breakfast possible of brown rice; that gives you over twice that at a total magnesium of 1477. And we haven't even begun to discuss quantities that are eaten.

Or let's take a " healthful" lunch of salad with lettuce and oil, and fried chicken, and a glass of milk, That gives you 102 plus 85 plus 6 plus 195, or a total of 388. And don't forget, if the person decides to have a soft drink in place of the milk, the phosphates in the soft drink actually inhibit magnesium absorption so you don't get all of the magnesium from the other foods. Phosphates are also hidden as other (chemical names) in most processed foods.

A problem with milk is that the ratio of calcium to magnesium is so disproportionately high that the calcium is preferentially absorbed many times over the magnesium. Also, if one is magnesium deficient and eating high calcium foods such as milk and cheese, this excessive calcium is often laid down inside blood vessel walls to create arteriosclerotic calcifications or plaques (coronary artery disease & Alzheimer's) as well as the creation of renal disease and gall stones.

Compare this 388 to a simple macrobiotic lunch of millet with some parsley and broccoli. This gives you a whopping total of 2,557. And heaven forbid if you threw in a little miso soup with seaweed which has 13,658 mcg/gm of magnesium, you really rev up the ailing system. Now you can begin to understand why and how macrobiotic diets are so healing. They are loaded with nutrients per gram of food. It is a nutrient-dense diet.

You can begin to appreciate that not only did we have none of this information in medical school when I graduated in 1969 when this paper was published, but this information and a plethora of information that has come out since that time, is still not stressed in medical school educations. No wonder physicians and lay people alike find it difficult to see how a diet could ever profess to heal anything. They are totally unaware of how deficient the average American processed diet is, and of how incredibly rich in healing minerals a macrobiotic diet is. And yet this information is coming out so fast, we can't write books fast enough. For this reason we have a newsletter (available through this publisher) so that we can keep people abreast (with referenced articles) of the current findings.

As a final point in this little lesson, you'll notice that it's much healthier to eat cat chow or cattle feed than it is the standard American diet. There are many reasons for this, both political and financial. Basically, Americans value a food that is quick and easy to prepare and looks colorful, far over a food's innate nutritional value. Whereas animals don't have such abnormal value systems.

The scary part of all this is that, as our nation becomes more magnesium deficient (which it inevitably has to as you can now appreciate from a look at a sampling of the nutrient levels for just one mineral), there is going to be progressively more cardiovascular disease.

As you probably know, the number 1 cause of death and chronic illness in the United States now is cardiovascular disease, relating to the heart, blood pressure, high cholesterol, etc. For example, if you do not have enough magnesium, the vessels can go into spasm and we call this hypertension. Low calcium, potassium or magnesium are just some of many causes of hypertension. Likewise, if you do not have enough magnesium, the cholesterol that your body must manufacture every day in order for you to live, cannot be metabolized properly and it lays down in the body's toxic waste dump, mainly the arterial wall and produces arteriosclerosis. Certainly high cholesterol comes from a high cholesterol diet in many people as well. But in a vast number, they have high cholesterol because they do not have the proper minerals (magnesium, chromium, copper, etc) in the enzymes to metabolize the cholesterol.

You can begin to appreciate that the American prescription of plastic foods such as margarines and synthetic egg substitutes to treat a cholesterol problem only worsen the problem, since it does not correct the underlying magnesium deficiency, but allows it to progress silently, unrecognized, until it creates a sudden heart attack or stroke. Likewise, when the underlying cause of hypertension has not been found (such as magnesium deficiency), medications are prescribed to lower the blood pressure. Many of the high blood pressure medications now are known to actually elevate the cholesterol and triglycerides. This has been well-published in the Archives Of Internal Medicine, Vol. 148, page 1280-1288, June 1988, in the article "The Effects of Anti-Hypertensive Agents on Serum Lipids and Lipoproteins" by Claude K. Lardinois, MD and Sherry L. Neuman. And to make matters triply worse, the cardiologists' prescribed foods, as you'll learn later, also contribute to arteriosclerosis. Furthermore, diuretics prescribed for high blood pressure actually cause a faster loss of magnesium.

Now you can begin to appreciate why once people have something diagnosed as wrong with them in American society, they tend to get sicker and sicker or require progressively more medication. (If they checked your magnesium and other minerals as routinely as they check your cholesterol and chemical profile, we would not have such an epidemic of sick people. All of the tests (with explanation and references) that you should request of your doctor, are spelled out in Tired Or Toxic?, Prestige Publishing, P.O. Box 3161, Syracuse, NY 13220).

Now you can also appreciate why the transition diet is so important, because it starts to correct the underlying biochemical deficiencies that are at the root of many common diseases. American medicine thinks that there should be a drug for every symptom and that a headache is a Darvon deficiency, when there is nothing further from the truth. We need to find the biochemical defect in people and correct that. And that's what you are going to be doing as you start eating more healthfully; correcting your biochemical deficiencies.

There is much more regarding the myths of cholesterol, for those who are interested in The Cure Is In The Kitchen, (same publisher).

Let's Make Arteriosclerosis

Arteriosclerosis begins as inflammation in the arterial wall and progresses to the eventual laying down of cholesterol and calcium and then hardening of this mixture, so that the accumulated material makes the vessel wall thicker, and more rigid and the opening in the vessel smaller. When it finally plugs off, the person usually has a stroke or a heart attack. If it plugs off only partially, then they begin gradual disease in a specific organ, like the pancreas which we then call diabetes, or in the kidneys which we then call renal disease, or in the blood vessels which we then call cardio-vascular disease, poor circulation, angina, or high blood pressure.

Since arteriosclerosis is the number 1 cause of disease and death in the United States, researchers need a model of an animal with arteriosclerosis so that they can experiment and find the treatment for it. Since animals eat more wisely than man and do not naturally get arteriosclerosis, researchers have had to find out how to give it to them. The formula was easy:

1. Increase the cholesterol and saturated fats in the diet.
2. Increase the sugar in the diet.
3. Decrease magnesium, chromium and/or copper.

Now, if you went to the F.D.A. (Food and Drug Administration) fifty years ago and said, "I want to do an experiment on foods that form the basis of the American diet. I want to see if processing (removing many vitamins & minerals so the food lasts longer on the shelf) just a few foods (by making white flour or white bread or white sugar) have an affect on disease. I want to see if making available a lot of processed foods high in fat and sugar adversely affects the body." Obviously, they would have said that would be too dangerous and they wouldn't have allowed you to do it. But they have allowed the food industry to do this. Hence, the high level of sickness that predominates.

However, research also shows that you can reverse arteriosclerosis by the exact same mechanisms that caused it. You can decrease the cholesterol, decrease the sugars, and increase the magnesium, copper and chromium. You can also do it by making

343

sure that you don't get too much vitamin D (homogenized milk from the grocery store is fortified with vitamin D and this accentuates calcifications in arteriosclerosis). So getting rid of excess vitamin D in the diet is very important as well (Ito, M., Sekin, I., Kummerow, F.A. - Dietary Magnesium Effect on Swine, Coronary Atherosclerosis Induced by Hypervitaminosis D, ACTA Pathologica Japonica 37, 6, 955-964 June 1987).

In this paper, they showed that supplementing magnesium even went so far as to prevent the coronary arteriosclerosis induced by hypervitaminosis D. Of course, the calcifications come from excessive calcium which in the United States there is now a craze for. Almost every woman is taking extra calcium in order to stave off osteoporosis. Since she doesn't know her levels of chromium, zinc, copper, and magnesium, and one or more of these nutrients is low in 80% of the population, she in essence is hastening arteriosclerosis and Alzheimer's pre-senile dementia (Tanimura, A., McGregor, D. H., Anderson, H. C., Calcification in Atherosclerosis. I. Human Studies, Journal of Experimental Pathology, 2, 4, 261-273, Summer 1986.)

Other studies show that lowering the blood glucose is very important in turning off atherosclerosis. Even more important, however, are other studies showing that dietary lecithin (which is high in beans, which people do not normally eat except in macrobiotic diets) actually returns the lipid levels to normal and removes lipids from established atherosclerotic plaques. In other words, it actually turns back the hands of time. This is something that medications do not do (Hunt, C. E., Duncan, L.A.- Hyperlipoproteanemia and Atherosclerosis in Rabbits Fed Low Level Cholesterol and Lecithin, British Journal of Experimental Pathology, 66, 1, 35-46, February 1985). Other publications have shown that there was a 50% reduction in the aortic intimal plaque (calcified cholesterol deposits in the aorta or the main artery leading out of the heart) in only 60 days when chromium was supplemented (Abraham, A. S., Sonnenblick, M., Eini, M.-The Action of Chromium on Serum Lipids and on Atherosclerosis in Cholesterol Fed Rabbits, 42, 2-3, 185-195, April 1982).

There is much further explanation and many more medical references in both books, but you understand the primary problem here. It is that a low cholesterol, low sugar, high magnesium, copper, chromium and lecithin diet is exactly what a macrobiotic diet is. And yet, the government is spending billions of dollars on health programs which focus on drug therapy while allowing people to continue to support the processing food industry, which supports diets to actually worsen the problem.

Even registered dieticians in hospitals, whose prime reason for being is to guide the sickest people in matters of diet control for their health, are not aware of these studies. For example, the August 16, 1990, New England Journal Of Medicine finally published what we have known and written about for years: that trans fatty acid, as found in corn oil margarines, grocery store hydrogenated oils and in most processed foods, cause worse arteriosclerosis than steak, butter, cheese or bacon. Yet it's margarines and corn oil that hospital dieticians and cardiologists erroneously recommend. Fortunately, it's an exciting time in medicine since you have an advantage over most dieticians and physicians, because you know how to make yourself healthy. The choice is now yours. Please read The Cure Is In The Kitchen even though you may not plan on ever doing the strict healing phase of macrobiotics. For in there is also all the latest information on your cholesterol. It has now been found that the level of cholesterol that is currently being recommended (200 mg/dl) is a level that gives a greater than one in four chance of dying of an early heart attack. But it will take years before the information gets to the public that 150 is the ideal level.

Also the evidence is there to show that taking drugs to lower cholesterol and blood pressure makes these blood measurements look normal, but does nothing to increase longevity or decrease heart attacks. In fact, it can raise the risk.

The major parameters that are described in more detail, that have not only decreased heart attack rate and lowered cholesterol without drugs and even reversed or dissolved cholesterol plugs in arteries (that regrew after surgery and drugs) are (1) a cholesterol of 150 mg/dl or less, (2) a diet of 5 mg cholesterol a day, (3) healing harmful feelings of isolation, anxiety, guilt, loneliness, fear, envy, hostility, anger and depression, (4) a regular walking (or other exercise) program, and (5) meditation and positive imagery, and more.

The point is, this program is within the realm of those who really want to be well, and it gets them better than they would be with drugs and/or surgery, but without any of the cost of side effects. What more could you ask for?

NUTRIENT DEFICIENCIES ARE RAMPANT
IN THE LAND OF PLENTY

It is rapidly becoming apparent that unless we make a concerted effort to eat more nutritionally complete foods, we are going to continue in the downward medical spiral: eat nutritionally inferior foods, develop nutrient deficiencies, which lead to more symptoms, which cause us to take more drugs, get more nutritional deficiencies from the drugs, eat more processed foods in attempt to boost ourselves up and save time because we're always so tired, then this in turn serves to escalate our deficiencies, which then cause more symptoms, so we take more drugs, etc.

The optimum solution is to eat whole foods. If you have the luxury of being able to discover and correct any deficiencies along the way, so much the better. But do not wait for the government or medicine to come along and rescue you, for the changes will occur too slowly to be useful in your lifetime.

You already know the government surveys show that the average American diet provides only 40% of the daily need for magnesium. And this is just an example of one out of several dozen nutrients upon which your health depends. Experts estimate 80% of the U.S. population is deficient (Science News, 133, 1988). They also know that in over 90% of the people who were magnesium deficient, their doctors   never   even   thought   of   checking   for   this (Journal Of The American Medical Association, 263, 1990). This is not routinely done or even checked for.

They also know that in people who present to an emergency room with chest pain, they can reduce the risk of it progressing on to a heart attack by giving magnesium injections.   But this is not routinely done. They know also, that after the person has had a heart attack, they can cut his chance of dying from 100% to 44% by giving magnesium (Annals Of Emergency Medicine, 16, 1987).

They know that in elderly hospitalized patients, the hospital stay, complications, and death rate can all be cut in at least half by giving supplements (Lancet, 335, 1990). But none of this is standard accepted therapy, because of the politics of medicine and big business.

PRESCRIPTION MEDICATIONS GUARANTEE
WORSE SYMPTOMS

If you haven't been eating enough greens and have silently become magnesium deficient, one of the first symptoms you could get is a little high blood pressure. So the doctor prescribes a diuretic (fluid pill) to solve that. The only problem is that the fluid pill fails to address the initial problem of magnesium deficiency, and in fact, it also causes the loss of further magnesium. So in a few months of escalating hidden and untreated magnesium deficiency, another magnesium-induced symptom can emerge, like chronic muscle pain and spasm, say in an old back injury site. Then you may start getting very tense and irritable, so a tranquilizer is prescribed instead of fixing the underlying cause, magnesium deficiency. And on and on the scenario goes, with more medication and surgery being piled on to an ailing system, until the ultimate magnesium deficiency symptom: smooth muscle spasm of the coronary blood vessel with resultant cardiac arrhythmia, and sudden death by heart attack.

Or take the fact that the majority or cases of arthritis have hidden food allergies. By prescribing the common anti-inflammatory drugs to quiet the pain, the underlying cause remains untreated. And the anti-inflammatory drugs themselves inflame the stomach and intestines and promote gastritis and bleeding ulcers. They can also inflame the entire lining of the gastrointestinal tract so that now the normal barriers in the gut that regularly protect us from developing food allergy are compromised and further food antigens are allowed across the gut wall to trigger even more food allergy. The arthritis escalates as the person hurts and is swollen more and more while the drugs do less and less and the prescriptions become stronger and more dangerous (references in the newsletter from this publisher).

One of the most dangerous drugs are calcium channel blockers, used for regulating cardiac arrhythmias. This is because any time you need to block calcium, you can bet you also have an undiscovered magnesium deficiency, since magnesium is nature's calcium channel blocker. Or look at the numbers of people who take tranquilizers. Magnesium is also nature's tranquilizer. But when one is magnesium deficient and merely takes tranquilizers, he risks getting sleepy, having an accident, and getting progressively more edgy and irritable to the point of nervous breakdown or criminal acts (references in <u>Tired or Toxic?</u>, from this publisher).

PARADIGM SHIFT

Man has always resisted changing his model of how he thinks the world works. He has, in fact, risked his reputation and even his life on it. History is full of examples of paradigm (preconceived notion or model) shifts that lead to death. The shift in thought was not any easier for those who believed that the earth was flat than it was for those who believed that the earth was the center of the universe. Columbus and Copernicus had no easier time than Semmelweiss (who told doctors they should wash their hands after performing autopsies, and before delivering babies so the women would not die of puerperal fever) or Pasteur, or the 21st century ecologist.

Whenever there is a war or political struggle going on in medicine, you can be sure there is also a paradigm shift. There is the old guard on one side who has a vested interest in hanging on to the old way regardless of how much evidence there is against it. They fear losing their prestigious position of power, losing any financial control, having to learn new techniques, and resent anyone else having scooped them. Consequently, they use every bit of political muscle they can muster regardless of how unethical or dishonest it is, but always being careful to cloak it in the disguise of something good for everyone. A common ploy is to continually bad-mouth all the evidence and insist it is unscientific and that they are protecting the masses from quacks.

Right now we are in one huge paradigm shift. Diseases have been until now, thought of as being caused by bacteria or mysterious viruses. Antibiotics have been the mainstay of medicine, while most other symptoms that cannot be controlled with antibiotics, have been covered up with drugs. In other words, the golden rule of medicine might be thought of as "A headache is a Darvon deficiency".

At this point in time, the most seemingly "incurable diseases like multiple sclerosis, rheumatoid arthritis, chronic fatigue, chronic Candidiasis, multiple chemical sensitivities and even cancer with metastases can be cleared. We now have the tools with which to do the "impossible" just as Jenner with his smallpox vaccine and other paradigm pioneers did.

We now have the capability to often identify the environmental trigger, the hidden food intolerance and the biochemical defect and correct these (Tired Or Toxic?, for details). So why is it not common knowledge? Why are we still confronted with only high tech medications and surgical procedures as our only options on T.V.? Because those with the bucks and the power are clinging desperately to the past to maintain their financial turfs. And they rely on the average man's shared fear of change and ignorance of the issues to support their chastisement of such "quackery". Just bear in mind that every place that a drug can work to produce a desired effect, there is probably a nutrient missing in that path that can do the job better.

Psoriasis is often due to an essential fatty acid deficiency. Fatigue is often due to hidden mineral deficiencies, carpel tunnel syndrome and other numbness and tingling problems are often due to vitamin lack. More importantly, one of the commonest causes of uncontrollable cravings is an unsuspected nutrient deficiency.

KNOW YOUR NUTRIENT LEVELS

You will always hear negatives when you embark on any diet to improve yourself. If brings out the guilt in others who know they too should take responsibility for their health, but do not want to. So if they can undermine your program, they feel a lot better because the threat of your success staring them in the face everyday can be crushed.

One of the first negatives is "You know vegetarian diets are known for vitamin B12 deficiency". Sure, they have been in the past because many vegetarians ate predominantly breads, honeyed baked goods, and vegetables. They neglected the seaweeds. B12 deficiency classically causes numbness and tingling, fatigue, depression, and even psychosis (New England Journal Of Medicine, 26, 1988). But wakame, a sea vegetable that you can cook into your soups is rich in B12 (American Journal Of Clinical Nutrition, 47, 1988). And if you don't want to know it's there, pass the soup through a blender. Also any animal flesh once every 1-4 weeks, (white fish is preferable) will provide enough B12 for most. But when in doubt, get a test.

If a person has a digestive complaint, we think nothing of ordering a full set of stomach and intestine x-rays and scopings. But for the same cost, you can obtain the majority of your nutrient levels.

Others query whether they get enough calcium from a diet devoid of milk and cheese. When I lectured in China, we did not see any dairy products for the whole month, and they had no osteoporosis worry like we do. We have to worry because (1) we eat a high phosphate diet when we eat processed foods, especially soft drinks. Phosphates inhibit the absorption of calcium. (2) We, as you saw, are missing many minerals like magnesium because of processed foods. These minerals are important to assure that the calcium we ingest gets deposited in the bone. If we don't have enough magnesium, manganese, zinc, copper, vanadium, boron, etc., we put the calcium instead in the toxic waste dump of the body: so the calcium that the uninformed physician recommends without checking your calcium and other minerals first, may end up depositing in your vessels and actually accelerating arteriosclerosis, early heart attack or Alzheimer's pre-senile dementia.

Two cups of greens contains as much calcium as a glass of milk, but the greens also contain the accessory minerals needed to assure that the calcium gets into the bone, whereas the milk does not.

Another frequently asked question is "Doesn't man really need meat?" The answer is that some people definitely do. Man is after all, a hunter as well as a gatherer. The brain neurotransmitters that determine our moods and emotions are made out of amino acids, the building blocks of proteins, as are the muscles. Many can get sufficient protein from the grains and beans, others cannot. There is tremendous biochemical individuality. This brings us to the last issue of...............

GUILT

In two words, FORGET IT. There is no useful purpose for guilt. You can only educate yourself so much. You can formulate a plan for health. You can periodically assess it to see if you are meeting your goals, if the goals were set too high for your schedule, if you should reassess your priorities, if the pace was set too fast, if a different plan with more support might be needed, perhaps you need to see the doctor for ruling out the causes of your hidden cravings, or if you should make a new plan of attack to overcome a serious addiction. But guilt only serves to undermine your confidence in you.

Let's look at a serious example of an addiction that can cause tremendous guilt and could stall your hopes of cleaning up your diet, getting rid of some long-standing symptoms, and feeling wonderful: alcoholism. First I hope you know that alcoholism is a medical disease, like diabetes or high blood pressure. It is NOT a sign of lack of will-power or poor moral fiber. Why, even the gene that is responsible for   alcoholism   has   been   identified

(Journal Of The American Medical Association, 263, 1990). Because many forms of food allergy also cause very strong addiction patterns, it is not surprising that most alcoholics have allergic people in their family history, and vice versa.

So it won't come as a surprise to you that there are environmental factors and biochemical defects that can be identified and corrected to terminate this problem as well. As a minute example, often an alcoholic will have a combination of a severe food allergy like corn sensitivity that drives him to drink, as well as a hidden Candida infestation of the bowel and multiple severe nutrient deficiencies. You will note that all three items are common causes of uncontrollable cravings, so no wonder they have such a tough time trying to break the habit.

And most alcoholics have all three, food allergies, Candida, and nutrient deficiencies plus they usually have psychological problems (Who doesn't? I haven't met a perfect person yet). If that were not enough of a burden of total load, most alcoholics also have unsuspected mold allergies and a biochemical defect in the synthesis of the "happy hormones" or brain neurotransmitters that are responsible for making us feel content and happy.

There is in the brain a cascade of reactions involving neurotransmitters that has to function in order for us to feel happy, content, and satisfied. But it can be blocked in several ways. One is through lack of the nutrients that make the pathway run. Another is by having the gene to promote dysfunction of the pathway. Another is to have a deficiency of the amino acid precursors that promote the synthesis of the neurotransmitters. Most alcoholics have a problem in all three of these areas.

So no wonder medicine has become frustrated in trying to help the alcoholic. As is true to form, when medicine is stumped as to how something works, and can't fix it with drugs, the blame is laid on the patient. It has happened for years. Lupus is a good example. They thought all the women who were complaining of rashes, severe body pain, chest pain, arthritis, headache and depression had too many symptoms at once. So they labeled them hypochondriacs.......until they discovered the anti-nuclear antibody that diagnoses the condition. Blaming the patient continues to this day with psychiatric cases and with the patient with environmental illness when the physician is stumped because he has failed to look for the causes: the biochemical defects and environmental triggers.

When the proper chemistry does not proceed in these areas of the brain, the person suffers poor self esteem, depression, anxiety, anger, and intense craving for the substance that makes these bad feelings go away, namely alcohol. But this abnormal chemistry in the brain of alcoholics can now be corrected (Integrative Psychiatry, 6, 1989). So no source of guilt should seem insurmountable in this area. Even though a problem may appear insurmountable to you and even to many medical experts. Always check around, for the artificial barriers between what is possible and what is not are being dissolved daily.

Guilt is a negative and destructive emotion that you have neither need of nor time for. If you can't get yours out of your life so that you can go full steam ahead in your plan to get healthier, find the appropriate help. And in the course of gradually switching over to a healthier lifestyle, remember every positive conquest is a step in the right direction that you hadn't taken yesterday. There is no room for guilt for not having reached your artificially erected goals. Remember, if you constantly flagellate yourself for not being perfect in the diet, you will fall into the guilt trap, since no one is perfect. So instead, commend yourself daily for each step, however small, you have made toward improving your health.

Instead, replace your dissatisfaction with laughter. It's healthier for the whole body. Keep in mind that when something seems really impossible, there is probably a medical explanation and solution. In the meantime, find the humor wherever possible as you steadfastly journey toward your goal.

If you don't feel great, it's important to know your nutrient levels. Any symptom, big or small is a natural body signal that something is amiss. One of those things is most likely a hidden deficiency, especially when you take into consideration the statistics already given for even one nutrient. But be sure to get the correct test for each nutrient.

CRUSHING CRAVINGS

Do you want to lose that urge to kill when someone gets between you and your favorite food? Do you want to stop being obsessed with where your next food fix will come from? Would you like to have days free of preoccupation with food so you could concentrate on more important things than when you'll get your next coke, coffee or goodie?" Then first you need to understand why you have cravings.

We rarely see animals in the wild walking on crutches or sucking down Darvons. That's because they live by instinct. If they are thirsty, they drink. If they are sick they fast or change their nests. But we have lost many of our protective instincts. If we are thirsty it is usually because we need to balance too much salt, or we drink to satiate a sweet craving, or we drink to wake up or drink to relax. We rarely live by instinct, because it has been submerged by our addictions.

Now say an animal has been grazing in an area where the soil is lacking a particular mineral. The animal will forage to replace that mineral. But what happens to man when he lacks a specific nutrient? He also forages. He is driven to find that something that makes him feel normal. But since we are surrounded by a myriad of processed foods, we often make an improper choice, and the craving never gets cured. And it can easily lead to overweight.

When you think about it, there are basically only five categories of causes for cravings commonly. One, the individual craves because he is eating out of balance. For example, the person who eats too many processed high salt foods will crave sugars to balance it. Too high a fat diet will also cause a craving of either sugars or salts or both. These people frequently disgust themselves because they eat to the point of pain even when they are not hungry. So to nip the cycle of too high a salt, fat, or sugar diet in the bud, one of the quickest things to do is start a diet of whole foods and greatly reduce the processed foods. What are whole foods? Things like brown rice and lots of vegetables and beans.

The second reason for cravings you could kill for is hypoglycemia, or low blood sugar. This can disguise itself as headaches, horrid fatigue, or vicious mood swings, for example. And hypoglycemia can have many causes, but the commonest is a combination of too many sweets, coffee, alcohol, and other processed foods.

A second cause is an overgrowth of a yeast called Candida in the intestines. This yeast often gets a head start in the gut after you have had a bout of antibiotics. But other medications such as ulcer and stomach prescriptions to decrease the acid in the stomach, birth control pills, and Prednisone can do it. Since the yeasts thrive on sugars, but also need them to survive, they can cause you to crave sweets, but at the same time these very sweets cause the yeast to grow even faster, thus causing you to crave even more. You can padlock the refrigerator door, but it will be futile, for you are mercilessly driven to satisfy that craving. The treatment is to go on the yeast program that is outlined in The E.I. Syndrome (Prestige Publishing, Box 3161, Syracuse, NY 13220), temporarily cut out all sweets (including fruits) and to replace processed foods with whole grains and vegetables.

The 4th commonest reason for wicked uncontrollable cravings is by far the sneakiest: unidentified nutrient deficiencies. At first you might think that couldn't apply to you, because you live in the land of plenty and eat a wide variety of foods. But we have the dubious distinction of being the first generation of man ever to eat so many processed foods.

Vitamin C, for example, has a structure similar to glucose (sugar) and a deficiency of this is sometimes the cause of sugar cravings. A gram or less of ascorbic acid 3 or 4 times a day in a buffered calcium/magnesium form will quickly tell you if this is the cause.

But many other deficiencies can be behind your cravings. For example, to make bread nowadays, you first need white flour. To make this highly processed food, you take whole wheat and grind it into flour, then bleach it to make it white. Unfortunately, though, the minerals such as magnesium, chromium, and copper are reduced 80%. And what can a chromium deficiency cause? The very hypoglycemia that caused your cravings, for starters. And a deficiency of all three minerals (which is very common, since most people eat bread every day) can cause high cholesterol.

In fact the reason many people have high cholesterol is because they do not have all the minerals needed to metabolize the cholesterol properly. But instead of discovering the biochemical cause behind the high cholesterol, diets of more processed foods (margarines, egg-beaters, etc.,) are prescribed along with expensive medications that can potentiate Alzheimer's (early senility) and early heart attacks through free radical-induced degenerative disease.

So how do you correct this? Have your doctor draw your vitamin and mineral levels as described for him and you in Tired or Toxic? (Prestige Publishing, Box 3161, Syracuse, NY 13220). And once they are diagnosed and corrected, make sure you are on a diet of whole real foods that are rich in these nutrients so you never get that way again.

There are other causes for cravings as well. But the fifth category is one of hidden or unsuspected food and chemical sensitivities. For example, it is common for many people to be driven by cravings when they eat any food containing wheat. And chemical overload can come from such common sources as from auto exhaust fumes, new carpet, paint, and other chemicals in the normal environment. They outgas formaldehyde, toluene, xylene and other hydrocarbons that abnormally stimulate the brain's appetite center in some of those affected.

All of the above has been detailed in Tired or Toxic? As well, it contains the scientific references for statements in this article for interested physicians.

So next time you have a craving, look at it as a gift or early warning. For it is the only way your body has of alerting you that you are eating wrong, have hypoglycemia, intestinal dysbiosis, or have an undiscovered nutrient deficiency or food or chemical sensitivity. And by discovering and correcting the cause early, you may just be staving off that first heart attack from an undiagnosed magnesium deficiency or whatever other symptom would have been next after having ignored the real cause and improperly fed your craving.

THE DREADED DISCHARGE

Some people fear the discharge so much that it has kept them from pursuing macrobiotics and even the transition phase. But in 22 years of medicine, with all the regrets I've heard, never even once have I heard anyone say they wish they had not done macrobiotics because of the results of their discharge.

Like any drug addict, you can go through some rough headaches or other withdrawal symptoms for a day or so when you discontinue receiving your daily fix of caffeine, nicotine, sugar, or chocolate, or whatever else you are hooked on.

But if it is that bad, just resume the food again and you'll be re-addicted and turn off the symptom until you gear up to get rid of it once and for all.

As for the discharge, even for those of us who went through actual gut-wrenching pain, all the while we had a simultaneous feeling of contentment that is hard to explain; except that you know you will be at a new level of wellness when it is done. And there are always medications to attenuate it or even turn it off if you don't choose to endure it. The vast majority, however do not go through a dramatic or particularly bad discharge. It is often less aggravation than a flu, which if you don't clean out your system, you will probably get each year anyway. Once you are clear, however, you'll be amazed, as most of us have, that year after year everyone around us gets the current flus while we are totally unaffected. Also there are macrobiotic remedies for these discharges that can attenuate them.

In essence, food is a major factor for optimum health. But in this era, because nutrient deficiencies are so prevalent, don't overlook this aspect of your health, especially if you are having problems of any sort. And just as there is no perfect diet for everyone, there is no perfect diet for each person forever. As you change, so do your dietary needs. We change with the seasons as well as throughout our journey for improved health.

Likewise, it goes without saying that body work (such as massage, shiatsu, yoga, chiropractic, cranial sacral manipulations, acupuncture, sports, energy balancing or therapeutic touch) as well as mind work (meditation, religion, friendship, psychotherapy, gardening, work, etc.) are also necessary to round out your life.

MACRO MELLOWNESS

And when you begin your macrobiotic adventure, within the first month or two, you should experience what we call macro mellowness. It can happen to many in just a few weeks of the diet as you have just learned. For others, it requires a more rigid, but temporary, program (The Cure Is In The Kitchen) to bring this about, as they are sicker. But whenever you get it, the feeling of macro mellowness is unmistakable. It's a feeling of serenity, tranquility, or calmness that many of us had never experienced before. The implications this has for people on tranquilizers, in detention homes, prisons, hyperactive children with learning disorders, or on a global scale involving waring nations are profound. Yes, it does indeed appear that not only does our personal health begin in the kitchen, but the health of the world just may begin there as well.

Be that as it may, we know that once you begin to experience your own personal macro mellowness, you'll realize you are now in control; that you possess the power to improve the health of yourself and your family. And that you can accomplish more than you ever dreamed of once you are macro mellow.

Bon appetite!

N.E.E.D.S
527 Charles Ave #12A
Syracuse, NY 13209
Phone 1-800-634-1380

Gold Mine Natural Foods
1047 30th Street
San Diego, CA 82102
1-800-475-FOOD

Jaffe Brothers
PO Box 369
Valley Center, CA 92082-0636
Phone (619) 749-1133

Lundberg Family Farms
PO Box 369
Richvale, CA 95974
Phone (916) 882-4551

Mt. Ark Trading Co.
120 South East Ave
Fayetteville, AK 72701
Phone 1-800-643-8909

Mendocino Sea Vegetable Co.
PO Box 372
Navarro, CA 95463
Phone (707) 895-3741

Maine Coast Sea Vegetables
Shore Road
Franklin, ME 04251
Phone (207) 565-2907

Walnut Acres
Penns Creek, PA 17862
Phone (717) 837-0601

COOKBOOKS

Cooking With Rachel by Rachel Albert 1989, Published by George Oshawa Macrobiotic Foundation, 1511 Robinson Street, Oroville, CA 95965

Working Chef's Cookbook for Natural Whole Foods by Jackson Blackman 1989, Published by Central Vermont Publishers, P.O. Box 700, Morrisville, VT 05661

Judy Brown's Guide to Natural Foods Cooking by Judy Brown and Dorothy R. Bates 1989, The Book Publishing Company, Summettown, TN 38483

The Book of Whole Grains by Marlene Bumgarner 1976, St. Martin's Press, 175 Fifth Avenue, New York, NY 10010

The Book of Whole Meals by Annemarie Colbin 1979, Ballantine Books a division of Random House, Inc., New York, NY

An Introduction to Macrobiotics by Oliver Cowmeadow 1987, Published by Thorsons Publishers Limited, Wellingborough, Northamptonshire, NN8 2RQ, England

Natural Foods Cookbook by Mary Estella 1985, Published by Japan Publications, Inc., Tokyo and New York Kodansha International/USA, Ltd., 114 Fifth Avenue, New York

Basic Macrobiotic Cooking by Julia Ferre' 1987, Published by George Ohsawa Macrobiotic Foundation, 1511 Robinson Street, Oroville, CA 95965

Complete Guide to Macrobiotic Cooking by Aveline Kushi with Alex Jack 1985, Published by Japan Publications Inc., Tokyo and New York

The Changing Seasons Macrobiotic Cookbook by Aveline Kushi and Wendy Esko 1985, Published by Avery Publishing Group Inc., Wayne, New Jersey

The Quick and Natural Macrobiotic Cookbook by Aveline Kushi and Wendy Esko 1989, Published by Contemporary Books, Inc., 180 North Michigan Avenue, Chicago, IL 60601

The Macrobiotic Community Cookbook by Andrea Bliss Lerman 1989, Published by Avery Publishing Group Inc., Garden City Park, New York

American Macrobiotic Cuisine by Meredith McCarty 1986, Published by Turning Point Publications, 1122 M Street, Eureka, CA 95501-2442

Fresh From a Vegetarian Kitchen by Meredith McCarty 1989, Published by Turning Point Publications, 1122 M Street, Eureka, CA 95501-2442

Practically Macrobiotic by Keith Michell 1987, Published by Healing Arts Press, One Park Street, Rochester, VT 05767

Macrobiotic Cuisine by Lima Ohsawa 1984, Published by Japan Publications, Inc., Tokyo and New York

The First Macrobiotic Cookbook formerly Zen Cookery by George Ohsawa Macrobiotic Foundation 1985

The Self Healing Cookbook by Kristina Turner 1987, Published by Earthtones Press, P.O. Box 2341-B, Grass Valley, CA 95945

The Book of Tofu 1975 William Shurtleff and Akiko Aoyagi, Published by Ballantine Books, A division of Random House, Inc., New York

The Book of Miso by William Shurtleff and Akiko Aoyagi 1976, Published by Ballantine Books a Division of Random House, Inc., New York

The Sweet Life by Marcea Weber 1981, Published by Japan Publications, Inc. Tokyo and New York

Macrobiotic Dessert Book by Anneliese Wollner 1988, Published by Japan Publication, Inc., Tokyo and New York

GARDENING BOOKS

One Straw Revolution, Masanoba   Fukuaha,   Rodale   Press   Inc.
Emmanus, PA 1976

60 Minute Garden, Jeff Bell, Rodale Press Inc., Emmanus, PA
1985

Square Food Gardening, Mel   Bartholomew,   Rodale   Press   Inc.,
Emmanus, PA 1981

SEED SUPPLIERS

Abundant Life Seed Foundation
P.O. Box 772
Port Townsend, WA 98368

The Cook's Garden
P.O. Box 65
Londonderry, VT 05148

Johnny's Selected Seeds
P.O. Box 2580
Albion, ME 04910

Pinetree Garden Seeds
Rt 100
New Gloucester, ME 04260

Fox Hill Farm
Box 9
Parma, MI 49269
Catalog $1.00

Shepards Garden Seeds
6116 Highway 9
Felton, CA 95018

Seeds Blum
Idaho City Stage
Boise, ID 83706
Catalog $3.00
Heirloom varieties

BOOKS BY S.A. ROGERS, M.D.

1. <u>The E.I. Syndrome</u> is a 650 page book that is necessary for people with environmental illness. It explains chemical, food, mold an Candida sensitivities, nutritional deficiencies, testing methods and how to do the various environmental controls and diets in order to get well. Many docs buy these by the hundreds and make them mandatory reading for new patients. In this way it increases the fun of practicing medicine because patients are on a higher educational level and time is more productive. It covers hundreds of facts that make a difference between E.I. victims versus E.I. conquerors. It helps patients become active partners in their care while avoiding doctor burn-out. It covers the gamut of the diagnosis and treatment of environmentally induced symptoms.

2. <u>Tired or Toxic?</u> is a 400 page book that describes the mechanism of chemical sensitivity, complete with scientific references. It is written for the layman and physician alike and explains the many vitamin, mineral, essential fatty acid and amino acid analyses that may help people detoxify everyday chemicals more efficiently and hence get rid of baffling symptoms. The program shows how to diagnose and treat the majority of everyday symptoms and use molecular medicine techniques. It is the best book of the 4 for the physician.

3. <u>You Are What You Ate</u> is a book to show patients how to begin the macrobiotic diet, with which so many universal reactors have lost their food, mold, Candida and chemical sensitivities.

4. <u>The Cure is in the Kitchen</u> is the first book to ever spell out in detail what all those people ate day to day who cleared their incurable diseases, undiagnosable symptoms, relentless chemical, food, Candida, and electromagnetic sensitivities, as well as terminal cancers. Dr. Rogers flew to Boston each month to work side by side with Mr. Michio Kushi, as he counseled people at the end of their medical ropes, as their remarkable case histories will show you. If you cannot afford a $500 consultation, why not learn first hand what these people did and how you, too, may improve your health.

5. <u>Macro Mellow</u> is a book designed for 4 types of people:
(1) For the person who doesn't know a thing about macrobiotics,

but just plain wants to feel better, in spite of the 21st century.

(2) It solves the high cholesterol/triglycerides problem without drugs and is the perfect diet for heart disease patients.

(3) It is the perfect transition diet for those not ready for macro, but needing to get out of the chronic illness rut.

(4) It spells out how to feed the rest of the family who hates macro, while another family member must eat it to clear their "incurable" symptoms.

The delicious low-fat whole food meals use macro ingredients without the rest of the family even knowing. It is the first book to dove-tail creative meal planning, menus, recipes and even gardening so the cook isn't driven crazy.

PRESTIGE PUBLISHING
P. O. Box 3161
Syracuse, NY 13220
(800) 846-ONUS ∽6687
(315) 455-7862

Please send the following books:	Quantity	Sub-total
The E.I. Syndrome.......................$14.95	/	
You Are What You Ate.....................9.95		
Tired Or Toxic?.. ....17.95	/	
Macro Mellow.............................. ..12.95		
The Cure Is In The Kitchen..............14.95		
Health Letter (quarterly newsletter)15/yr	/	
Mold Plates 20.00		
Formaldehyde Spot Test 40.00		

Sub-total _____

*Discount _____

NY State residents add 7% sales tax _____

**Shipping/handling each _____

Total Enclosed _____

*Discounts available on ten or more books.

**Ship/hand $3.00 each in the continental U.S., $6.00 each elsewhere.

364

Northeast Center For Environmental Medicine
Statement of Purpose

The goal of the Northeast Center for Environmental Medicine is to help people realize their full health potential, through diagnosis, treatment and extensive education. It especially specializes in difficult to diagnose or apparently incurable medical problems. It does this by taking up where 20th century medicine leaves off by using 21st century molecular and environmental medicine to identify the hidden or unsuspected environmental triggers and biochemical deficiencies that cause most diseases. If there is enough interest in this type of information, we plan to publish it for a nominal sum to cover costs on a quarterly basis initially and then bimonthly.

The health letter is but one facet of our educational thrust, and we welcome your questions, requests, and comments to help us fashion this into the most meaningful health newsletter for you and your family.

- -

═RENEWAL═
NORTHEAST CENTER FOR ENVIRONMENTAL MEDICINE
HEALTH LETTER
P.O. Box 3161, Syracuse, NY 13220
(315) 455 - 7862

_____ Please renew my subscription for_____ years.

Subscription rates:

(United States) One year, $15.00 Two years, $28.00

(International) One year, $20.00 Two years, $36.00 (U.S.)

_____ Charge to: _____ VISA _____ MasterCard

#_____ Exp._____

Signature: _____

Name _____

Address _____

City _____State _____ Zip _____

Telephone _____

Northeast Center For Environmental Medicine Health Letter is published quarterly by Prestige Publishing, P.O. Box 3161, Syracuse, NY 13220

COOKING NOTES:

COOKING NOTES:

COOKING NOTES:

COOKING NOTES:

COOKING NOTES:

INDEX

-A-

Aduki, about, 20,33
Agar-agar, 20,34,37
Almonds, 33
Almond Butter Cookies, 241
Almond Dip, 221
Almond Custard, 62, 261
Almond Milk, 40, 273
Amaranth, 27, 42
Anasazi, 33
Apple, 35
Apple Crisp, 59, 262
Apple Crunch Pie, 66, 256
Apricot, 35
Arame, 20, 31
Arame w/Root Vegetables, 89
Arrowroot, 20, 37, 44
Autumn Apple Pilaf, 77
Autumn Baked Vegetables, 66, 90

-B-

B-B-Q Burgers, 115
Bancha Tea, 20, 39
Barley, 26, 43
Barley Cookies, 242
Barley Lentil Loaf, 116
Barley Malt, 20, 37, 42
Barley Nut Salad, 169
Barley Pilaf, 78
Basic Oat Bran Muffins, 196
Basic Vegetable Broth, 143
Bean Salad w/ Spring Veggies, 168
Bechamel Sauce, 209
Beets, 30
Blanched Vegetable Salad w/Arame, 59
Black Soybean, 33

Blueberry, 35
Blueberry Pie, 70, 257
Blueberry Sauce, 72, 285
Boston Baked Beans, 117
Bread Pudding, 263
Broccoli, 29
Broccoli-Walnut Stir Fry, 62, 118
Brown Rice, 25, 43
Brussel Sprouts, 29
Buckwheat, 28, 43
Buckwheat & Barley Pancakes, 72, 284
Buckwheat Noodles w/Scallops, 119
Buckwheat Pilaf, 58
Bulgur, 26
Burdock, 21, 29
Butternut Surprise Soup, 66, 148

-C-

Cabbage, 29
Cabbage & Arame w/Mustard Sauce, 91
Cantaloupe, 35
Carrot, 29
Carrot Raisin Cookies, 243
Cauliflower, 29
Cauliflower Bouquet, 92
Celebration Salad, 170
Celery, 30
Celery Root, 29
Chestnut, 34
Cherry, 36
Chinese Cabbage, 29
Chinese Cabbage Pressed Salad, 171
Collards, 29
Coleslaw w/Celery Seed Dressing, 172
Corn, 27, 54
Corn Muffins, 197
Corn Free Baking Powder, 203
Cooked Grain Milk, 274
Couscous, 20, 25
Couscous Vinaigrette, 173

Cream of Broccoli Soup, 149
Cream of Carrot w/Dill, 63, 150
Creamed Greens, 93
Creamy Garbanzo Soup, 59, 69, 151
Creamy Ginger-Miso Dressing, 234
Creamy Noodle Casserole, 57, 120
Creamy Split Pea Soup, 67, 73, 152
Crunchy Crust, 250
Cucumber, 30, 54

-D-

Daikon, 21, 29
Dandelion, 29
Dessert Shortcakes, 247
Dill Dressing, 235
Dulce, 31
Dynamic Duo, 59, 69, 79

-E-

Endive, 29
Escalloped Cabbage, 94
Escarole, 29

-F-

Filled Oat Bars, 60, 244
Fish, 35
Fish Stock, 144
Fit for a Queen Quinoa, 286
Flaky Pie Crust, 251
Flaxseed, 34, 41
Flaxseed Egg Substitute, 203
French Onion Soup, 60, 153
Fresh Cucumber Pickles, 185
Fried Rice w/Tofu, 121
Fruit Jell Dessert, 264
Fu, 33

-G-

Garbanzo Bean, 33
German Style Tempeh w/Cabbage, 59, 69, 122
Ginger, 21, 37
Ginger Sauce, 210
Gingerbread Cake, 248
Ginger-Miso Sauce, 211
Ginger Pumpkin Butter, 223
Gingered Carrots & Snow Peas, 95
Gingered Leek & Lentil Soup, 57, 69, 154
Glazed Onions, 68, 96
Golden Loaf, 70, 80
Golden Stuffed Onions, 97
Goldilock Porridge, 286
Gomashio, 21
Gourmet Oatmeal, 287
Grain, Green & Bean Soup, 155
Granola Crust, 252
Grape, 36
Grated Daikon Radish, 218
Great Granola, 288
Great Northern Bean, 33
Green Beans, 30, 54
Green Beans Almondine, 98
Green Goddess Dressing, 69, 236
Green Peas, 30, 33
Green Split Pea w/Barley Soup, 156

-H-

Harvest Stuffing, 68, 200
Hearty Miso Gravy, 230
Hearty Vegetable Stock, 145
Herbs, 37
Heavenly Pears, 58, 72, 265
Hijiki, 21, 31
Hijiki w/Creamy Dressing, 66, 174
Home Remedies, 303, 304, 305, 206, 307
Horseradish, 37
Hummus, 63, 224

-I-

Italiano Red Sauce, 71, 212
Italiano White Sauce, 213

-J-

J.A. Vichyssoise, 157
Jiffy Vegetable Stock, 146

-K-

Kale, 29
Kanten, 21, 31
Kasha, 21
Kidney Bean, 33
Knishes w/Veggie Rice Filling, 295
Kohlrabi, 29
Kombu , 21, 31
Kombu Broth w/Tofu & Lemon, 158
Kombu Mushroom Stock, 147
Kombu Vegetable Bake, 99
Kosher Dill Pickles, 186
Kukicha Tea, 21, 39
Kuzu, 21, 37, 41

-L-

Leeks, 29
Lemon Dessert Sauce, 68, 215
Lemon Miso Soup, 61, 73
Lemon-Oil-Herb Dressing, 237
Lemon Sauce w/Dill, 214
Lentils, 33
Lentil Pate, 64, 124
Lentil-Walnut Loaf, 66, 123
Lentil Stew, 73, 125
Light Miso Soup w/Wakame, 159
Lotus Root, 21, 29

-M-

Macro Macaroni & Cheese, 73, 126
Maple Syrup, 37, 42
Maple Cheesecake, 258
Marinated Broiled Snapper, 127
Mediterranean Greens & Beans, 100
Meat, 34
Meatless Tofu Balls, 71, 128
Menus, 57-73
Menu Planning, 44-56
Midas Root Soup, 160
Millet, 26
Mirin, 21, 37
Miso, 21, 37
Mocha Pudding, 71, 266
Mochi, 21
Mock Egg & Olive Spread, 72, 225
Mock Mashed Potatoes, 81
Molded Cranberry Salad, 175
Mugichi, 21
Mung, 33
Mustard Greens, 29
Mustard Dressing, 237
My Garden Stew, 58, 101

-N-

Navy Bean, 33
Nishime, 21
Nori, 21, 31
Nori-Pumpkin Seed Treats, 218
Nori Rolls, 69, 297
Nut Sauce, 216
Nutty Walnut Drops, 245

-O-

Oats, 26, 43
Oatmeal Raisin Cookies, 69, 73, 246
Oil, 56

Olive, 56
Olive-Walnut Dip, 222
Onion, 29
Onion Gravy, 70, 231
Onion-Mushroom Gravy, 232
Oriental Fish Stew, 129

-P-

Parsley, 29
Parsnip, 29
Party Pecan Pie, 259
Pasta w/Greens & Beans, 73, 130
Peach, 36
Peach Dream Couscous Cake, 72, 249
Peach Frosty, 277
Pecan, 34
Peanut, 34
Pear, 36
Pepper, 30
Perfection Salad, 176
Pickled Vegetables w/Dulse, 187
Pine Nut, 34
Pink Sparkle Punch, 276
Polenta, 82
Popcorn Balls, 279
Potato, 30
Pressed Cabbage Salad, 57
Pressed Crust, 253
Pumpkin, 29
Pumpkin Pie, 67, 260

-Q-

Quiche For All Seasons, 60, 131
Quinoa, 28
Quick & Easy Bulgur Pilaf, 73, 83

-R-

Radish, 29

Rainbow Stir Fry, 102
Raisin, 36
Raw Pressed Salad, 177
Rice, brown, 23
Rice Syrup, 21, 37, 42
Rice vinegar, 21
Roasted J.A. & Onions, 103
Romaine, 29
Rosy Bean Roll, 132
Rosy Salad, 62, 178
Russian Pickle Relish, 188
Rutabaga, 29
Rye, 26

-S-

Salsify, 29
Sauerkraut, 37
Scallions, 29
Scrambled Tofu, 289
Scrambled Tofu w/Millet, 73, 290
Sea Salt, 37
Sea Food, 35
Sea Palm, 21, 31
Seitan, 21, 33
Seitan Stroganoff, 133
Sesame Milk, 40, 275
Sesame Salt, 21, 37, 219
Simple Millet w/Vegetables, 73, 84
Shiitake Mushroom, 21
Shoyu, 22, 37
Shrimp Fried Quinoa, 61, 134
Snow Peas, 30
Soba, 21
Soda "Pop", 275
Somen, 22
Sourdough Bread, 192
Soybean, 33
Soy Yogurt, 204
Special Cabbage Rolls, 104
Special Puff Pastry, 296

Special Rice Pudding, 267
Spiced Cranberry Relish, 189
Spinach, 30
Split Pea, 33
Spring Chive Dip, 222
Spring Green Pea Soup, 161
Sprouts, 30
Squash, 29, 54
Steamed Pudding, 68, 268
Stir & Roll Pie Crust, 254
Strawberries, 35
Strawberry Dream, 61, 269
Stuffed Acorn Squash, 67, 72, 73, 105
Summer Couscous, 73, 85
Summer Green Bean Salad, 179
Summer Fruit Crisp, 270
Summer Minestrone, 70, 162
Summer Squash Soup, 163
Summer Squash Special, 64, 106
Summer Vegetables w/Kuzu Ginger Sauce, 107
Summer Time Corn Chowder, 65, 164
Sunny Condiment, 220
Sunshine Salad, 73, 180
Sunshine Turnips, 108
Sweet Dessert Sauce, 216
Sweet Potato Muffins, 72, 199
Sweet Sour Cabbage, 109
Sweet Sour Sauce, 217
Sweet & Tangy Tempeh, 135
Sweet Vegetable Butter, 69, 228
Swiss Chard, 30

-T-

Tabouli, 63, 72, 181
Tahini, 22, 34
Tahini Gravy, 233
Tamari, 22, 37
Tapioca Quinoa Pudding, 271
Teff, 28
Teff Treat, 291

Tekka, 22, 37
Tempeh, 22, 33
Three Color Veggie Combo, 67, 110
Three Way Rice & Lentils, 136
Tofu Cheese, 53, 205
Tofu French Toast, 70, 292
Tofu Mayonnaise, 207
Tofu Rice Croquettes, 137
Tofu Ricotta Cheese, 40, 206
Tofu Sour Cream, 40, 208
Tofu Swiss Steak, 138
Tofu Turtles, 280
Tofu Veggies Spread, 226
Transition Turkey, 140
Trail Mix, 281
Tuna Style Tempeh, 227
Turnips, 29

-U-

Umeboshi, paste, plum, vinegar, 22, 37
Umeboshi Vegetable Pickles, 190

-V-

Vegetable Barley Soup, 72, 165
Very Berry Shake, 282

-W-

Wakame, 22, 31
Walnut Butter, 229
Walnut Oil Vinaigrette, 238
Watercress Winter Salad, 182
Watermelon, 36
Wheat, 26
Wheat Free Muffins, 198
Wheat Free Pie Crust, 255
Whole Grain Rice Bread, 194
Whole Meal Salad, 183
Whole Wheat Herb Bread, 195

Wild Greens, 30, 111
Wild & Tame Rice Pilaf, 66, 86
Winter Root Salad, 184

-Y-

Yam, 30

-Z-

Zucchini, 30